*Michael Widener*
*Editor*

# Public Services Issues with Rare and Archival Law Materials

*Public Services Issues with Rare and Archival Law Materials* has been co-published simultaneously as *Legal Reference Services Quarterly*, Volume 20, Numbers 1/2 2001.

*Pre-publication REVIEWS, COMMENTARIES, EVALUATIONS . . .*

"**I**mpressive . . . surveys the state of research in legal history, provides practical advice for those charged with the care of legal research materials, and lays out sound guidelines for improvement in the education of legal curators and archivists. THERE IS MUCH TO BE LEARNED FROM THIS VOLUME."

**John N. Jacob**
*Archivist*
*Lewis F. Powell, Jr. Archives*
*Washington and Lee University*
*School of Law*
*Lexington, Virginia*

*More pre-publication*
*REVIEWS, COMMENTARIES, EVALUATIONS . . .*

"**L**ONG OVERDUE . . . an easy one-volume introduction to the library public service issues involved with providing access to rare law books and legal archives. A useful adjunct to classes on American legal history in law schools or graduate history departments, as well as a principal text or reader for courses in rare book and archival training. I HEARTILY RECOMMEND IT."

**Jim Paulsen, LLM, JD**
*Professor of Law*
*South Texas College of Law*
*Houston*

The Haworth Information Press
An Imprint of The Haworth Press, Inc.

# Public Services Issues with Rare and Archival Law Materials

*Public Services Issues with Rare and Archival Law Materials* has been co-published simultaneously as *Legal Reference Services Quarterly*, Volume 20, Numbers 1/2 2001.

# The *Legal Reference Services Quarterly* Monographic "Separates"

Below is a list of "separates," which in serials librarianship means a special issue simultaneously published as a special journal issue or double-issue *and* as a "separate" hardbound monograph. (This is a format which we also call a "DocuSerial.")

"Separates" are published because specialized libraries or professionals may wish to purchase a specific thematic issue by itself in a format which can be separately cataloged and shelved, as opposed to purchasing the journal on an on-going basis. Faculty members may also more easily consider a "separate" for classroom adoption.

"Separates" are carefully classified separately with the major book jobbers so that the journal tie-in can be noted on new book order slips to avoid duplicate purchasing.

You may wish to visit Haworth's website at . . .

### http://www.HaworthPress.com

. . . to search our online catalog for complete tables of contents of these separates and related publications.

You may also call 1-800-HAWORTH (outside US/Canada: 607-722-5857), or Fax 1-800-895-0582 (outside US/Canada: 607-771-0012), or e-mail at:

### getinfo@haworthpressinc.com

---

**Public Services Issues with Rare and Archival Law Materials**, edited by Michael Widener, BJ, MLIS (Vol. 20, No. 1/2, 2001). *An essential reference for law librarians and archivists, this helpful book gives practical advice and information on providing access to rare and archival law collections and promoting their use by scholars, teachers, and students.*

**Teaching Legal Research and Providing Access to Electronic Resources**, edited by Gary L. Hill, JD, MLL, BA, Dennis S. Sears, JD, MA, MLIS, MBA, and Lovisa Lyman, MA, MLIS, BA (Vol. 19, No. 3/4, 2001). *"A unique mixture of historical, theoretical, and practical approaches to legal research instruction in one convenient location."* (Gail A. Partin, MSLS, JD, Associate Law Librarian, Sheely-Lee Law Library, The Dickinson School of Law of the Pennsylvania State University)

**Emerging Solutions in Reference Services: Implications for Libraries in the New Millennium**, edited by John D. Edwards, JD, MALS (Vol. 19, No. 1/2, 2001). *"The authors provide practical advice on how to cope with everything from tight budgets to training needs to knife wielding patrons. I highly recommend that law school reference librarians purchase and read this outstanding work."* (Bill Draper, BA, MS, JD, Reference Librarian and Lecturer, Biddle Law Library, University of Pennsylvania, Philadelphia)

**Law Librarians Abroad**, edited by Janet Sinder, AB, JD, MS (Vol. 18, No. 3, 2000). *"A pure pleasure! Law librarians seeking information on how to find professional work abroad and useful advice on how to survive in a foreign land will be amply rewarded. Delightful."* (Peter C. Schanck, JD, MLS, Law Library Director and Professor of Law, Marquette University Law Library, Milwaukee, Wisconsin)

**The Political Economy of Legal Information: The New Landscape**, edited by Samuel E. Trosow (Vol. 17, No. 1/2, 1999). *Through this informative book you will gain new insights into such important issues as how industry consolidation will affect small legal publishers and the possibility that the law that governs public access to judicial opinions mandates citation reform.*

**Symposium of Law Publishers**, edited by Thomas A. Woxland, MLS, JD (Vol. 11, No. 3/4, 1991). *"Librarians involved in collection development would find the symposium useful as it provides an insider's view of the legal publishing industry."* (Canadian Law Libraries)

**The Legal Bibliography: Tradition, Transitions, and Trends**, edited by Scott B. Pagel, JD, MLS (Vol. 9, No. 1/2, 1989). *"An excellent introduction to major bibliographic titles and future concerns for the novice law librarian or student of legal librarianship. . . . A useful addition to the reference shelf of the private law or acquisitions librarian."* (Legal Information Alert)

**Practical Approaches to Legal Research**, edited by Kent C. Olson, JD, MLS, and Robert C. Berring, JD, MLS (Supp. #01, 1988). *"A long overdue book–a legal research manual for librarians. . . . A readable and entertaining text on locating and using law books. . . . Almost everything a law librarian needs to know about legal research is covered in this book."* (Legal Information Alert)

# Public Services Issues with Rare and Archival Law Materials

Michael Widener
Editor

*Public Services Issues with Rare and Archival Law Materials* has been co-published simultaneously as *Legal Reference Services Quarterly*, Volume 20, Numbers 1/2 2001.

The Haworth Information Press
An Imprint of
The Haworth Press, Inc.
New York • London • Oxford

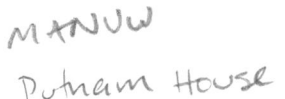
MANUW
Putnam House

Published by

The Haworth Information Press®, 10 Alice Street, Binghamton, NY 13904-1580 USA

The Haworth Information Press® is an imprint of The Haworth Press, Inc., 10 Alice Street, Binghamtom, NY 13904-1580 USA.

*Public Services Issues with Rare and Archival Law Materials* has been co-published simultaneously as *Legal Reference Services Quarterly*™, Volume 20, Numbers 1/2 2001.

© 2001 by The Haworth Press, Inc. All rights reserved. No part of this work may be reproduced or utilized in any form or by any means, electronic or mechanical, including photocopying, microfilm and recording, or by any information storage and retrieval system, without permission in writing from the publisher. Printed in the United States of America.

The development, preparation, and publication of this work has been undertaken with great care. However, the publisher, employees, editors, and agents of The Haworth Press and all imprints of The Haworth Press, Inc., including The Haworth Medical Press® and Pharmaceutical Products Press®, are not responsible for any errors contained herein or for consequences that may ensue from use of materials or information contained in this work. Opinions expressed by the author(s) are not necessarily those of The Haworth Press, Inc.

Cover design by Thomas J. Mayshock Jr.

### Library of Congress Cataloging-in-Publication Data

Public services issues with rare and archival law materials / Michael Widener, editor.
    p. cm.
  Co-published simultaneously as Legal reference services quarterly, v. 20, no. 1/2, 2001.
  Includes bibliographical references and index.
  ISBN 0-7890-1407-6 (alk. paper) – ISBN 0-7890-1408-4 (pbk. : alk. paper)
   1. Law libraries–Special collections–Rare books. 2. Law libraries–Special collections–Archival materials. 3. Law–Information resources. I. Widener, Michael. II. Legal reference services quarterly.

Z675.L2 P795 2001
026.34–dc21
                                          2001039007

# Indexing, Abstracting & Website/Internet Coverage

This section provides you with a list of major indexing & abstracting services. That is to say, each service began covering this periodical during the year noted in the right column. Most Websites which are listed below have indicated that they will either post, disseminate, compile, archive, cite or alert their own Website users with research-based content from this work. (This list is as current as the copyright date of this publication.)

Abstracting, Website/Indexing Coverage......... Year When Coverage Began

- *BUBL Information Service: An Internet-based Information Service for the UK higher education community* <URL: http://bubl.ac.uk/>................................. **1994**

- *CNPIEC Reference Guide: Chinese National Directory of Foreign Periodicals* ........................................ **1995**

- *Current Awareness Abstracts of Library & Information Management Literature, ASLIB (UK)*..................... **1997**

- *Current Cites [Digital Libraries] [Electronic Publishing] [Multimedia & Hypermedia] [Networks & Networking] [General]* ............................................... **2000**

- *Current Law Index* ....................................... **1992**

- *FINDEX <www.publist.com>* ............................. **1999**

- *Hein's Legal Periodical Checklist: Index to Periodical Articles Pertaining to Law <www.wshein.com>* ................ **1992**

- *IBZ International Bibliography of Periodical Literature* ......... **1995**

- *Index Guide to College Journals (core list compiled by integrating 48 indexes frequently used to support undergraduate programs in small to medium sized libraries)* ....... **1999**

(continued)

- *Index to Legal Periodicals & Books* .......................... 1992
- *Index to Periodical Articles Related to Law* .................... 1992
- *Information Science Abstracts* ............................. 1992
- *Informed Librarian, The* <http://www.infosourcespub.com> ....... 1993
- *InfoTrac Custom* <www.galegroup.com> ..................... 1996
- *INSPEC* <www.iee.org.uk/publish/> ........................ 1992
- *Journal of Academic Librarianship: Guide to Professional Literature, The* ............................................ 1997
- *Konyvtari Figyelo (Library Review)* ......................... 2000
- *LegalTrac on InfoTrac web* <www.galegroup.com> .............. 1984
- *Library & Information Science Abstracts (LISA)* ................ 1992
- *Library and Information Science Annual (LISCA)* <www.lu.com/arba> .......................................... 1998
- *Library Literature & Information Science* ..................... 1992
- *OCLC Public Affairs Information Service* <www.pais.org> ....... 2000
- *Sage Public Administration Abstracts (SPAA)* ................. 1992

*Special Bibliographic Notes related to special journal issues (separates) and indexing/abstracting:*

- indexing/abstracting services in this list will also cover material in any "separate" that is co-published simultaneously with Haworth's special thematic journal issue or DocuSerial. Indexing/abstracting usually covers material at the article/chapter level.
- monographic co-editions are intended for either non-subscribers or libraries which intend to purchase a second copy for their circulating collections.
- monographic co-editions are reported to all jobbers/wholesalers/approval plans. The source journal is listed as the "series" to assist the prevention of duplicate purchasing in the same manner utilized for books-in-series.
- to facilitate user/access services all indexing/abstracting services are encouraged to utilize the co-indexing entry note indicated at the bottom of the first page of each article/chapter/contribution.
- this is intended to assist a library user of any reference tool (whether print, electronic, online, or CD-ROM) to locate the monographic version if the library has purchased this version but not a subscription to the source journal.
- individual articles/chapters in any Haworth publication are also available through the Haworth Document Delivery Service (HDDS).

# Public Services Issues with Rare and Archival Law Materials

## CONTENTS

Public Services Issues with Rare and Archival Law Materials:
   An Introduction     1
    *Michael Widener*

GENERAL

A Portrait of Research in Legal History     5
    *Ann D. Gordon*

Helping Historians Write Legal History "From Below":
   Collecting New Sources, Teaching New Strategies     17
    *David Warrington*

Training Law Librarians in the Use of Rare Legal Materials     29
    *Morris L. Cohen*

Rare and Archival Law Materials: Exhibits and Outreach,
   Traditional and Electronic     41
    *Mark W. Lambert*

Rare and Archival Law Materials on the World Wide Web:
   An Evaluation of Selected Sites     67
    *Carole Prietto*

Bibliography on Rare and Archival Law Materials     79
    *Mark W. Lambert*
    *Michael Widener*

## RARE BOOKS

The Role of Rare Books in Law Libraries     85
    *Joel Silver*

Rediscovering Rare Books in an Electronic Age     93
    *Claire M. Germain*

Roman and Canon Law Research     99
    *Lucia Diamond*

## ARCHIVES

Lawyers, Archivists and Librarians: United or Divided
    in the Pursuit of Justice?     113
    *Menzi L. Behrnd-Klodt*

Using the Tom Clark Papers for a Seminar: A Faculty
    Member's Perspective     135
    *Michael J. Churgin*

Access to the Working Papers of State Supreme Court
    Justices: A Case Study from Texas     139
    *Michael Widener*

Providing Access to Lawyers' Papers:
    The Perils . . . and The Rewards     151
    *Akiba J. Covitz*

Lawyer-Client Files: A Historical Source, But Can We
    See Them?     181
    *Victor Tunkel*

Index     191

## ABOUT THE EDITOR

**Michael Widener, BJ, MLIS**, has been the Archivist/Rare Books Librarian at the Tarlton Law Library, University of Texas at Austin, since 1991. In 1994 he was named a Joseph D. Jamail Fellow in Law Librarianship. He holds a Master's Degree in Library and Information Science from the University of Texas at Austin. Mr. Widener serves on the Board of Trustees of the Texas Supreme Court Historical Society and the Editorial Board of H-LAW, the legal history listserv sponsored by the American Society for Legal History. He is active in the Society of American Archivists and has served on its publications board and committee on legal and legislative affairs. Mr. Widener's publications include a number of articles. He edited four published oral history interviews and bibliography of the current faculty of the University of Texas School of Law. In addition, Mr. Widener was a consultant on the cataloging, housing, and public services for the rare book collection at the law school of the Universidad Nacional Autónoma de Mexico.

 ALL HAWORTH INFORMATION PRESS BOOKS AND JOURNALS ARE PRINTED ON CERTIFIED ACID-FREE PAPER

# Public Services Issues with Rare and Archival Law Materials: An Introduction

Michael Widener

In the past few years I have perceived a modest but definite growth in rare book and archival collections in academic law libraries in the U.S. In addition, legal history remains a vital field of study, not only within law schools but also in the legal profession as a whole and outside the legal community. I thus think it's timely to devote a special volume to the topic of public services for rare books and archives. I am grateful for the invitation to edit this volume.

I have always felt that the primary value of these special collections lie in their use, both actual and potential. Rare books and archives come alive when consulted by readers and researchers.

In the administrative and budgetary environment of law librarianship, outstanding reference service is crucial to the survival and growth of special collections in law libraries. Rare book collections and archives must demonstrate that they are pulling their weight and contributing to the mission of their libraries and parent institutions. I hope that this special volume will demonstrate the importance of these contributions to law librarians in general, and in particular to our colleagues in public services and our library directors. In addition, the following arti-

---

[Haworth co-indexing entry note]: "Public Services Issues with Rare and Archival Law Materials: An Introduction." Widener, Michael. Co-published simultaneously in *Legal Reference Services Quarterly* (The Haworth Information Press, an imprint of The Haworth Press, Inc.) Vol. 20, No. 1/2, 2001, pp. 1-4; and: *Public Services Issues with Rare and Archival Materials* (ed: Michael Widener) The Haworth Information Press, an imprint of The Haworth Press, Inc., 2001, pp. 1-4. Single or multiple copies of this article are available for a fee from The Haworth Document Delivery Service [1-800-342-9678, 9:00 a.m. - 5:00 p.m. (EST). E-mail address: getinfo@haworthpressinc.com].

© 2001 by The Haworth Press, Inc. All rights reserved.

cles provide examples of best practice and solutions to common problems.

This volume focuses on those aspects of public services that are peculiar to rare book and archival collections with a legal focus, particularly those in academic law libraries and other repositories maintained by the legal profession. With three notable exceptions, the authors of the following articles also come from the world of law librarianship. The contributions fall into three sections: an opening set of articles that span both rare books and archives, followed by those dealing more specifically with rare law books and law-related archives.

The "General" section begins with a focus on a primary clientele for rare and archival legal materials, legal historians. Ann D. Gordon presents the only detailed survey in existence of the research habits of legal historians, extracted from a nationwide study that Gordon prepared for the National Historical Publications and Records Commission in 1992. Both legal historians and law librarians have remained largely unaware of this study, which will help law librarians and archivists to better serve their users. Harvard Law Library's David Warrington follows with an overview of current trends, methodology, and guides to the literature of legal history.

Morris L. Cohen of Yale, the leading authority on special collections in law libraries, provides a model curriculum for training law librarians in the care and use of rare legal materials. In the absence of formal training programs, his article is a virtual "do-it-yourself" course for archivists and rare book librarians in law libraries. In his discussion of exhibits and outreach activities, Mark W. Lambert of South Texas College of Law views these activities as not just teaching tools, but as important assets in marketing a special collections department and in furthering institutional goals. Today, exhibits and outreach make increasing use of the Internet. I called on a legal "outsider," Carole Prietto (university archivist at Washington University) to evaluate some of the online efforts of involving law-related collections. Prietto has been a frequent speaker on the World Wide Web at meetings of the Society of American Archivists and related organizations. The "General" section closes with a bibliography on law-related archives and rare book librarianship.

Joel Silver, curator of rare books at the Lilly Library, is well-known in the rare book world as a lecturer and as a columnist in the now-defunct trade journal, *AB Bookman's Weekly*. He opens the "Rare Books" section with a vigorous argument for the role of rare books in law libraries and legal education. Claire M. Germain, director of Cornell's law library, shows how rare books have contributed to the curriculum at her law school. Early books on Roman and canon law are found in many law libraries, but librarians are often not equipped to understand or make use of them. Lucia Diamond of Berkeley's Robbins Collection guides the reader through the literature of this fascinating field of legal research.

The final section, on "Archives," leads off with an article that will be useful for any archivist whose patrons include attorneys. Menzi L. Behrnd-Klodt, herself both an attorney and corporate archivist, explains how archives can be used in litigation and suggests ways in which archivists and attorneys can learn to work with each other. Michael J. Churgin describes how the personal papers of U.S. Supreme Court Justice Tom C. Clark bring constitutional law to life for his students at the University of Texas School of Law.

One aspect of law-related archives that set them apart is the question of access to papers that document judicial decision-making or communications between attorneys and their clients. These records are among the best evidence for the inner workings of our legal system, but they raise difficult issues for archival public services. The archivist must strike a balance between research needs, on the one hand, and the requirements of the judiciary and attorneys to protect the confidentiality of their deliberations.

The three concluding articles address these access issues. I describe how my library worked with the Texas Supreme Court and the Texas State Archives on access to the case files retained by justices when they leave the court. Regarding the attorney-client privilege and its implications, we have both U.S. and British perspectives. Akiba J. Covitz (now a professor at the University of Richmond) explains the background of the attorney-client privilege in U.S. law, and the guidelines that Yale University developed to deal with privileged materials in its archival collections. Victor Tunkel, the secretary of the Selden Society, traces the development of the attorney-client privilege in British law, and proposes a model act that would protect both the historical record and lawyers' confidentiality.

## *ACKNOWLEDGMENTS*

I wish to thank Publisher Bill Cohen, Editor-in-Chief Sul Lee, and all the staff of The Haworth Information Press for their support, assistance and patience. Mike Chiorazzi, the editor of *Legal Reference Services Quarterly*, reviewed the initial drafts and gave editorial advice. The suggestions from Arleen Dallachiesa, Production Editor at Haworth Press, contributed significantly to the clarity of the text. I owe special thanks to two people. Roy M. Mersky, the director of the Tarlton Law Library at The University of Texas at Austin, encouraged me to take on this project. Professor Mersky and my wife, Emma Molina Widener, also provided me with the time I needed to complete this work.

# GENERAL

# A Portrait of Research in Legal History

Ann D. Gordon

**SUMMARY.** In 1991, members of the American Society for Legal History were surveyed about their research habits as part of the Historical Documents Study, which explored the large and diverse demand for historical sources in the United States and Canada. The data offer a suggestive portrait for librarians, archivists, and others delivering legal and historical sources and reference services. While answering questions about their current research, the legal historians, like other respondents, described their training, research practices, and needs. Less directly, they revealed the extent to which they avail themselves of services provided to enhance the use of historical sources. *[Article copies available for a fee from The Haworth Document Delivery Service: 1-800-342-9678. E-mail address: <getinfo@haworthpressinc.com> Website: <http://www.HaworthPress.com> © 2001 by The Haworth Press, Inc. All rights reserved.]*

Ann D. Gordon is Editor of *Papers of Elizabeth Cady Stanton and Susan B. Anthony* and Associate Research Professor, Department of History, Rutgers, the State University of New Jersey. She directed the Historical Documents Study for the American Council of Learned Societies and the National Historical Publications and Records Commission in 1990 and 1991.

[Haworth co-indexing entry note]: "A Portrait of Research in Legal History." Gordon, Ann D. Co-published simultaneously in *Legal Reference Services Quarterly* (The Haworth Information Press, an imprint of The Haworth Press, Inc.) Vol. 20, No. 1/2, 2001, pp. 5-15; and: *Public Services Issues with Rare and Archival Law Materials* (ed: Michael Widener) The Haworth Information Press, an imprint of The Haworth Press, Inc., 2001, pp. 5-15. Single or multiple copies of this article are available for a fee from The Haworth Document Delivery Service [1-800-342-9678, 9:00 a.m. - 5:00 p.m. (EST). E-mail address: getinfo@haworthpress inc.com].

Nine years ago, members of the American Society for Legal History took part in a survey about their research that explored the large and diverse demand for historical sources in the United States and Canada. Though the data are not fresh, they are unique, and they offer a suggestive portrait for librarians, archivists, and others delivering legal and historical sources and reference services. While answering questions about their current research, the legal historians, like other respondents, described their training, research practices, and needs. Less directly, they revealed the extent to which they avail themselves of services provided to enhance the use of historical sources.[1]

A word, first, about the Historical Documents Study itself and why members of the American Society for Legal History were asked to take part. The study originated in a desire on the part of the National Historical Publications and Records Commission to learn more about the researchers who consult sources made available through projects it funds.[2] Recognizing that a study of users of the historical record addressed a larger audience than the Commission itself, the American Council of Learned Societies joined in a cooperative agreement to sponsor the study. By 1990, a number of archives and libraries had launched studies of the users within their walls, but none of those studies could contextualize their results within the universe of repositories or within the population of researchers. The Historical Documents Study set out to explore that larger context by focusing on the researcher and the paths he or she followed to conduct research.

Historical agencies, libraries, and archives serve large and varied populations. At no earlier time in its history have so many people sought historical information in and about the United States. The largest generation of historians ever trained in the nation's graduate schools are in the prime of their intellectual lives. Genealogy ranks as one of the top two or three hobbies in the nation. Historic places and museums report unprecedented numbers of visitors, and concern for the natural and built environments translates into countless studies about the prior use of specific sites. No matter what their purpose or how broad the impact of their research, people should have access to an historical record of the highest quality. Good service to this complex population must be based on good information.

The Historical Documents Study, with the aid of a professional research firm (the Response Analysis Corporation of Princeton, New Jersey), polled 2,225 individuals selected by random samples of members in five historical and genealogical societies. Those societies were chosen to represent some of the known variety among users of the historical record. In members of the Organization of American Historians, the study tapped the largest group of scholars of American history, dominated by professors and graduate students but also encompassing public historians and secondary school teachers. In the American Association for State and Local History and in the National Council on Public History, non-academic professionals dominate. The enormous presence of genealogists in historical archives and libraries led to including the National Genealogical Society and its 12,500 members.

In this company, the American Society for Legal History represented a group of historical specialists based for the most part in academic life, but including legal professionals who pursue history on the side. A sample of 325 people was drawn from the membership of the American Society for Legal History. Completed surveys were received from 145 people, for a response rate of 55.3 percent.

Who are these potential users of law libraries? They are active users of the historical record, with research projects underway. Measured in the number of years engaged in historical research, the American Society for Legal History's membership is tilted toward experience, with few students and a low number of beginners. Indeed, this was the most experienced group in the survey and the one with the smallest number of novices. Two-thirds of them studied history in a doctoral program, a percentage topped in the survey only by members of the Organization of American Historians (OAH). More than three-quarters of the respondents describe their research as occupational rather than avocational, and overwhelmingly that group identify themselves as professors. The percentage of professors exceeds the percentage in the OAH.

To focus only on the clear majority in this group of researchers is, however, to overlook important minorities. Nearly one quarter of the legal historians last studied history in their undergraduate course work, and a similar percentage pursue historical work as an avocation. Against the background of the entire survey population those percentages are not high. Overall, the world of historical researchers tapped by the Historical Document Study's survey divided quite evenly between people who last attended a course in history as a high school or college student and those whose study of history extended into graduate courses for masters or doctoral students. A similar balance existed between those pursuing their avocation and those performing their occupation.

But like many statistics drawn from the survey, these change if the large sample of National Genealogical Society members is removed.

When the legal historians are compared just to the other historical associations, their minorities in training and purpose are distinctive. In the Organization of American Historians and the National Council on Public History, only five percent of the members pursued no graduate training in history. Legal historians report historical education like that of the researchers in the American Association for State and Local History, where twenty-six percent of the members report no graduate courses in history. Presumably, it is the presence of professionals trained in law rather than history that accounts for these numbers. The same comparison, between local and legal historians, holds up with respect to the prevalence of avocational researchers. In those two groups, the percentages of avocational researchers are three to four times higher than in the Organization of American History and the National Council on Public History. Here the difference seems to stem from the presence of lawyers and judges who pursue legal history for pleasure.

The legal historians, by and large, prepare the same biographies, scholarly articles, and monographs produced by members of the Organization of American Historians, but they reported a smattering of applied research: a brief to an appellate court, an exhibit marking the bicentennial of the Bill of Rights, a commissioned history of a circuit court, class lectures for a survey course, and an edition of letters. There are, however, differences in how they define their topics. Where public historians and members of the OAH concentrate on the twentieth century, and even on the latter half of that century, legal historians are asking questions that spread more evenly across the span of American history. They show more interest in the nineteenth century and less inclination to take up topics after 1890. They are most like the local historians in this regard. At the same time, history with a national perspective dominates. Only about one quarter of the legal historians sought to document local events.

Within those broad parameters, legal historians described themselves as particularly interested in studying institutions (30 percent) without reference to informal groups in society. Asked if they were interested in the study of people as individuals, the legal historians, compared to others, were at the high end but only at fifteen percent. When asked to indicate the social characteristics of people in their research, legal and public historians alike were more likely than other groups to indicate that the question was inapplicable. Nonetheless, nearly half of the legal historians indicated that their topic focused solely on men.

One of the ways that the survey sought to explore the practice of historical research was to ask about people's use of libraries and archives. Where did they begin their quest? What was their primary library? And then, over the course of a specific project, what kinds of libraries did they visit? It was an important finding of the study that researchers expect every library to function in some respects as a research institution, regardless of scope and budgets. They begin their inquiries where they can, at a local library, an academic library nearby, an institutional library at their place of work, a special library for genealogical research, or their state library. Much of the time this primary library acts as a switchboard, routing the researcher beyond itself to more specialized institutions. The better the library, the better the research.

The group most confident that they begin their research at the top are members of the American Society for Legal History, sixty-one percent of whom described their primary library as a major research library. A rough category, distinguished in the survey from "library at college or school," it can be said to meet the highest standards for service to researchers. By way of contrast, among members of the Organization of American Historians, nearly three-quarters of whom teach at academic institutions, only half recognized their primary library as a major research library.

Like all researchers in the survey, legal historians will rely, over the course of a project, on numerous libraries and repositories of different types to locate sources and complete their research. But the legal historians display some distinctive patterns in where they choose to go and where they do not venture. They are the dominant users of law libraries. Indeed, given the depth of historical sources within law libraries, it is striking how infrequently other researchers use them. Compare the seventy-six percent of members of the American Society for Legal History visiting law libraries to the next highest reported usage: fourteen percent of members of the Organization of American Historians.

With so many of the legal historians working at academic institutions, it is not surprising to find them also making heavy use of college and university libraries. All of the academic historians show similar use. But the legal historians have not ventured in any great numbers off that path, even to repositories which might be expected to retain records related to law. Their use of the National Archives, any state archives, and branches of local government is, in each case, the lowest of any association; only five percent of them indicated use of presidential libraries; and they rarely turn to independent research libraries (Table 1).

TABLE 1. Types of Libraries Used in Research

| Types of Libraries or Repositories | All Respondents | Without Genealogists | ASLH Members |
|---|---|---|---|
| National Archives | 53% | 35% | 22% |
| Library of Congress | 33% | 32% | 30% |
| Historical societies | 67% | 56% | 35% |
| State archives | 51% | 36% | 25% |
| Local/state government | 37% | 22% | 17% |
| College/university | 60% | 80% | 84% |
| Independent research | 32% | 27% | 17% |
| Law libraries | 10% | 16% | 76% |

It should be added to this discussion that legal historians share with other researchers the limitations imposed by distance and cost of travel in the conduct of their research. Restrictions on their ability to travel to sources was identified by all respondents to the survey as the most frequent obstacle to their use of sources, far out-distancing such well-known obstacles as security classification, privately held sources, poor physical condition, and lack of arrangement and description. Interlibrary loan is one way that researchers try to overcome the difficulties of travel, and eighty-five percent of the legal historians reported that they accessed sources by this means. No doubt some of the considerable use of microfilmed sources (86 percent) also addresses the difficulties of travel. Clearly the more ways that archivists and librarians can integrate the distribution of primary sources into the lending system, the better the chance that the sources will be used.

Most historical researchers turn to a common core of sources long recognized as the basic material of historical research: records and manuscripts from the private sector, government records and documents, and newspapers. But to that core, researchers bring different frames of reference on history and evidence, and they rely upon the sources in different proportions and select different parts of the whole. Legal historians, ninety percent of whom turn to government records, rely heavily on a small range of legislative and judicial sources. The historians least likely to use the census and vital statistics, they are most likely to consult published court cases (77 percent), unpublished records of the courts (53 percent), legislative proceedings (53 percent), and unpublished records of legislatures (20 percent). Their use of newspapers is the lowest among historians, but nonetheless fifty-eight percent of the legal historians look there for evidence (Table 2).

Librarians and archivists often ask if historians choose the best sources for their projects and criticize them as unsystematic in their search. It is possible that the selection of sources follows the path of least resistance. Legal historians' preference for published texts of court decisions over other judicial sources, for instance, allows them to use the indexing and retrieval systems designed for the legal profession, which is no small advantage. According to the results of the Historical Documents Study's survey, researchers have their own systems which may not be recognizable as such to librarians and archivists. When researchers want to locate sources, they piece together the information that they need from a variety of systems. Most of all they rely on their own past experience (64 percent). At lower rates they depend on leads from reference librarians and archivists (48 percent), information gleaned from footnotes (44 percent), and published guides to sources (40 percent).

Researchers relied most of all on their own experience in related research. They regard the hunt for sources, in other words, as an acquired skill. Confidence that past experience proves vital to the search grows with years of practice; newcomers credited experience only

TABLE 2. Usefulness of Sources to Legal Historians

| Types of Sources | Percentage Not Using | Percentage Rating Indispensable |
|---|---|---|
| Artifacts | 81% | 5% |
| Audio materials | 86% | 3% |
| Government records | 10% | 68% |
| Institutional records | 25% | 36% |
| Machine-readable data | 72% | 6% |
| Maps | 57% | 6% |
| Moving images | 84% | 4% |
| Newspapers | 28% | 28% |
| Oral histories | 73% | 9% |
| Pamphlets/published ephemera | 33% | 12% |
| Personal interviews | 64% | 11% |
| Photographs/still images | 56% | 15% |
| Records/manuscripts | 24% | 50% |

thirty-seven percent of the time, while seventy-eight percent of the veterans of twenty or more years did so. But researchers run the risk of restricting themselves to variations on an old theme, while limiting the impact of innovative reference services.

Among members of the American Society for Legal History and the Organization of American Historians, leads from footnotes and citations mark the most common path to sources. The system is conservative by its very nature, and it too may draw too close a circle around a subject and blind researchers not only to other finding aids but also to new sources. When seventy-nine percent of the legal historians say they rely on footnotes (the highest percentage in the survey) and only thirty-two percent rely on either guides or reference professionals (the lowest percentages), it is difficult to see how their pool of sources will expand. At the same time, the footnotes are the core of the discipline, documenting the cumulative knowledge about sources and marking the boundaries of intellectual debate.

Members of the American Society for Legal History are exceptional in the survey for how few of them (32 percent) credited reference librarians or archivists with leading them to sources. Since the same group also credits reference staff least with teaching them skills, there may be a special problem about reference in law or the relationship between "legal" and "historical" reference services that deserves separate investigation.

Any conversation about intervening in the research behavior of historians needs to recognize the rather complicated picture of how they first learned their skills and acquire new skills over the course of their careers. Significant numbers of researchers did not pursue graduate work in history at any level, and to the extent that departments of history omit research methods from their undergraduate courses, pushing such instruction upward into graduate programs, it is a fact that many active researchers never received formal instruction in the conduct of historical research. In the American Society for Legal History, that number is twenty-two percent of the membership.

Even the academically trained historian cannot rely on graduate training as in itself sufficient preparation for a lifetime of research. Tools, topics, and interests change. There are historians active today whose formal education predates the start of national guides to unpublished sources forty years ago, for example. The explosion of related finding aids and computerized networks for sources since that time has challenged successive waves of historians to augment their skills after leaving school. Changing interests also push individuals beyond the limits taken for granted when they first studied their craft.

The Historical Documents Study's survey asked participants to indicate how they acquired their skills for finding and using historical sources. Members of the American Society for Legal History reported a unique and rather self-reliant pattern. Only genealogists relied more on self-instruction, yet the legal historians were five times as likely as genealogists to have studied history in graduate school and six times as likely to credit graduate courses with teaching them skills. No other group relied less on friends and colleagues with similar interests to learn research, and no other group turned to librarians and archivists less often. Participants in special workshops or institutes were so few as barely to register in a small sample (Table 3).

Legal librarians are probably in a better position than I am to speculate about what in this profile of historians might have changed in the last decade. At the time of the survey in 1991, Lawrence M. Friedman's optimistic report on legal history's growth and sophistication was still fresh.[3] There is no reason to suspect any setbacks since that time, but insofar as Friedman described competing schools of legal history, there is reason to uncover where growth occurred since he wrote.

As a reader of legal history, I would venture to say that the percentage of historians declaring that they studied only men would be lower today if the survey were repeated. More than a decade ago, the Research Libraries Group, in the course of a study about the cutting edge of research in the humanities, uncovered a need, among others, for legal historians to retrieve unofficial contemporary accounts of trials. Although that need was not evident in the Historical Documents Study's data on the sources used by legal historians, it indicates the kind of changes in evaluating evidence that can occur in a field. If it proved to be an accurate prediction, or if other shifts in evidence have occurred, significant num-

TABLE 3. Ways of Learning Research Skills

| Ways of Learning Research Skills | All Respondents | Without Genealogists | ASLH Members |
|---|---|---|---|
| Self-instruction | 79% | 71% | 74% |
| Reference services | 67% | 65% | 53% |
| Colleagues/friends | 57% | 53% | 46% |
| Graduate courses | 45% | 77% | 64% |
| Workshops/institutes | 39% | 17% | 7% |

bers of legal historians may be seeking new sources and tackling new means of identification and retrieval.

Indubitably, the rapid expansion of electronic finding aids and library catalogues since 1991 has changed the steps that all historians take in the course of their research. Owing to the early use of electronic media for legal references, legal historians were in 1991 already ahead of their colleagues in their ability and willingness to use electronic databases to find their sources.

None of these changes would render the basic portrait of research in legal history irrelevant. Librarians and archivists can still usefully contemplate many of the needs identified in the survey. Most important may be to realize and address the disparity in training, the fact that a significant number of workers in legal history lack formal training in historical research. At the same time, those responsible for reference services in law libraries may be called upon to serve disparate needs–those of legal practice and scholarship, on the one hand, and those of legal history, on the other. If librarians and archivists can define for themselves what distinguishes the questions those two groups ask, they will be better able to assist the historians. Many law libraries are also in a position to offer workshops in historical research that would highlight their own holdings, display their reference capabilities, and offer valuable opportunities for legal historians to continue their education. If librarians taught ways to retrieve a more varied record, the historians might be encouraged to use more varied sources. Finally, such workshops aimed at a wider audience might address the larger challenge facing law libraries with good historical sources, and that is, the remarkably low use of their facilities and resources by historians other than those identified as legal historians.

## NOTES

1. The Historical Documents Study published a report in 1992, *Using the Nation's Documentary Heritage: The Report of the Historical Documents Study*, authored by Ann D. Gordon. Recently and inexplicably, the National Historical Publications and Records Commission destroyed its remaining supply of the report, but in response to new requests for copies, the Executive Director has indicated that the agency will post the report on its web site. You may contact the staff at <nhprc@archl.nara.gov>. Ann Gordon also published a series of articles with findings from the study and survey. These are: "A National Study on the Uses of Historical Documents: An Inside Story," *Carolina Comments* 40 (May 1992), 70-75; "Learning Skills to Find Historical Evidence," *OAH Newsletter*, May 1992; "Framing Questions and Seeking Answers: OAH Members Conduct Research," *OAH Newsletter*, Nov. 1992; "A Mirror on the Associa-

tion [of State and Local History]: Some Findings of the Historical Documents Study," *History News* 47 (Nov./Dec. 1992), 14-18; "Who's Minding the Sources? Recommendations from the Historical Documents Study," *Perspectives: American Historical Association Newsletter* 30 (Nov. 1992), 7-8; and "The Historical Documents Study and Members of the National Genealogical Society," *NGS Newsletter* 18 (July-Aug. 1992), 97-99.

2. Created by Congress in 1934, the National Historical Publications and Records Commission has a mandate to undertake activities for the publication, preservation, and use of documentary sources relating to the history of the United States. Since 1950, it has carried out that charge by the encouragement and support of documentary publications. In 1975, Congress added to its responsibilities programs to ensure the preservation of non-federal historical records.

3. Lawrence M. Friedman, "American Legal History: Past and Present," 34 *Journal of Legal Education* 563 (1984).

# Helping Historians Write Legal History "From Below": Collecting New Sources, Teaching New Strategies

David Warrington

**SUMMARY.** In the past fifty years, legal history has turned from a concentration on legal texts to a broader view of the social, political, and economic conditions that affected a particular legal system at a given time in the history of a nation. To assist scholars in realizing the potential of these new methodologies, law librarians who work with historical materials must have a firm grasp of the developing trends in legal historiography. This article outlines the information sources that a librarian may use to become familiar with the literature in legal historiography and, using practices at the Harvard Law School Library as examples, suggests ways that a library can form collections of non-traditional genres of research materials that support these new approaches to legal history. *[Article copies available for a fee from The Haworth Document Delivery Service: 1-800-342-9678. E-mail address: <getinfo@haworthpressinc.com> Website: <http://www.HaworthPress.com> © 2001 by The Haworth Press, Inc. All rights reserved.]*

---

David Warrington, Librarian for Special Collections at the Harvard Law School since 1986, co-teaches a course, "Collecting the History of Anglo-American Law," with Morris Cohen, Librarian Emeritus of the Yale Law School, at the University of Virginia's Rare Book School.

[Haworth co-indexing entry note]: "Helping Historians Write Legal History 'From Below': Collecting New Sources, Teaching New Strategies." Warrington, David. Co-published simultaneously in *Legal Reference Services Quarterly* (The Haworth Information Press, an imprint of The Haworth Press, Inc.) Vol. 20, No. 1/2, 2001, pp. 17-27; and: *Public Services Issues with Rare and Archival Law Materials* (ed: Michael Widener) The Haworth Information Press, an imprint of The Haworth Press, Inc., 2001, pp. 17-27. Single or multiple copies of this article are available for a fee from The Haworth Document Delivery Service [1-800-342-9678, 9:00 a.m. - 5:00 p.m. (EST). E-mail address: getinfo@haworthpressinc.com].

© 2001 by The Haworth Press, Inc. All rights reserved.

Legal history has traditionally been written from the perspective of the custodians of the law. The decisions of judges, the enactments of legislators, and the interpretations of treatise writers and legal educators are the raw materials from which, until very recent times, our knowledge of the history of the law was principally constructed. Underpinning this mainstream legal history is a positivist vision of the law that assumes that "law is embodied in authoritative, official texts called statutes, cases, and treatises"; to discover what the law was at a particular time in history, "legal historians typically begin (and often end) by learning what legal texts say was the law."[1] Much of our basic understanding of the history of the law comes from the monuments erected by this approach, Sir William Holdsworth's sixteen-volume *History of English Law* (1922-1966) being perhaps the most prominent.

Beginning in the 1950s with the work of J. Willard Hurst and his colleagues at the University of Wisconsin and in the 1960s in England with the work of E. P. Thompson, the writing of legal history took a new turn. Scholarship in the field over the past half-century has focused on the social, political, and economic conditions that affected a particular legal system at a given time in the history of a nation. "From the bottom up," in Thompson's phrase, or "from below" in Hendrik Hartog's, legal scholars are investigating how those who were not primary stake holders in a legal culture "learned to shape their own meanings and public values to conform to a language recognized as legal discourse."[2] In this pursuit, researchers have drawn not only on cases, laws, and the literature of bench, bar, and academe but also on economic and business records, sociological data, newspapers, and the dockets, case files, and other records preserved by courts. They have turned to manuscript sources such as the personal and professional papers of lawyers and judges and to such quasi-legal materials as the constitutions and by-laws of voluntary associations, manuals of parliamentary procedures, and popular accounts of sensational trials. New insights into the role of the law in the life of the ordinary citizen have even come from such unlikely sources as the diaries and letters of emigrants on the Overland Trail and ships' logs and seamen's records.[3] Using these new sources, legal historians are now writing legal history not only from the perspective of a legal culture's establishment but also from that of those whom the law was intended to regulate.

To assist scholars in realizing the potential of these new methodologies, law librarians who work with historical materials must themselves have a firm grasp of the developing trends in legal historiography. Moreover, they must be aware of non-traditional genres of research materials that can be used for research in legal history. If their library has the capability to collect primary research materials, they should advocate the formation of collections that their institution may be uniquely positioned to acquire. This article outlines the information sources that a librarian may use to become familiar with the literature in legal historiography and, using practices at the Harvard Law School Library as examples, suggests ways that a library can form collections of materials that support these new approaches to legal history.

A concise overview of current trends in legal history–particularly good, I think, for those new to the field–can be found in Dan R. Ernst's survey article, "Law and American Political Development, 1877-1938."[4] Ernst does an excellent job in tracing the development of the main strands of legal historiography over the past half century, and his footnotes point to the principal landmarks in the literature. The author's scope encompasses not only the scholarship written by professional historians and law professors but also that of social and political scientists, and while his article focuses on the history of the development of legal institutions in America during the late nineteenth and early twentieth centuries, his discussion surveys recent methodologies that have been applied to a wide variety of topics in Anglo-American legal history. Students lament the cessation in the mid-1980s of William Nelson and John P. Reid's exhaustive annual survey, the *Literature of American Legal History*; Professor Ernst helps fill the gap with his examples of leading articles in such trends of the past decade as critical legal history and cultural and gender studies.

Terry Fisher's "Texts and Contexts: The Application to American Legal History of the Methodologies of Intellectual History" is a thorough examination of a major strand in current legal historiography and a fine example of the work of a leading legal historian.[5] One of several essays in a special issue of the *Stanford Law Review* inspired by a November, 1996 symposium on the critical use of history, the article describes and applies "four methodologies derived from Intellectual History–Structuralism, Contextualism, Textualism and New Historicism–to nine possible projects that legal historians might seek to advance through their research and writings."[6] The discussion and footnotes in Fisher's opening sections on modern American intellectual history and how the principal methodologies in the field have influenced the study of legal history serve as an excellent introduction to the current issues in historiography that confront legal historians. The concluding portion of the article "argues that these methodological innovations are best evaluated from a purposive or pragmatic standpoint; it considers nine possible uses of history in general and legal history in particular, [e.g., explain why events transpired as they did and why they did not come out differently], then considers which of the four methodologies, if any, is best suited to the attainment of those ends."[7] Even though his examples are drawn solely from intellectual history, Fisher is particularly successful, I believe, in his treatment of what legal historians should consider when selecting a methodology.

The major law reviews and the principal journals in history and the social sciences publish legal history illustrative of the new methodologies in the field. Only a handful of these, however, publish this research consistently. *Law & Social Inquiry,* until 1988 the *American Bar Foundation Research Journal,* is a leading forum for this scholarship. The journal regularly publishes a "review section symposium," a feature in which several specialists survey and criticize the current literature on a topic; this is frequently followed with commentaries by other scholars conversant with these developments. Recent symposia have examined feminist jurisprudence, the legacy of *Lochner,* and the Wisconsin influence on sociolegal scholarship.[8] A similar feature, the review essay, often includes a response by the author whose book is being reviewed and a rejoinder by the reviewer. Recent examples are Lawrence M. Friedman's review of Peter Karsten's *Heart versus Head: Judge-Made Law in Nineteenth-Century America* (1997) and Brook Thomas's review of Michael Grossberg's *A Judgment for Solomon: the D'Hauteville Case and Legal Experience in Antebellum America* (1996).[9] Other exemplary articles on legal history published by the journal in recent years are Michael Grossberg's "Crossing Boundaries: Nineteenth-Century Domestic Relations Law and the Merger of Family and Legal History," Matthew J. Lindsay's "Reproducing a Fit Citizenry: Dependency, Eugenics, and the Law of Marriage in the United States, 1860-1920," and Susan D. Carle's "Lawyers' Duty to Do Justice: A New Look at the History of the 1908 Canons."[10]

The *Law & History Review,* the scholarly journal of the American Society for Legal History (ASLH), is another excellent source of articles in the fields of the social history of law and the history of legal ideas and institutions. Reflecting the intellectual interests of the Society's membership, the journal covers topics from all periods and legal traditions. Like *Law & Social Inquiry,* it frequently contains a cluster of articles, called the "Forum," devoted to a particular topic. Recent issues have featured fora on eighteenth-century English legal history, the intellectual history of law and economics, legal culture in eighteenth-century New York, and the inception of case method teaching at the

Harvard Law School.[11] Occasionally an entire issue will be devoted to a single topic; the recent "Engaging Willard Hurst: A Symposium" assesses the work and influence of the most prominent American legal historian of the twentieth century.[12] Two related journals, the *American Journal of Legal History* and the *Journal of Legal History,* also publish articles in the field.

Among the student-edited law reviews that consistently publish legal historiography are those at Yale, Chicago, Wisconsin, and Stanford. Of these, the *Yale Law Journal* is clearly the leader. From Robert W. Gordon's seminal article, "Historicism in Legal Scholarship" (1981), to last year's symposium issue, "Moments of Change: Transformation in American Constitutionalism," its editors have selected trend-setting scholarship in legal historiography.[13] Recent articles have theorized on interdisciplinary studies and on the pitfalls of according judicial history the same weight as legislative history.[14] Also produced in New Haven is the *Yale Journal of Law & the Humanities,* a semiannual journal devoted to interdisciplinary investigations of the law and the liberal arts, which often publishes incisive articles on legal history.

The two mainstream journals for academic historians, the *Journal of American History* and the *American Historical Review,* frequently publish in the field. The former has a regular section, "Recent Scholarship," which annually lists some 5,000 books, articles, dissertations, and CD-ROMs. Its usefulness to scholars will be greatly enhanced next year, as its cumulative database is placed online, searchable by topic, keywords, and dates. The American Historical Association and the Organization of American Historians, publishers of the *American Historical Review* and the *Journal of American History,* respectively, have formed a cooperative to make current issues of the journals available online and to provide access to special databases including "Recent Scholarship."[15]

Another good source of bibliographical essays covering American legal history is *Reviews in American History.* Current issues are available online through Project Muse; issues before 1995 can be found on JSTOR, the online journal storage project.[16] In addition to Dan Ernst's fine article discussed above, recent issues of *Reviews in American History* have included comprehensive surveys of such historiographical topics as methodological approaches to American conservatism and the role of problem-oriented historical inquiry.[17]

Librarians who wish to acquire a working knowledge of current trends in legal historiography should regularly examine the journals discussed above. Most of these publications have web sites that reproduce the tables of contents of recent issues (often with abstracts of the articles). Bookmarking these and checking the pages periodically makes it easy to maintain awareness of developments in the field.

Another good way of learning about trends in legal history is to subscribe to H-Law, an on-line discussion list dealing with constitutional and legal history. Sponsored by the ASLH, the moderated list not only posts "material relevant to the intellectual, professional, and scholarly concerns of legal and constitutional historians" but also contains conference announcements, book reviews, calls for papers, and updates on archives, libraries, and museums.[18] The discussions recorded on the list are a barometer of research trends and topics. Contents are archived and both keywords and discussion threads are accessible through the H-Law web page. Incidentally, anyone with more than just a passing interest in legal history should join the ASLH. In addition to *Law & History Review* and H-Law, the Society sponsors "Studies in Legal History," a series of book-length monographs, and publishes a semiannual newsletter. Its annual conferences are a lively mixture of lectures, panel discussions, and networking.

A firm grasp of the methodologies of legal history, coupled with a knowledge of how to locate primary materials beyond those genres typically found in law libraries, make it possible for librarians to assist patrons working on contemporary problems in legal history. But librarians can and should go a step further. They should be advocates for the formation of research collections that their libraries may be in a good position to assemble. Among these may be the archives of their own institution, the professional papers of their faculty, genres of legal or quasi-legal materials that support the research needs of faculty, and primary legal materials generated by local institutions not otherwise likely to be collected.

All law schools preserve at least some of their records. Librarians interested in legal history will appreciate that the history of their own institution is a part of the general history of legal education. Even if the archives of the school are subsumed in those of the parent institution, librarians should be familiar with what is collected and ensure that records documenting the history of the school are being preserved.[19] Similarly, the professional papers of law school faculty reflect the intellectual, administrative, and social environment of the institution. They supplement published works by providing information on the faculty member's teaching style, scholarly and professional interests, and collaboration with others. Correspondence, memoranda, meeting notes, and drafts of articles and books offer a valuable perspective on the life of the institution as well as on the creative processes of the individual. Preserving the papers of faculty, particularly of those who have made major contributions to scholarship, the profession, or the institution, ensures the availability of primary research materials for tomorrow's historians.[20] My own library has collected the papers of more than fifty members of the Harvard Law School faculty, spanning the history of the School from the days of Joseph Story and Simon Greenleaf to the present.

Historians are increasingly making use of other types of materials produced in law schools, such as student notebooks. These notebooks can encompass any written record that a student has compiled from her own reading, from lectures that she has heard, and from discussions she has had with fellow students in preparation for moots and other exercises. In the history of the common law, these notebooks stretch from the accounts of the readings and moots of early English legal history to those being compiled by law students today on countless laptops. For over a century the Harvard Law School Library has collected such notebooks, from those of students taught by famous legal educators such as William Blackstone and Tapping Reeve to those compiled by students in law schools associated with colleges and universities. Today the collection numbers more than two hundred sets, of which more than 160 were created by students at Harvard. Many others were compiled in the nineteenth century by students at law schools in Albany, Ann Arbor, Litchfield, New Haven, New York, and Northampton, Massachusetts.

Student notebooks record exactly what was being taught in the classroom (discounted, of course, for student inattention). A number of notebooks recording Blackstone's lectures have survived; and an analysis of these provides information on the way he presented his course of legal studies later commemorated in the *Commentaries.* With the development of the case method of law teaching, student notebooks from the Harvard Law School of the last decades of the nineteenth century disclose the patterns of doctrinal logic Langdell and his disciples wished to inculcate through their analyses of appellate decisions.

In many cases notebooks survive of students who themselves became prominent legal educators. Not only is the Harvard Law School Library fortunate in owning all of the notes that Felix Frankfurter took in his classes as a Harvard law student, but it also has more than twenty notebooks recorded by his own students. In at least one instance, we have notes taken by two of Frankfurter's students who were in the very same class. A compilation of the two allows the researcher to overcome even the vagaries of student inattention!

Legal historians draw on these materials in imaginative ways. At the Harvard Law School Library, Bruce Kimball has used lecture notes and annotated casebooks from the papers of Christopher Columbus Langdell and James Barr Ames, along with student notes taken in Langdell's and Ames's classes, to reconstruct "three class discussions from the period 1870-1883, when case method was introduced into legal and professional education in the United States."[21] For example, a class discussion from Langdell's course in the fall of 1875 on jurisdiction and procedure in equity is reconstructed from five heavily annotated copies of Langdell's *Cases in Equity Pleading*: Langdell's own copy annotated with his teaching notes; two copies in which students recorded their extensive notes; and two copies annotated by Ames, one when he audited this class, and another annotated later for use when he co-taught the course with Langdell in 1877.[22]

In addition to advocating the preservation of school archives and faculty papers, librarians who wish to foster research in legal history at their institutions may also want to build collections that support the specialties of their faculties. If a school has a strong program in environmental law, for instance, it may well wish to complement the acquisition of faculty members' papers with collections of materials relating to important trials, organizations, or events in environmental law in which those faculty were involved.

If a professor specializes in a particular topic in legal history, it may be possible for the library to form collections that support that faculty member's research. Faculty are often aware of research materials in their specialty—family papers, the records of an organization, a genre of research material—that the library may be able to acquire. A professor who is studying the legal history of a local industry, for example, may know of the existence of records of companies in the field no longer in business. Within its ability to care for such records, the library may wish to acquire them or to assist in their relocation to another local repository. Willard Hurst and his colleagues certainly would not have been able to write their trail-blazing legal histories of the lumber industry in Wisconsin without access to such records.

In his recent inaugural lecture as Downing Professor of the Laws of England at Cambridge University, John Baker discussed the "basic truth that history cannot be written in any reliable way until the best evidence has been harvested." Speaking of the founder of the modern discipline of legal history, Professor Baker noted that "[F. W.] Maitland's approach to legal history, which we all now take for granted, was to uncover as far as possible the original records and writings that constitute the body of contemporary evidence, and then to interpret them according to the social and intellectual setting in which they were produced."[23] The uncovering of these records and writings is a task far from completion, he continued, and observing the situation in England, reported:

> There are collections of cause papers, solicitors' archives, and the papers of government departments, organizations and individuals involved in litigation, not to mention printed pamphlets, newspapers, and (as we reach modern times) oral evidence. Little has yet been done with this kind of material, though the pioneering work of Professor Simpson has shown how it can shatter traditional illusions. For the centuries nearest our own we ought to have the most complete picture of all; but it has only been sketched in outline.[24]

The situation is arguably better in the United States, but much remains to be done here, too. We as research librarians have the rewarding task of helping to identify and preserve the materials from which reliable legal history will be written, and through our awareness of the new approaches to the discipline, of assisting in the education of those who will write it.

## NOTES

1. Hendrik Hartog, "Introduction: Legal Histories From Below," 1985 *Wisconsin Law Review* 761 (1985).

2. E.P. Thompson, *The Making of the English Working Class* 12 (1963); Hartog, *supra*, note 1 at 765.

3. J. Reid, *Law for the Elephant: Property And Social Behavior on the Overland Trail* (1980); A.W. Brian Simpson, *Cannibalism and the Common Law: The Story of the Tragic Last Voyage of the Mignonette and the Strange Legal Proceedings to Which It Gave Rise* (1984).

4. 26 *Reviews in American History* 205 (1998); available on the Internet through Project Muse.

5. William W. Fisher, III, "Texts and Contexts: The Application to American Legal History of the Methodologies of Intellectual History," 49 *Stanford Law Review* 1065 (1997).

6. "Introduction," 49 *Stanford Law Review* 1021 (1997). The other articles in this issue contribute to what its editor, Robert Gordon, believes "may well be the most exciting work currently being done on law": R. Gordon, "Foreword: The Arrival of Critical Historicism" (noting trends in this methodology since his pioneering 1981 *Yale Law Journal* article, "Historicism in Legal Scholarship"); J. Rakove, "The Origins of Judicial Review: A Plea for New Contexts" (re-examining traditional views of *Marbury v. Madison* as the source for judicial review); R. Siegel, "Why Equal Protection No Longer Protects: The Evolving Forms of Status-Enforcing State Action" (examining how standard interpretations of nineteenth-century race and gender status law

affect our understanding of current manifestations of gender and racial subordination); and G. Binder & R. Weisberg, "Cultural Criticism of Law" (advocating a "New Historicist" approach to placing legal disputes and transactions in context).

7. *Id.* at 1065.

8. Adelaide H. Villmoare, "Feminist Jurisprudence and Political Vision," 24 *Law & Social Inquiry* 443 (1999); Linda C. McClain, "The Liberal Future of Relational Feminism: Robin West's *Caring for Justice*," 24 *Law & Social Inquiry* 477 (1999); Jonathan Boyarin, "Law, Literature, and the Resurrection of Contract," 24 *Law & Social Inquiry* 195 (1999); Gary D. Rowe, "*Lochner* Revisionism Revisited," 24 *Law & Social Inquiry* 221 (1999); William J. Woodward, "Clearing the Underbrush for Read-Life Contracting," 24 *Law & Social Inquiry* 99 (1999); Jonathan Simon, "Law after Society," 24 *Law & Social Inquiry* 143 (1999).

9. Lawrence M. Friedman, "Losing One's Head: Judges and the Law in Nineteenth-Century American Legal History," 24 *Law & Social Inquiry* 253 (1999); Brook Thomas, "Michael Grossberg's Telling Tale: The Social Drama of an Antebellum Custody Case," 23 *Law & Social Inquiry* 431 (1998).

10. 1985 *American Bar Foundation Research Journal* 799 (1986); 23 *Law & Social Inquiry* 541 (1998); 24 *Law & Social Inquiry* 1 (1999).

11. "Symposium: English Legal History in the Age of Mansfield," 12 *Law & History Review* 93 (1994); "Forum: On the Intellectual History of Law and Economics," 15 *Law & History Review* 275 (1997); "Forum: Constitutions on Edge: Empire, State, and Legal Culture in Eighteenth-Century New York," 16 *Law & History Review* 257 (1998); "Forum: That Impecunious Introvert from New Hampshire: Re-Imagining Langdell," 17 *Law & History Review* 57 (1999).

12. 18 *Law & History Review* 1 (2000).

13. 90 *Yale Law Journal* 1017 (1981); 108 *Yale Law Journal* 1917 (1999).

14. Jane B. Baron, "Law, Literature, and the Problems of Interdisciplinarity," 108 *Yale Law Journal* 1059 (1999); Adrian Vermeule, "Judicial History," 108 *Yale Law Journal* 1059 (1999).

15. Information about the cooperative is available at <http://www.historycooperative.org>.

16. Information about Project Muse can be found at <http://muse.jhu.edu; and for JSTOR at <http://www.jstor.org>.

17. Leonard J. Moore, "Good Old-Fashioned New Social History and the Twentieth Century American Right," 24 *Reviews in American History* 555 (1996); Michael Kammen, "An Americanist's Reprise: the Pervasive Role of Histoire Problieme in Historical Scholarship Concerning the United States Since the 1960's," 26 *Reviews in American History* 1 (1998).

18. Information about H-Law, including instructions for subscribing, is available at <http://www2.h-net.msu.edu/~law>.

19. A good overview of issues related to the preservation of records of educational institutions can be found in W. Maher, *The Management of College and University Archives* (1992).

20. Research using faculty papers and other manuscripts has been greatly facilitated in the past few years with the development of encoded archival description, a technique that allows finding aids to these collections to be placed on the Internet. A good example is the finding aid to the papers of the University of Michigan law professor and dean, Thomas McIntyre Cooley (1824-1898), housed at the Bentley Library: <http://www.umich.edu/~bhl/bhl/uarphome/tcooley.htm>.

21. Bruce A. Kimball, "'Warn Students That I Entertain Heretical Opinions, Which They Are Not to Take as Law': The Inception of the Case Method Teaching in the Classrooms of the Early C.C. Langdell, 1870-1883," 17 *Law & History Review* 57, 77 (1999).

22. *Id.* at 99.

23. J. Baker, *Why the History of English Law Has Not Been Finished* (1999), 4.

24. *Id.* at 22.

# Training Law Librarians in the Use of Rare Legal Materials

Morris L. Cohen

**SUMMARY.** Librarians and archivists need special training in the use of rare law books and manuscripts that includes not only the protective functions with respect to rare materials but also education in the history of law, its literature, and its historical methodology. The article describes two different training programs: one, at Yale, trains law students in the use of historical legal materials; and the other, at the University of Virginia Rare Book School, trains librarians, archivists, historians, collectors and dealers in the care and use of rare law books and manuscripts. The article concludes with suggestions for model curricula for law librarians in the use of rare materials. *[Article copies available for a fee from The Haworth Document Delivery Service: 1-800-342-9678. E-mail address: <getinfo@haworthpressinc.com> Website: <http://www.HaworthPress.com> © 2001 by The Haworth Press, Inc. All rights reserved.]*

---

Morris L. Cohen has been Professor Emeritus of Law and Professorial Lecturer in Law at Yale Law School since 1992. He holds a BA from the University of Chicago, a JD from Columbia University, an MLS from Pratt Institute Library School and an Honorary LLD from Dalhousie University. Mr. Cohen previously headed the law libraries at SUNY-Buffalo, the University of Pennsylvania, Harvard, and Yale. He has also taught in the library schools at Simmons College, Columbia University, and Drexel University, and in the summer Rare Book Schools at the University of Virginia. He has authored numerous works on legal research and legal history, most recently the landmark *Bibliography of Early American Law* (6 vols., 1998).

[Haworth co-indexing entry note]: "Training Law Libraries in the Use of Rare Legal Materials." Cohen, Morris L. Co-published simultaneously in *Legal Reference Services Quarterly* (The Haworth Information Press, an imprint of The Haworth Press, Inc.) Vol. 20, No. 1/2, 2001, pp. 29-39; and: *Public Services Issues with Rare and Archival Law Materials* (ed: Michael Widener) The Haworth Information Press, an imprint of The Haworth Press, Inc., 2001, pp. 29-39. Single or multiple copies of this article are available for a fee from The Haworth Document Delivery Service [1-800-342-9678, 9:00 a.m. - 5:00 p.m. (EST). E-mail address: getinfo@haworthpressinc.com].

The profession of law librarianship has been shaped significantly by the materials within its charge. Subject specialization has been a major focus of training for law librarianship, for planning of legal reference services, for design of law classification, and for collection development. More law librarians have had formal training in their subject discipline than is true in other library fields.

Similarly, more time is spent on bibliographic instruction in law schools than in training for other professions. Electronic storage and retrieval of research information became available in law at about the same time that it became available for medical science, but the attention given to training both law librarians and lawyers in the new technology has been far greater than comparable efforts in health sciences.

With a strong tradition that emphasizes the importance of specialized training in both research methods and legal bibliography, it is therefore not surprising that special training in the use of rare law books and manuscripts for both librarians and readers is necessary. The centrality of legal history in both the study and the practice of law can be seen in its growing presence in the law school curriculum, in the pages of academic journals, and in the decisions of our appellate courts. Many of the major debates in constitutional law, jurisprudence, and other areas of law today are arguments over historical interpretations.[1] The complexity of the history of our law and legal system adds further to the need for special training.[2] Such training therefore must include not only the protective functions of the librarian's special custodial role with respect to rare materials but also education in the history of law, its literature, and its historical methodology.

Since law librarians and legal researchers deal with historical materials in very different ways, it should not be surprising that the preparation required for their respective roles would differ. Law librarians define collection parameters for rare and other historical materials; within those parameters, they select materials for acquisition; they also catalog materials, provide reference services, offer bibliographic instruction, establish and implement policies for use, and for preservation and conservation. In addition, while carrying out those functions, they perform many of the same research activities as do other readers. Legal researchers, on the other hand, carry on more limited functions. They identify and locate specific documents; read, analyze and interpret them; and use them in the development of an argument or as justification for a particular position, action or forbearance. The training of these two classes of people overlap to a minor degree, but are quite different. Training general librarians for the administration of rare materials and special collections has been discussed in the periodical literature,[3] but there has been little attention given to preparing law librarians for this work.

I have been involved in two quite different programs relating to such training: one, at Yale, training law students in the use of historical (not necessarily rare) legal materials; and the other, at the University of Virginia Rare Book School (with David Warrington), training librarians, historians, collectors and dealers in the care and use of rare law books and manuscripts. This paper will briefly describe each of these programs and then suggest model curricula for law librarians in the use of rare materials.

For each of the last three years, I have taught a seminar to a few law students on Research Methods in American Legal History. It is described in the Yale Law School catalog as follows:

> Research Methods in American Legal History. This seminar will examine the methods and major materials used in American historical legal research. It will cover judicial, statutory, and constitutional sources; government documents; biographical materials; manuscript collections; crime literature; court records; and early American international law.

I developed the course when I realized that students interested in historical research (and that was an ever-increasing group at my law school) were not equipped for such work even if they had taken our advanced legal research offering. Several judges had also indicated to me that weakness in law student training generally. My goal was to give the students a good introduction to the bibliographic sources of American legal history, regardless of format or date of publication, so that, when faced with a research problem, they would know roughly what types of material might be available and how they could identify and locate specific materials relevant to their problem. The treatment of methodology included comparative analysis of alternative research approaches; criteria for determining the priority order of research steps; and training in the use of various search strategies. Class discussion of hypothetical research problems and the writing of a term paper on a substantive topic or a pathfinder on a specific field of legal history gave the students opportunities to apply and test the knowledge gained from their reading and from the instructional presentations.

The seminar focuses equally on historical sources of American law and research methods in American legal history–that is, what are the sources and how do we research them. Electronic sources, micro-facsimiles, and modern reprints have been dealt with as much as old leather and buckram since our concern is with the content of the material, not its form. Today, of course, much legal history can be researched without recourse to old books and manuscripts, but original texts do heighten interest and can refocus wandering minds and reopen eyes that are glazing.

The areas covered in this seminar, week by week, have been as follows:

- Historical sources of American law; American law during the colonial period.
- Overview of bibliographic sources (general and legal), including RLIN, OCLC, E.S.T.C., E.A.I., N.U.C., periodical indices, historical abstracts, etc.
- Research in early (pre-1880) case law.
- Research in early statutory law and legislative history.
- Constitutional research (federal and state).
- Research in federal government documents (including the *Serial Set*).
- Biographical materials (general and legal); manuscript collections and personal papers.
- Researching crimes and criminal law (including trials).
- Legal ephemera (including student notebooks, commonplace books, court calendars and dockets, almanacs, advertisements, broadside notices, etc.).
- Court records (federal and state).
- Practice materials (court rules, legal forms, legal manuals); secondary sources for reconstructing the legal and public context (treatises, periodicals, newspapers, law lectures and student texts).
- Early American sources of international law and relations.
- Historical research in legal language.
- Coordinating historical research.

Selected readings from various published sources were assigned and often discussed in class. George Grossman's *Legal Research: Historical Foundations of the Electronic Age* was assigned for several classes. Guest lecturers gave the class presentation in four of the specialized sessions. A reference librarian from the University Library who specializes in American history participated throughout the term as a resource person for electronic databases on history. She was an invaluable co-teacher, in part because of the increasing value of non-legal, particularly historical, databases in legal research, and also because of her teaching skill and ability to bring in the perspective of a trained historian. Despite my intent and design that the seminar be a form of skills training, the historical content of the readings, the hypotheticals, and much of the class discussion imparted a substantive flavor to the proceedings. That was probably on balance a good thing and stimulated more interest on the part of the students. I believe (and students who took the course agreed) that it was successful for the stated purposes, but it has never attracted more than a handful of takers.

The second program relevant to this topic is a five-day course usually called "Rare Law Books and Manuscripts," co-taught with David Warrington, Head of Special Collections in the Harvard Law School Library. We offered this course at the Rare Book School, directed by Terry Belanger, in 1989 and 1990, when the school was at the Columbia University Library School, and then in 1993, 1995 and 1998, when it had moved to the University of Virginia. The students were not matriculating for a degree, and included librarians (usually from law libraries), antiquarian booksellers, collectors of law books, and (at its last offering) legal historians. These were intensive programs, meeting for almost seven hours a day, with work on library problems during at least two of the evenings. Preparatory readings were assigned before the program began and some reading was expected during the week of classes. Two written problems were completed and the results presented in class. There was much show-and-tell of rare books and manuscripts, slides were projected, and class discussion was also lively.

The following topics were covered over the five days:

- The book as physical object.
- Terminology of rare books and manuscripts.
- Role of legal materials in the development of Anglo-American law.
- Overview of Anglo-American legal bibliography.
- English law books and manuscripts to 1700–their production, distribution and bibliography.
- English law books and manuscripts since 1700–their production, distribution and bibliography.
- American law books and their production, distribution and bibliography.
- The antiquarian market for Anglo-American legal materials.
- English and American legal manuscripts, including legal ephemera.
- Strategies and techniques for forming a focused collection.
- Institutional and private collections of legal materials.
- The physical well-being of rare materials.
- Techniques of research in legal history.

Because the students included non-librarians, the program did not deal seriously with those aspects of library administration that are usual topics in courses for rare book librarianship, e.g., special cataloging requirements, security considerations, photocopying and other reproduction limitations, insurance, physical environment, binding policies, etc.

While neither of these offerings constituted an ideal (or even an adequate) instructional program for law librarians charged with the administration of rare materials, each included elements essential to such a program. The research skills which were the focus of the Yale Law School course would be an important component of the law librarian's instruction. The bibliographic core of the Rare Book School course would be an equally central element of the law librarian's training as would the book history, collection development and antiquarian market topics. The description of a proposed program which follows is not premised on a particular course length or format but merely suggests the desirable areas to be included. It is hoped that, to a greater or lesser extent, they would constitute the heart of the new course. Instructional methods would consist of some combination of the following: lectures; class discussion of readings and assigned problems; and research, analysis, and presentation of results of case studies.

The program would include the following components:

1. Brief history of English and American legal materials; production and distribution of law books in different time periods in England and America.
2. Brief history of Continental legal materials (including Roman and canon law); production and distribution of law books in different time periods on the European continent.
3. Overview of bibliographic sources and reference aids (general and legal; traditional and electronic) for English, American and Continental materials.
4. The book as a physical object; terminology of rare books and manuscripts; fundamentals of descriptive bibliography and analytical bibliography.
5. Defining rare materials and special collections (everything old is not necessarily rare; everything rare is not necessarily old); establishing collection parameters and a collecting scope.
6. Drafting policy statement on budgeting, donations, rules for use; staffing; strategies and techniques for developing collections.
7. The antiquarian market for books and manuscripts generally and for law books and manuscripts in particular.
8. Collecting, recording and administering legal ephemera, e.g., broadsides; court dockets and rules; diaries, journals and common-

place books; legal forms; publishers' and booksellers' catalogs; law student notebooks.
9. Physical well-being of materials; principles and techniques of preservation and conservation; security considerations; space planning and physical environment; insurance.
10. How and why historical law materials are used; research methods in Anglo-American legal materials–primary and secondary, traditional and electronic; the role of the librarian in historical legal research. At least two class sessions should be devoted to this unit. It is in fact the subject of the whole Yale Law School seminar described above. The following approaches to historical legal research (and perhaps others) can provide the framework for this important segment of the course:

   a. doctrinal research–the traditional analytic study of a rule, legal concept, series of decisions and/or statutes;
   b. document or event analysis–study of a specific legally significant document or event, including its background, causes and meaning;
   c. impact analysis–study of the economic, political or social impact of an event or rule, usually by social science techniques (e.g., data collection and analysis; interviewing; statistical surveying; model simulation, etc.); and
   d. biographical study of an individual or group of individuals in order to understand a legally significant event, condition or rule.[4]

The optimum length of such a program should include approximately twenty-four classroom hours with additional time for reading and assigned problems. Substantial reading for each class hour along the lines suggested below should be assigned. The curriculum need not be limited to a formal classroom situation. It can be the basis of a self-guided learning program since it seems unlikely that such a program will be offered anytime soon, unless, of course, the American Association of Law Libraries or the Virginia Rare Book School could be persuaded to give it. For either a self-taught or classroom program, I would suggest the following tentative list for both general, preliminary reading and for session-by-session assignment.[5]

### *PRELIMINARY READING*

John Carter, *ABC of Book Collecting* (7th ed. 1994).
Morris L. Cohen, *Administration of Rare Materials*, in *Law Librarianship, a Handbook* 603-688 (1983).
Roy M. Mersky, ed., *Collecting and Managing Rare Law Books* (1981).
Thomas H. Reynolds, *Rare Books for Law Libraries* (1983).

## FIRST SESSION:
## ENGLISH AND AMERICAN LEGAL MATERIALS

### English

John Baker, *Legal Literature*, Ch. 11 in *Introduction to English Legal History* 200-222 (3d ed. 1990).

W. W. S. Breem, *Historical Sources*, Ch. 7 in *Manual of Law Librarianship: The Use and Organization of Legal Literature* 249-292 (Elizabeth M. Moys ed.; 2d ed. 1987).

Percy H. Winfield, *The Chief Sources of English Legal History* (1925).

### American

Lawrence M. Friedman, *A History of American Law* 90-104; 322-333; 621-632 (2d ed., 1985).

Jenni Parrish, *Law Books and Legal Publishing in America, 1760-1840*, 72 *Law Library Journal* 355 (1979).

A. W. B. Simpson, *The Rise and Fall of the Legal Treatise: Legal Principles and the Forms of Legal Literature*, 48 *University of Chicago Law Review* 632 (1981).

Erwin C. Surrency, *A History of American Law Publishing* (1990).

## SECOND SESSION:
## CONTINENTAL LEGAL MATERIALS

Claire M. Germain, *Germain's Transnational Law Research: A Guide for Attorneys* (1991 & suppl.)

M. H. Hoeflich, *Roman and Civil Law and the Development of Anglo-American Jurisprudence in the Nineteenth Century* (1997).

Ralf Rogowski, ed., *Civil Law* (1996).

## THIRD SESSION:
## BIBLIOGRAPHIC SOURCES AND REFERENCE AIDS

Morris L. Cohen, *Bibliographic Control of Early American Law*, in *Collecting and Managing Rare Law Books* 119 (Roy M. Mersky ed., 1981).

Robert G. Logan, *The History of English Legal Bibliography Before 1900*, 10 *The Law Librarian* 43 (1979).

*Symposium: Bibliographic Control and Guides to Historical Sources*, 69 *Law Library Journal* 347-368 (1976).

## FOURTH SESSION:
## BOOK AS A PHYSICAL OBJECT AND TERMINOLOGY

Terry Belanger, *Descriptive Bibliography*, in *Book Collecting, a Modern Guide* 97-115 (Jean Peters, ed., 1977).

Ann Fidler, *"Till you understand them in their principle features": Observations on Form and Function in Nineteenth Century American Law Books*, 92 *Papers of the Bibliographical Society of America* 427 (1998).

Philip Gaskell, *A New Introduction to Bibliography* (1972; reprinted with corr., 1974; frequent reprintings).

Library of Congress, *Descriptive Cataloguing of Rare Books* (1991).

## FIFTH SESSION:
## DEFINITIONS AND COLLECTING PARAMETERS

Deborah Mayo-Jefferies, *Special Collections in Law School Libraries*, 86 *Law Library Journal* 503 (1994).

Marsha Trimble, *Archives and Manuscripts: New Collecting Areas for Law Libraries*, 83 *Law Library Journal* 429 (1991).

## SIXTH SESSION:
## POLICY STATEMENT FOR ADMINISTRATION

Christopher Anglim, *Special Collections: Policies, Procedures and Guidelines: A Model Plan for the Management of Special Legal Collections* (1993).

Susie R. Bock & Susan T. Dean, *Records Management for Special Collections Departments*, 11 *Rare Books & Manuscripts Librarianship* 73 (1996).

Judith A. Overmier & Elaine M. Doak, *Provenance Records in Rare Book and Special Collections*, 11 *Rare Books & Manuscripts Librarianship* 91 (1996).

Henry Raine & Laura Stalker, *Rare Book Records in Online Systems*, 11 *Rare Books & Manuscripts Librarianship* 103 (1996).

## SEVENTH SESSION:
## THE ANTIQUARIAN MARKET

Jean Peters, ed., *Book Collecting, a Modern Guide* (1977).

William S. Reese, *The Rare Book Market Today*, 74 *Yale University Library Gazette* 146 (2000).

Thomas H. Reynolds, *Collection Development and Acquisition of Rare Law Books*, in *Rare Books for Law Libraries* (1983) 60-100.

## EIGHTH SESSION:
## LEGAL EPHEMERA

Karen S. Beck, *One Step at a Time: the Research Value of Law Student Notebooks*, 91 Law Library Journal 29 (1999).

M. H. Hoeflich, *Legal Ephemera: A Window on Society and the Law*, Antiquarian Bookman, Mar. 10, 1997, at 785.

## NINTH SESSION:
## PHYSICAL WELL-BEING

AALL Special Committee on Preservation Needs of Law Libraries, *Preservation Treatment Options for Libraries*, 84 Law Library Journal 259 (1992).

Guy Petherbridge, ed., *The Conservation of Library and Archive Materials and the Graphic Arts* (1980).

Hedi Kyle, *Library Materials Preservation Manual* (1983).

Symposium: *Preservation of Law Library Materials & Disaster Planning*, 73 Law Library Journal 831 (1980).

## TENTH SESSION:
## USE OF MATERIALS AND RESEARCH METHODOLOGY

Peter de Cruz, *Techniques of Comparative Law*, Ch. 7 in *Comparative Law in a Changing World* 213-241 (2d ed. 1999).

Buckner F. Melton, Jr., *Clio at the Bar: A Guide to Historical Method for Legists and Jurists*, 83 Minnesota Law Review 377 (1998).

Jenni Parrish, *A Guide to American Legal History Methodology with an Example of Research in Progress*, 86 Law Library Journal 105 (1994).

Francis Paul Prucha, *Handbook for Research in American History* (2d ed. revised, 1994).

No one should think that a course like this is the be-all and end-all of rare book education for law librarians. Whether taken in a formal setting or as self-instruction, it should be supplemented by following current developments in the journal, *Rare Books & Manuscripts Librarianship* (Association of College and Research Libraries), unfortunately soon to be renamed *RBM: A Journal of Rare Books, Manuscripts, and Cultural Heritage*. The materials discussed may be old, but the discipline is constantly renewing itself and encompassing the latest developments in information technology. The continuation and expansion of one's formal training can be pursued in the many offerings of the Rare Book School at the University of Virginia. That lively and varied program is fast becoming the intellectual center of the rare book and manuscript library world in America and beyond.

## NOTES

1. These debates, particularly when ideological in nature, are discussed in the following articles: Stephen B. Presser, *"Legal History" or the History of Law: A Primer on Bringing the Law's Past into the Present*, 35 Vanderbilt Law Review 848 (1982); Robert W. Gordon, *The Past as Authority and as Social Critic: Stabilizing and Destabilizing Functions of History in Legal Argument*, in The Historic Turn in the Human Sciences (Terence J. McDonald ed., 1996); and Laura Kalman, *Border Patrol: Reflections on the Turn to History in Legal Scholarship*, 66 Fordham Law Review 87 (1997).

2. That complexity is shaped in part by the development of our law from the English common law system, supplemented (depending on the region involved) by Dutch, French, and Spanish sources, and by the federal structure of our government with three law-making branches at both the federal and state levels.

3. Examples of such discussions include: Rollo G. Silver, *The Training of Rare Book Librarians*, 9 Library Trends 446 (1961); Ann Bowden, *Training for Rare Book Librarianship*, 12 Journal of Education for Librarianship 223 (1972); and William L. Joyce, *Educating and Training Special Collections Librarians*, 10 Rare Books & Manuscripts Librarianship 73 (1995).

4. This might include *prosopography*, the investigation of the common background characteristics of a group of actors in history.

5. The growing literatures of legal history and rare book librarianship make this only a tentative list. It is likely that there will be many new relevant publications available by the time anyone decides to undertake a program of this kind.

# Rare and Archival Law Materials: Exhibits and Outreach, Traditional and Electronic

Mark W. Lambert

**SUMMARY.** Exhibits allow you to be creative, to use your imagination, and educate the viewer. In fact, exhibitions are one of the only areas that allow you to project the personality of your law library in both intellectual and physical assets. Online exhibits, when done correctly, can impact and affect significant numbers of people, exposing them to historical subjects and objects they never knew existed, or would never have traveled to view in the originals. Outreach can be defined as anything that contributes to a greater awareness about what we do. Today's online outreach allows us to reach many more people than ever before, in a far easier way. Exhibits and outreach, both in traditional forms and in the electronic age, are the special collection librarian's main tools in marketing. *[Article copies available for a fee from The Haworth Document Delivery Service: 1-800-342-9678. E-mail address: <getinfo@haworthpressinc.com> Website: <http://www.HaworthPress.com> © 2001 by The Haworth Press, Inc. All rights reserved.]*

For a department normally banished to a far corner, top floor, or even the basement of a law library, exhibits and outreach can be the very life-

---

Mark W. Lambert is Special Collections and Government Documents Librarian, South Texas College of Law Library, Houston, TX.

[Haworth co-indexing entry note]: "Rare and Archival Law Materials: Exhibits and Outreach, Traditional and Electronic." Lambert, Mark W. Co-published simultaneously in *Legal Reference Services Quarterly* (The Haworth Information Press, an imprint of The Haworth Press, Inc.) Vol. 20, No. 1/2, 2001, pp. 41-65; and: *Public Services Issues with Rare and Archival Law Materials* (ed: Michael Widener) The Haworth Information Press, an imprint of The Haworth Press, Inc., 2001, pp. 41-65. Single or multiple copies of this article are available for a fee from The Haworth Document Delivery Service [1-800-342-9678, 9:00 a.m. - 5:00 p.m. (EST). E-mail address: getinfo@haworthpressinc.com].

© 2001 by The Haworth Press, Inc. All rights reserved.

blood of an institution's rare books and archives department. Do not think of exhibits and outreach as something you have no time for, or something that takes you away from your primary duties. Exhibits and outreach are probably required to accomplish your department's written goals. What is preserved in your repository is special, but you need to get the word out in order to insure that your mission survives, and to educate and attract a wider range of patrons.[1] Today, even with the advent of the Internet, history and art museum attendance figures are on the rise. Perhaps because of the ever increasing complexity of modern society, and the vast distances now separating families, people still want to see cultural resource items for themselves, to connect in some way with the past.

An active exhibits and outreach program for a Special Collections department, including use of the Internet, targeted at the right people, can not only insure your department's survival, but can make asking for budget increases easier. Exhibits and outreach allow you to create and maintain a presence outside of your law school, in the larger legal community, as well as in non-legal environments, especially among people who normally view themselves outside of the legal sphere. All people sooner or later find themselves affected by such legal areas as Constitutional rights, zoning ordinances, the state penal code, or the state, local or federal tax code. Thoughtful exhibits and outreach can educate people in these important areas. You can remind people that we live in a country governed by laws, not men. You can suggest to people who say they do not like lawyers, why we still need lawyers. Through your exhibits and outreach, you can help to improve the law's tattered image. These are powerful messages that not only appeal to practicing lawyers and academics, but also to corporate leaders and politicians who may hold formal or informal power over law library budgets. Many corporate leaders and politicians come from legal backgrounds. Therefore, departmental "marketing," through exhibits and outreach, can reap your department strong benefits in financial or moral support.[2]

## DEPARTMENT MISSION STATEMENT

Your written department mission statement should include the use of exhibits and outreach to accomplish departmental goals.[3] Even the noblest mission can die on the vine if no one is its caretaker. Preserving and providing access to your treasures is not enough. You must also be an advocate for archives and rare books' important role in providing people, and society as a whole, with knowledge about their past in order to make better, more effective, informed decisions in the future. One of the best ways to advocate for the continued important role of archives and rare books in the future is to show their present relevance to people who normally see no reason to consult the past. If not presently part of your department's mission statement, the use of exhibits and outreach should be added as soon as possible. It does not have to be a very detailed section. That can wait for time and reflection. But make sure it is mentioned. You do not want to be accused of wasting precious departmental resources by someone who does not see the need for exhibits or outreach. Your justification for the hard work you do on exhibits and outreach should be in your mission statement.

## *EXHIBIT POLICY*

It is a good idea to have a written exhibit policy. While this might sound like more paperwork that takes months of work which no one will ever read, a policy on paper, approved by your library director, can give you freedom and direction. Putting on paper and getting approved by management what the purpose of your exhibits are, who the audience should be, and your library's preservation and security policies concerning exhibits, including the potential for loaning your exhibits, can save you from potential problems later. Be sure to mention your primary and secondary audiences and the frequency and ways you will attempt to appeal to both groups in your use of exhibits and outreach opportunities. Your primary audience should be the students, faculty and staff of your law school. Your secondary audience, however, can be as broad as your imagination and resources allow. It can include the lawyers of the local bar; all people involved in the legal sphere of your community; or even the average citizen. This can be influenced by where you choose or attempt to place your exhibits. Also be sure to mention preservation and security requirements for your exhibits. An exhibit policy that does not mention preservation and security requirements for your exhibits may lead to trouble later. Someday you may find your Dean has promised your prized exhibit to someone outside of your target audience, or at an inappropriate site, leaving you with no policy to stand on.

## AUDIENCE AND IDEAS

Exhibits allow you to be creative, to use your imagination, and to educate the viewer. In fact, exhibits are one of the only areas that allow you to project the personality of your law library in both intellectual and physical assets.[4] It is ironic that exhibits are usually the stepchildren of a library's activities. Exhibits first and foremost can educate the rest of the library's own staff to what is held in the Special Collections department.[5] In most libraries, if the Special Collections Librarian does not do exhibits for the library, they will not get done.

Each exhibit and its topic must be tailored to the audience you have in mind. The topic must be drawn from the available subject matter covered in your collections. However, there lurk within your collection topics you might never have considered. Ideas can come from any number of places. Topics can include persons, subjects, or events represented in your collections. If you hold the papers of a United States Supreme Court Justice, devising exhibit topics can be fairly easy. Other prominent individual's papers in your archive may also be as straightforward to work with, but mining exhibit topics out of some of the lesser materials in your department may take a good amount of creative thinking. Ask your co-workers for ideas. A different insight might prove helpful. Check your calendar and newspaper. National Something Month might be coming up, and you just might have the perfect materials in your collection to do an exhibit. State legislators and federal officials are forever naming things like "Official Pickle Day"! You just might have that collection of papers from a local attorney who later became a pickle magnate! A topic of interest presently being discussed in your local paper might be hiding in your stacks. Also ask colleagues in the archive and rare book profession. With the advent of e-mail and professional electronic discussion lists, good ideas can come from anywhere around the globe. An old idea in Australia may be the freshest idea in Texas!

It is possible to develop writer's block in regards to exhibit topics. No audience wants to see the same subjects or objects in exhibits over and over again, year in and year out. Do not be afraid to use the ideas of other librarians, staff members, law students, library science students, or history students to give you a fresh outlook on what are good topics. Unique exhibit ideas can include the following:

- Oddities of your collection, e.g., the lock of hair from one collection, the x-rays from another, or the smallest to largest books in the collection.
- School letterhead over the years.

- The products derived from research in your collections.
- Antiquated laws of your state/the laws of your state over time. (Everyone has heard about the "it's illegal to walk your alligator without a leash" laws, or other legal legends.)
- Art of the book/techniques of the handpress period. (While legal rare book collections are not often strong in the art of the book, there are sure to be some real winners in even a collection of 500 books, such as interesting bindings, marbled boards, textblocks, vellum bindings, gilt bindings, etc.)
- See Appendix A for additional ideas for exhibit topics.

Once you have the idea, the next step is to select the items themselves. Not only must the items support the theme; they must also be exhibitable. This can mean either easily understandable, or readable. If the item in mind will not fit into the exhibit case you have, or is not easily distillable to a short explanation, it is simply not exhibitable. Also, if the item or concept is too esoteric for the average viewer, then it is not exhibitable. Any manuscript or typescript that is not readable due to legibility, type size, or length, should also not be exhibited.[6]

## *EXHIBIT LOCATIONS*

Exhibits located in your Special Collections area can work well, if advertised effectively. However, some reading rooms may be too small to host exhibits. Also, use of this location for exhibits is like preaching to the choir. If your archives and rare books department has a fairly visible location in your library, an exhibit outside the front door of your department can help to pull people into the reading room. However, for departments with out-of-the-way locations in their libraries, other exhibit locations may need to be used as well to increase awareness of the department.

It is important to insure that your department has a presence at the entrance to your law library. The less scholarly minded of the law school management (e.g., financial types) can easily forget the existence and needs of your department up there, or down there, in the shadows of the stacks. Another excellent exhibit location would be at the most prominent entrance to your law school. An attractive, well-maintained exhibit can even become a stopping point for VIP tours of the law school. Another prime location is by heavily used elevators, if there is space nearby that can accommodate floor cases or small wall-mounted cases. With the use of small wall-mounted cases, and surrogates for display items, even the interiors of elevators, with their captive audiences, can be used for exhibit locations.

It also would be clever to locate exhibit cases in the main administration building of your campus. Then you would be able to attract a wider variety of viewers, as well as catch the attention of the school leadership. Your department could purchase an exhibit case in part with other departments, and use could be rotated among the purchasers. Other good building locations would be in social sciences or humanities buildings, or by the undergraduate pre-law advisor's office.

Significant times to have an important exhibit displayed could include during important Moot Court Trials, homecoming or graduation weekends, during alumni events, or at school honor banquets. Alumni weekend displays can be erected easily using school annuals, law reviews from the period, and school newspapers, among other things.

A display opportunity unique to law schools would be during Continuing Legal Education (CLE) training sessions. A well-thought-out exhibit could attract the attention of long-lost alumni, significant members of the bar who are potential donors, or legal historians not aware of the research opportunities at your facility.

It might even be worthwhile to look into the possibility of setting up exhibits in other law libraries in your area that have no special collections, such as smaller academic law libraries, or city, county or state law libraries. Other public buildings strongly associated with the law are also options. These locations can include state appellate court buildings; the state attorney general's office, the governor's office or mansion, the state capitol, or state supreme court building.

Do not forget one of the best places for exhibits is at local or state bar association annual meetings. Much like vendors, you have information to impart, and customers to attract. The bar also performs honor dinners and banquets, where you could volunteer to create an exhibit concerning an honoree's life, and/or his significance to the law. Work like this could help to strengthen your department's ties to the local practicing bar.

Other significant interest groups to approach would be historians or political scientists at local, state, regional or national meetings. Many historians or political scientists are intimidated by the complexity of the law and legal archives. Displaying an exhibit, and answering questions and highlighting research opportunities in areas such as social history or lawmaking in your collection, can attract new users to your department.

Even large law firms in your area may enjoy having attractive exhibits in the lobby of their building or office. These firms would appreciate well-done exhibits that can convey the history and majesty of the law.

The firm might even underwrite the costs associated with an exhibit. The logistics could be fairly easy, since most large office buildings and public buildings have loading docks for deliveries and constant security in their lobbies or at their entrances. Some of these law firms, due to their longevity, house rare items in their own libraries. They may find it appropriate to donate these items to your department for the better care and more frequent use they would receive there. All it may require is their awareness of your department's mission, a public announcement of the gift, and creation of attractive bookplates for the volume to identify the donor firm.

It certainly doesn't hurt that lawyers are well-represented in politics, and are powerful, well-paid professionals. A mailing list obtained from either your law school's development or alumni affairs office can be used to mail out flyers announcing new exhibits. The local bar association newsletter would probably be eager for content such as an announcement of your department's upcoming exhibit. Even making friends with the legal affairs writer of the local newspaper can do no harm. They may not be able to write about the exhibit, but they could pass the information on to the entertainment writer or someone else who could. In fact, good relations with the local press can turn them into customers. Almost any current story has an antecedent in the past. If there exists in your archive a story similar to current news, let the reporter know. They could end up reporting on this historical information, becoming customers and advertisers for your collections at the same time.[7]

## *EXHIBIT FILES*

Make sure to keep records of the exhibits you display. It may seem obvious, but make sure you have a complete list of the items displayed, text of the labels used, the location of the exhibit, as well as the actual dates of display (and not just the proposed dates). Even better is to photograph the erected exhibit, and file the photographs in their own subject filing system, separated either intellectually or physically from the rest of your photograph collection. Using text and/or photographs, the more detail about the exhibit preserved the better. In the future, it would be nice to know how the exhibit had been illuminated, its exposure to temperature extremes and outside air, as well as the duration of the exhibit. Also, if a burglar were to clear out your case or cases, it could be difficult and very time-consuming to determine what was stolen after the fact, without detailed exhibit records.

Exhibit files will also be invaluable in the future to create exhibits without much work. It is possible to use the same subject again, after a decent interval has passed (hopefully at least three years, the length of a law school class). This will normally require at least new exhibit labels. (It is amazing how typography styles change over time, and old fonts can look rather dated.) When using the same subject over again, also be sure to represent new ideas in thinking on the subject which may not have existed the last time around, or changes in the law.

Preservation information can also be gleaned from exhibit files. Knowing how long a specific object has been on display in the past, and under what conditions, can let you know if or when it should be exhibited again. (Archival preservation knowledge is founded in scientific research, which is constantly being updated, but it is a good rule of thumb to limit display of archival or rare book materials to at the most six months at a time, and then only once every several years. This is assuming that during storage, items are stored in the dark, or are boxed, and are stored in the best environmental conditions available at your facility.)

Last but definitely not least, should a disaster occur at your facility or campus, your exhibit records, including photographs, may be required to prove to insurance adjusters just what exactly a rare 16th century manuscript or volume was doing in the lobby of the central administration building![8]

## *IDEAS FOR GOOD EXHIBITS*

Exhibits must be well thought out, informative, factually correct, aesthetically pleasing, and tell a good story, or they can do more harm than good. Sloppy, poorly maintained exhibits can lead others to think poorly of your department and your library. It is important to have enough white space in your labels, and the right amount of information, or they will never be read. Plan on having an introductory label, known as a didactic panel, to impart whatever general knowledge the viewer needs to have to understand the exhibit. Your didactic panel should probably not be more than a paragraph or two, so being concise and precise is important. Also, each object label should probably be a brief paragraph or less. A well-done exhibit is a pleasant diversion for patrons, a time of relaxation, a break in their routine. Good exhibits can impart to viewers a pleasant feeling, making them re-energized for work, even if they have walked away having learned something![9]

It is also important not to overcrowd exhibit cases with artifacts, and to tailor your exhibits to your audience. Too many objects to look at can cause a patron to visually skip over a majority of the exhibit, while their eyes look for something "worthwhile" to view. Better to have less to look at, and more space between objects, so a patron's eyes will glide from one object to another. Imagine you are the average patron on a short break from your work, and have the option of looking at *Life* magazine, or the dictionary. Which would you choose? Just as important, tailor your exhibits to your audience. The evolution of tort theory in the United States as told through your famous professor's papers is probably too esoteric to be exhibited in the college's main administration building, but very appropriate for your law students.

Consistently good exhibits can begin to attract a local following, even leading to such events as lecturers taking their students out of the classroom to stimulate their thinking by walking them by your latest exhibit. It is hard to consistently do great exhibits year round, especially when you are doing many. With other demands on your time, you should not commit to so many exhibits a year that they are rushed and sloppy. If you are lucky enough to have student workers or paraprofessionals working for you, involving them with the planning, design and exhibit creation can keep them motivated, maintain their morale, and improve their overall work product. Almost everyone likes to be creative and challenged at work.

## *EXHIBIT PREPARATION AREA*

To efficiently create exhibits, you will need an area solely dedicated to exhibit preparation. Having to clear off a place to work every time you need to mount an exhibit will quickly get old. Tools to help you create suitable exhibits can include a laser printer, a digital camera, a mat cutter, mat board, a digital scanner, foam core board, a glue stick, polyester sleeves, polyester ribbon, cardstock that will pass through your laser printer, and various sizes of acrylic photo and label holders.[10]

## *EXHIBIT CREATION*

Computers, word processing programs, and desktop publishing programs have made exhibit creation relatively painless ventures. Even in the information age, however, there are some good old-fashioned tips to follow on exhibit design. More detailed ideas on this subject can be found in the Smithsonian Institution's "Accessible Exhibition Design," mounted on their web site. It may seem obvious, but make sure labels are in an easily readable font, and in a size large enough for the visually impaired to read. Also make sure that there is plenty of white space around the text on your labels, or the print will look like it is crowded and floating in the exhibit case. The most important thing to remember is to not put too much text on a panel or label. Viewers will probably skip introductory didactic panels with more than a few paragraphs, and object labels with more than a few sentences. Just like any other type of storytelling, your exhibit should also have a beginning, middle, and an end. Make sure to clearly identify each artifact on display, and its source, including the source for loaned items. No one likes to leave an exhibit with questions about the items on display. If your library is located in an area where there are a high number of non-English language speaking patrons, you should create brochures in the other language, so patrons can read along with the exhibit, or you could even produce the panels and labels themselves in that alternate language. Brochures would also be a good place to include extra information you might have cut from labels due to brevity. Any brochure should also include your location, address, departmental hours and contact information.

You should also keep in mind mobility-impaired patrons when creating and erecting your exhibit. Labels in exhibit cases should be displayed so wheelchair-bound visitors can view them. Exhibit cases should be spaced so wheelchair-bound patrons can go all the way around deep flat exhibit cases. Labels or documents should never be laid flat in a case. As a general rule, the higher the object sits on the shelf, the closer the angle of the document and label should be to the vertical (90 degrees). This is so that standing and sitting visitors can both read a document or label while at the same spot on the floor. For instance, in flat cases, or in the bottom of upright cases, documents and labels should be mounted at a small degree of angle from the horizontal, such as 30 degrees; so that standing visitors and those in wheelchairs can both see the label from the same point. Documents and labels that are above this height, such as in upright cases, but below the average standing viewer's eye level, should be at a greater angle, such as 60 degrees. Documents and labels in upright cases, around eye level to the standing viewer, should be mounted near the vertical (90-degree angle), so that sitting visitors may also read them.

## EXHIBIT OPENINGS

It is a good idea to have an exhibit sign-in or guest book, if it is feasible, for the length of the exhibit, or at least for the exhibit opening. Major exhibit openings can be advertised by mailing press releases or invitations using addresses obtained from the school development or alumni office. Another way to advertise your exhibits is through articles or advertisements in such publications as the school newspaper and other student, faculty, staff, or alumni publications. Press releases to local newspapers or in bar association publications well in advance of the opening date also have a chance of getting published. From a guest book can also come the start of a departmental mailing list.

## EXHIBIT CATALOG

Major exhibits should have an exhibit catalog. Catalogs no longer need to be produced in a print shop by professionals. There are now inexpensive software programs that can make your in-house produced catalogs look professionally done. Production of exhibit catalogs is a good job for a student worker or paraprofessional who gets easily bored, wants to learn something new, and would like to gain a valuable job skill. The catalog is also the place to include text dropped from exhibit labels for brevity. Also be sure to include a bibliography covering the exhibit topic, and your department's hours and contact information. Patrons may walk away from an exhibit with their curiosity piqued, and want to find out more on the subject, or they may even become a future researcher in your department.

## PRESERVATION CONCERNS

Preservation should be a major concern in creating and displaying exhibits. The use of surrogates, or duplicates of materials, should always be considered. However, always be sure to identify items that are not originals used in an exhibit. You do not want to be accused of attempting to deceive viewers. If possible, copies of photographs, and never originals, should be used. These can easily be produced at any professional photography lab in the area. However, it is wisest to use the photo lab which best understands the nature of archival images, whether your own campus photo lab, or the lab used by other cultural resources collections in the area. This is to insure that no crop lines are used, and that original images are never altered in any way. Call the largest local museum, or the college's art department, for suggestions on photographers. Preservation is also an area in which digitization can be utilized. If digital surrogates can be produced internally with sufficient quality to suit your purposes, you can save on photo lab reproduction costs by creating the surrogates in-house.

Exhibit of archival materials and rare books should only be done with the proper equipment. Book supports, page weights, or polyester ribbon tape is usually needed to properly exhibit rare books. Ultraviolet light inhibiting polyester sleeves should be used when possible to house archival documents. Condition reports should be prepared on all rare books before and after they are displayed, so that any damage done during exhibits can be spotted and evaluated.[11]

Exhibition of archival materials is a trade-off, with better exposure of your collections on one hand, and the potential for theft, acceleration of aging and damage to the materials on the other. If precautions are taken, however, exhibitions can make the risks worthwhile. Some things to consider when planning exhibits are the light source to be used in the area, its location, and hours of operation; exposure to temperature and light extremes and exposure to airborne contaminants. Carefully consider the use of non-archival display materials such as book supports and matting of materials, since they can damage rare and archival materials over time. Also consider the potential for patrons to lean or drop books on exhibit cases, causing damage or breakage of the case glass. Judge also the potential for spillage of liquid or food items on the cases, with the chance of seepage and damage to the case's contents. In certain instances like these, upright cases are better to use than flat cases, although for many materials, flat cases allow patrons to better linger over and study the materials. Having access to both styles of cases for exhibits is ideal.[12]

## *SECURITY*

Security should be another of the concerns when planning and displaying exhibits. Few exhibits will be affected as drastically as the recent armed robbery of an early Jonathan Swift text in Ireland by a terrorist group, but the range of things that can happen to exhibits is almost limitless.[13] All exhibits should be in well-traveled areas, under constant surveillance, even if only by a secretary. The cases should lock, and be large enough so they are not easily carried away. It is also suggested that you erect and take down exhibits during times when the public is not present in the area, since these are the times ripest for theft.[14] It is also important to have reliable records of what is on display. This is where your exhibit file can assist you. An inventory, or even better, photographs of the exhibit when it is mounted, can help insure the return of the materials should they be stolen, and an insurance claim needs to be filed.[15]

## *LOANS AND TRAVELING EXHIBITS*

Loaning of your exhibits, or exhibition of loaned items, can be of great assistance your exhibit program. Perhaps your state law library has traveling exhibits they would be able to loan, or you could develop a reciprocal arrangement with another academic law library in your area, state, or even across the country. Insist on lending arrangements with only those institutions that are also known to produce exhibits of high quality, and have the same understanding of preservation and security issues that you do. Make sure you have condition reports done on items before they are lent, to be better able to judge new damage to returned items. Keep in mind when considering cooperative arrangements that not all of your exhibits have to be law-related. In fact, an exhibit unrelated to the law can be a breath of fresh air to law students and patrons who spend a large amount of time surrounded by law-related materials.[16]

## *EXPENSES*

Creation and display of exhibits does cost money in staff time and supplies. There are one-time expenses for items such as exhibit cases, book supports and mat cutters, and recurring costs for supplies such as mat board and photo-reproduction. However, the relatively small amount of money expended on exhibits has the potential for reaping large rewards by raising your department's visibility in the law school and in the larger community.

## *OUTREACH*

Exhibits are one aspect of a broader outreach program. As with exhibits, outreach opportunities are only limited by your imagination. Outreach can be defined as anything "that contributes to a greater awareness of archives and what they do."[17] It is important to look at outreach opportunities as a way to provide "meaningful service or aesthetic and intellectual experience to an extended audience," and not just as a publicity stunt or circus act.[18] A simple start would be the creation of a mailing list, either obtained from the school development or alumni affairs office. Be sure to include your own department user sign-in sheets or exhibit guest books to obtain names.[19] Comparison of lists and guest books after library events or programs can identify a solid core of potential supporters of your department. The list can be used for distribution of newsletters or postcards of exhibit announcements. Simple desktop publishing programs can now create flyers or bookmarks touting your department, which you could station at the circulation desk of your law library, or the main library on campus. Christmas cards with photographs of the department and important acquisitions of the past year can be easily created from digital photography kiosks found at major pharmacies and department stores.

One easy way to raise your exposure is to remember to thank your donors. Use your library or school newsletter to post notices publicly thanking them. Create simple bookplates from computer clip-art and archival paper to place in books to acknowledge donors. Also be sure to send donors a thank-you letter on departmental letterhead.

Work with the rest of your library to create a "Friends of the Library" program, with benefits being circulation privileges, insider tours, or better access to the staff. Target heavy users such as the larger law firms in town, which consistently use your collection at no cost to themselves. Become involved with a state or local history society, start a legal history section within one, or host a meeting of the local historical society. Speak about your collections to the local historical or genealogical society. Talk to the faculty in graduate history programs and suggest research topics that are supported by your collections. Offer tours to interested groups. Help push aside the old special collections snobbery of desiring only "serious researchers," meaning academics or the well-to-do. This is elitist, and out of date with the times.

Host a lecture, conference, workshop, or reception at your library. These can serve to announce new collections or exhibits, to honor a colleague upon retirement, or to cover topics from genealogy, preservation, rare books, archives, manuscripts, or history. Tap local writers and historians to appear. Get prominent professors to assist. If all else fails, do it yourself. As a trained professional, you have knowledge that others lack. Doing some education, along with advocacy, can help make your department known more widely in the local and surrounding areas.

The largest law libraries can even endow a visiting scholars program to encourage use of their special collections. This would require providing a fellowship to selected individuals who apply yearly so they may travel to your institution to use your collections. The fellowship should offset their travel, and hotel expenses, and perhaps even provide a daily per diem for them.[20]

In the Internet age, archives and rare books departments need anybody and everybody we can attract to our institutions. It is elitist to require researchers to be "serious," or to require them to prove their "scholarliness" before allowing them admittance to your archive. The curious undergraduate today may be the "serious" researcher of tomorrow. It should be apparent in this age of tight budgets, that departments, even in private institutions, which are not seen as "democratic" or of use to society at large, can be viewed as irrelevant by school, community and state leaders and resource allocators, and be allowed to wither and die.

The easiest way to insure you are reaching every potential customer is to think like one. When you see a patron outside the Special Collections department door with a puzzled look on their face, ask if you can help them. They are curious. Utilize their curiosity. Offer to give them a tour, and explain your department's mission. Make them feel special. They can now know what goes on in "that" room, and what a "special" collection is. They will not forget it. They will probably tell other people what is contained in there, and how nice you were. Sometimes it is just that simple.

## *OUTREACH AND EXHIBITS IN THE ELECTRONIC AGE*

The biggest step in the electronic age is the first one. You should have your own departmental page on the library's web page. This may sound basic to most, but some schools at this point still do not have much more than an introductory page to their library on the Internet, much like not all libraries yet have their electronic catalog available through their web site. With at least an informational page on the Internet, more people potentially will be able to find you than without one. To increase the chances of being discovered, advocate having your departmental link on the front page of the library's web site. If you are really persuasive, have a direct link straight from your school's main web page. In both instances, you increase the chances of web search engines indexing your page, allowing more people to find you.

This introductory page should at least include your department's mission statement, an overview of the types of materials that reside within your department, and hours of operation with contact information, so that even the uninitiated will have a general idea of what lies within your departmental walls. Scholars and genealogists aren't the only ones doing historical research anymore. With the advent of the Internet, many more people have taken to writing on various and sundry subjects. Someone's next research topic may be found within your walls.

It would be wise to have an explanation of archives, manuscripts and rare books included on your page, how they are treated differently from materials in the main collection, and instructions on using each of these resources. There is no need to re-invent the wheel in this instance. There are already some good web sites on this subject. Simply ask the creator for permission to add a link to their site from yours.[21]

The next step would be to post all of your departmental policies and procedures on the Internet. These average Special Collections rules may sound draconian to the average person, so some gentle wording on why these measures are important can go a long way towards preventing people from being scared off when they read things like the requirement to fill out forms, or that pens are forbidden.

More specific descriptions of your collections are needed on your web page to assist patrons in far off places in determining if it is worth a trip to visit your library. Publishing a guide of your collections in the Internet age is less troublesome than previously. Before the Internet, publishing a guide to your collections was time-consuming and expensive, and it was obsolete as soon as you acquired a new collection. Today, on the other hand, you can add features to your web page as you go, making it easier for patrons to find out what your collections contain.[22]

Your next step is to mount finding aids for individual collections on your web site. Be sure to delete archival jargon from them first. "Creator Sketch" and "Scope and Contents Notes" have no meaning for the average person, and their use serves no legitimate purpose but to intimidate potential users. Utilize more patron friendly terms, such as "Biographical Sketch," and "Outline of the Collection." Your patrons will have enough to deal with slogging through legal terminology. Make it easier for them whenever possible, such as including a glossary of archival terms on your web site.[23] To provide superior service, add links on your page to repositories that hold related or similar collections. This makes it easier on potential patrons, since you should already know how to work the national bibliographic entities, and most of your patrons don't.

The next step into the Information Age is probably the biggest: creation of online exhibits. All the previous steps hopefully utilized information already available from printed documents, which required little new work beyond HTML coding and mounting on a computer server. Creation of online exhibits, however, takes all of the previous information on creating exhibits, and moves it several steps further. You will now need to utilize digital technology, and evaluate your potential exhibit items a little bit differently, whether you are converting existing exhibits to a digital medium, or creating them wholly new for the Internet.

The main ideas behind good exhibits do not change, however. Having a good topic, and being able to exhibit and explain it properly are still paramount. Exhibit items, especially three-dimensional ones, must now be evaluated using slightly different aesthetics, since all items will be presented only in two dimensions on a computer screen. Can the item still be interpreted successfully in this new medium? Can the item be visually understood in this new medium? A photograph of a three-dimensional object may just supply shadow and ambiguity where there once was shape and realization in the original. Additional text in labels may help to explain confusing images. Remember, however, that the exhibit should still be informative and entertaining. Too much text can still cause your days and months of work to be stillborn, as few viewers will take the time to read all the information you have worked hard to impart.

New concerns in the digital environment include creation of the digital files, and dealing with their bulk. With most persons accessing the Internet by way of modem, exhibits with large amounts of images, or complicated formatting, can cause online exhibits to load very slowly on home computers. So the decision on how many images to have, and how they are displayed, is an important one. There is no easy answer. People love to view images, but hate to wait for them to load. There is a middle ground to be found somewhere.[24]

Online exhibits, when done correctly, can impact and affect significant numbers of people, exposing them to historical subjects and objects they never knew existed, or would never have traveled to view in the originals.[25] The leader in presenting online exhibits is "American Memory," part of the National Digital Library Project of the Library of Congress.[26] Grant money is issued each year by the Library of Congress to facilitate mounting of online exhibits of historical materials of regional or national significance. Other projects have managed to gain corporate funding, and private donations, as well as public funding.[27]

Online exhibits have the ability to shorten distances and to reveal the hidden. A recent project is the creation of the 'Bach Digital' Project, which will reunite many of composer Johann Sebastian Bach's works on the Internet. These works have long been locked away from the average person. Scattered throughout Europe by sale and war, eight institutions have collaborated to bring Bach's compositions together again. One composition has in fact been divided between two institutions for the entire 250 years since Bach's death, and will now be reunited in cyberspace.[28] It takes little imagination to envision what could be done with this technology. Already being created are subject or state-specific archival finding aids online, such as the "Online Archive of California."[29] The next step would be to mount scanned images of historical documents themselves. This is the vision behind the Texas History Internet Consortium. This is collaboration between five small history museums in the Gulf Coast region of Texas, using standards developed from the Library of Congress' American Memory Project. The first step is to unite all five museums' online catalogs, and then later to add scanned images of historical documents. While none of the institutions envisions scanning, or being able to afford to scan, all of their collections for display on the Internet, they plan to mount small, important collections together at their unified site.[30] There is potentially a large amount of grant funding available at this time for digitization projects. It might be possible for interested law libraries to form a consortium around a legal subject area of great interest, such as constitutional law or Supreme Court Justice papers, and obtain a large amount of funding to get the unified collection online.

Perhaps one of the most compelling reasons to put primary source historical materials online is because they are "real." Children of all ages are being encouraged by their teachers to perform historical research online. Students will turn to whatever information is out there. They are doing it now, using things such as suspect secondary sources, and unverifiable oral histories. Your institution holds "real," verifiable, unquestionable, unimpeachable primary sources of history in its collections. And while by now most scholars can manage to track down an important source during their research, students and many others do not have access to this information network of archivists, librarians and scholars. Putting collections online, at least samples, can inform many more people about your collections, fulfilling the part of your mission which changes your school and library to perform a needed, useful service to society.

Realizing that the technology and skills to create online exhibits are expensive, talk to academic departments and local schools about obtaining interns, or sponsoring practicums. You can offer something valuable in return for this cheap form of labor, since the experience students can get digitizing historical materials and creating web sites for them is usable now in almost any profession.

Knowing if Internet users are actually finding and using your web pages is difficult to determine. Programs that can count the amount of hits on a web site can be useful, but are not foolproof. There is no way to know how many persons have accessed your page accidentally. If you are notifying all telephone reference callers about your web site, and noticing a drop in actual walk-in reference service, that might be the clearest indication of your website's usefulness.

## *OUTREACH IN THE ELECTRONIC AGE*[31]

Outreach in the electronic age allows you to keep in touch with people easier and quicker. A good start would be the creation of an electronic mailing list, obtained from your reading room sign-in sheets, exhibit guest books, and/or your school's development or alumni affairs office. You can also ask visitors to your website to sign in. Through these means you can give notices of your upcoming exhibits, both online and in your facility. This medium also allows you to create a virtual "Friends of the Special Collections Department" mailing list, through which you can notify interested parties if collections or rare books are presently on the market that would be a good addition for your department. This may be all that is needed to raise the funds to purchase significant items for your department.

To insure that the widest possible audience can view your online exhibits, ensure that the proper metatags are included in your web site. Ask other history and archives people to add a link to your web site on their site. Announce your web site and new exhibits on professional discussion lists, and send the information to local newspapers. To insure that your site is as good as it can be, ask other professionals for constructive criticism and suggestions on how to make it better. Every special collections librarian will sooner or later deal with this subject, some just might get there before the rest. Monitor and make contributions to online evaluation sources such as the *Internet Scout Report*,[32] and view well-liked and well-reviewed sites to get ideas for improvements to your departmental site. Write about your own experiences setting up online exhibits in newsletters and professional journals, and volunteer to do a column on online exhibits for your library, school, or professional publication, which then gives you an excuse to consistently view online exhibits. Attend Internet conferences, read the professional literature concerning the Internet, and participate in discussion groups at work and at conferences to find out what others are doing in the field.

## *CONCLUSION*

Exhibits and outreach, both in traditional forms and in the electronic age, are the special collection librarian's main tools in marketing.[33] Ignoring the new tools that the Internet offers to make our collections more widely known is begging to become irrelevant in the information age. With some imagination, and of course hard work, exhibits and outreach can not only insure your department's future success, but almost guarantee it. With no more than a handful of new exhibits a year, and successful outreach opportunities, this small part of your duties can have a huge impact on your department. In fact, a large amount of this work can be handed over to work-study students and paraprofessionals, who can gain valuable job skills working with digital technology, while at the same time improving their morale and work habits through the release of creative expression. Do not look at exhibits and outreach as a drain on time and departmental resources, but as an opportunity for advocacy and education. Today's online exhibits and outreach allow us to reach many more people than ever before, in a far easier way. In the end, the technologies of the 20th and 21st centuries will allow us to make more widely known our treasures of the 16th-19th centuries, thus insuring our mission is accomplished and perpetuated.

## NOTES

1. The standard sources in the field, both produced before the age of the Internet, are: Gail Farr, *Archives and Manuscripts: Exhibits* (Chicago: Society of American Archivists, 1980); and Ann Pederson & Gail Farr, *Archives and Manuscripts: Public Programs* (Chicago: Society of American Archivists, 1982).
2. David B. Gracy II, "Reference No Longer Is a 'P' Word: The Reference Archivist as Marketer," *Reference Services for Archives and Manuscripts* (Binghamton, NY: The Haworth Press, Inc., 1997), 175.

3. The best general introduction to law library Special Collections, including missions, is: Christopher Anglim, *Special Collections Policies, Procedures and Guidelines: A Model Plan for the Management of Special Legal Collections* (Buffalo, NY: William S. Hein & Co., 1993).

4. Edward J. Bander, "Library Exhibits–Two Proposals," *Law Library Journal* 58:1 (February 1965), 15-17.

5. Erika S. Chadbourne, "Part III–Library Administration of Historical Materials: Exhibits," 69:3 (August 1976), 321-325.

6. Shawn Aubitz & Gail F. Stern, "Developing Archival Exhibitions," *Mid-Atlantic Regional Archives Conference Technical Leaflet Series Number 5* (New York: Mid-Atlantic Regional Archives Conference, 1990), 4.

7. Bruce W. Dearstyne, "Archival Reference and Outreach: Toward A New Paradigm," *Reference Services for Archives and Manuscripts* (Binghampton, NY: The Haworth Press, Inc., 1997), 189.

8. For more on disaster plans for law library Special Collections, please consult: Julius J. Marke, et al. "Preservation of Law Library Materials & Disaster Planning–A Panel," *Law Library Journal* 73:4 (Fall 1980), 831.

9. Chadbourne, *supra* note 5.

10. For more information on the supplies needed, consult the following: Jane Greenfield, *The Care of Fine Books* (New York: The Lyons Press, 1988), and Mary Lynn Ritzenthaler, *Preserving Archives and Manuscripts* (Chicago: Society of American Archivists, 1993).

11. Greenfield, *supra* note 10, at 125.

12. Three good sources on this topic are Greenfield and Ritzenthaler, *supra* note 10, and also Catherine Nicholson, "What Exhibits Can Do To Your Collections," *Restaurateur* 3:3 (1992), 5-113.

13. "Irish Library Plundered," *Houston Chronicle,* Dec. 12, 1999: A35.

14. Joan Rabins, "Archival Exhibits: Considerations and Caveats," *A Modern Archives Reader: Basic Readings on Archival Theory and Practice* (Washington, D.C.: National Archives and Records Service, 1984), 292.

15. For more information, please consult: ACRL Rare Books and Manuscripts Section's Security Committee, *Guidelines for the Security of Rare Book, Manuscript, and Other Special Collections* (Association of College and Research Libraries, Sept. 15, 1999).

16. For guidelines on borrowing or lending Special Collections materials, please consult: ACRL Rare Books and Manuscripts Section's Ad Hoc Committee for Developing Guidelines for Borrowing Special Collections Materials for Exhibition, *ACRL Guidelines for Borrowing and Lending Special Collections Materials for Exhibition* (Association of College and Research Libraries, June 23, 1999).

17. Cathy Henderson, "Negotiating New Borders for Special Collections," *Rare Books & Manuscripts Librarianship* 14:1 (1999), 9.

18. *Id.,* 10.

19. Elsie Freeman, "Education Programs: Outreach as an Administrative Function," *A Modern Archives Reader: Basic Readings on Archival Theory and Practice* (Washington, D.C.: National Archives and Records Service, 1984), 284.

20. A good example of this idea is the *Visiting Scholars Program* of the Carl Albert Congressional Research and Studies Center at the University of Oklahoma. My thanks to Todd Kosmerick, Assistant Curator at the Center, for discussing this program at the Society of Southwest Archivists Annual Meeting in May 2000.

21. See "Using Manuscripts & Archives: A Tutorial," available from the Yale University Library Manuscripts and Archives Department, at <http://www.library.yale.edu/mssa/tutorial/>.

22. A recent article on this subject is: Jeanne Holba Puacz, "Bringing Archives to Life on the Web–The History of People Long Gone Finds New Life in This Library's Web-Based Archival Index," *Computers In Libraries*, 20:3 (February 2000).

23. This idea is from James Cross, "Generation Warriors: Access and Reference Service to the Next Wave of Researchers," presentation given at the Society of Southwest Archivists Annual Meeting, Fayetteville, Arkansas, May 19, 2000.

24. Two texts to consult before embarking on digitizing photographs are: Stephen E. Ostrow, *Digitizing Historical Pictorial Collections for the Internet* (Washington, D.C.: Council on Library and Information Resources, Feb. 1998), and the just-released *Guides to Quality in Visual Resource Imaging* (Council on Library and Information Resources, July 2000), available at <http://www.rlg.org/visguides/>.

25. Especially powerful is the online exhibit of early twentieth-century images of lynching victims in the United States, entitled "Without Sanctuary: Photographs and Postcards of Lynching in America," available at: <http://www.journale.com/withoutsanctuary/intro_body_main.html>.

26. Located at <http://lcweb2.loc.gov/ammem/ammemhome.html>.

27. A recent article on a significant digitization project by a history professor at the University of Virginia, is: Jeffrey R. Young, "A Historian Presents the Civil War, Online and Unfiltered by Historians," *New York Times*, June 29, 2000.

28. For more on the Bach Digital Project: <http://www.bachdigital.org>.

29. Available at <http://www.oac.cdlib.org/cgi-bin/oac>.

30. The five institutions are the Brazoria County Historical Museum, the Fort Bend Museum, the Matagorda County Museum, the Rosenberg Library, and the Star of Republic Museum. For more information, contact the Information Access Institute at <http://Information.org>.

31. A good paper on the subject is Terry Abraham's "The Next Step: Outreach on the World Wide Web," available at <http://www.uidaho.edu/special-collections/papers/outreach.htm>.

32. The Scout Report can be viewed at <http://scout.cs.wisc.edu/report/sr/about.html>.

33. Gracy, *supra* note 2, at 171.

## APPENDIX A
## ADDITIONAL IDEAS FOR EXHIBIT TOPICS

- School history/change in physical plant
- Deans and former deans
- Board of Trustees, past and present
- Benefactors
- Prominent faculty members, past and present
- Collection strengths/school subject strengths
- Famous law books and their others, national and regional
- Famous cases, national or regional
- Regional reporter system v. old systems in your state housed in special collections
- Law book collections of old; law on the frontier
- The business of law in the past, revealed in old law firm collections
- American legal history/English legal history/Spanish legal history
- Highlight an important case used for illustration in the law school's legal history classes
- The law school's founder; the person whom the building is named after
- Famous or notorious alumni
- The important legal work of an individual or an organization
- That street, building on campus no one alive now ever heard of
- A particularly well-covered subject area in a collection or across your collections
- Highlight a famous legal writer, e.g., Joseph Story
- Inscriptions and markings in books, past ownership of collections, impressive rubrics
- Literature and the law, e.g., Shakespeare and the law, Dickens and the law, etc.
- Fiction and the law, e.g., Harper Lee's *To Kill A Mockingbird,* Edgar Alan Poe, Sherlock Holmes, Hercule Poirot, John Grisham, Scott Turow
- Movies and the law
- Legal dictionaries across time
- The law of countries that have influenced your law

# APPENDIX B
## SELECT BIBLIOGRAPHY ON EXHIBITS AND OUTREACH

Abraham, Terry. "The Next Step: Outreach on the World Wide Web." Available at <http://www.uidaho.edu/special-collections/papers/outreach.htm>.

ACRL Rare Books and Manuscripts Section's Ad Hoc Committee for Developing Guidelines for Borrowing Special Collections Materials for Exhibition. *ACRL Guidelines for Borrowing and Lending Special Collections Materials for Exhibition.* Association of College and Research Libraries, June 23, 1999.

ACRL Rare Books and Manuscripts Section's Security Committee. *Guidelines for the Security of Rare Book, Manuscript, and Other Special Collections.* Association of College and Research Libraries, September 15, 1999.

Aubitz, Shawn, & Gail F. Stern. *Developing Archival Exhibitions.* New York: Mid-Atlantic Regional Archives Conference, 1990.

Bander, Edward J. "Library Exhibits-Two Proposals," Part of "Library Exhibits–Panel Discussion," *Law Library Journal* 58:1 (February 1965), 15-17.

Casterline, Gail Farr. *Archives and Manuscripts: Exhibits.* Chicago: Society of American Archivists, 1980.

Chadbourne, Erika S. "Part III–Library Administration of Historical Materials: Exhibits," *Law Library Journal* 69:3 (August 1976), 321-325.

Cohen, Laura B. ed. *Reference Services for Archives and Manuscripts.* Binghamton, NY: The Haworth Press, Inc., 1997. [Also published as *The Reference Librarian* 56 (1997).]

Coles, Laura M. *A Manual for Small Archives.* Vancouver: Association of British Columbia Archivists, 1988.

Cross, James. "Generation Warriors: Access and Reference Service to the Next Wave of Researchers." Presentation given at the Society of Southwest Archivists Annual Meeting, Fayetteville, Arkansas, May 19, 2000.

Daniels, Maygene F., & Timothy Walch, ed. *A Modern Archives Reader: Basic Readings on Archival Theory and Practice.* Washington, D.C.: National Archives and Records Service, 1984.

Farr, Gail. *Archives and Manuscripts: Exhibits.* Chicago: Society of American Archivists, 1980.

Freeman, Elsie. "Education Programs: Outreach as an Administrative Function." In *A Modern Archives Reader: Basic Readings on Archival Theory and Practice* (Washington, D.C.: National Archives and Records Service, 1984).

Greenfield, Jane. *The Care of Fine Books.* New York: The Lyons Press, 1988.

Henderson, Cathy. "Negotiating New Borders for Special Collections." *Rare Books & Manuscripts Librarianship* 14:1 (1999), 9-17.

"Irish Library Plundered." *Houston Chronicle,* Dec. 12, 1999. A35.

Marke, Julius J., et al. "Preservation of Law Library Materials & Disaster Planning–A Panel," *Law Library Journal* 73:4 (Fall 1980), 831-852.

Morris, Leslie A. "Beyond the Books: Programs for Exhibitions," *Rare Book and Manuscript Librarianship* 6:2 (1991), 89-99.

Nicholson, Catherine. "What Exhibits Can Do to Your Collection," *Restaurateur* 13:3 (1992), 95-113.

Ostrow, Stephen E. *Digitizing Historical Pictorial Collections for the Internet.* Washington, D.C.: Council on Library and Information Resources, 1998.

Pederson, Ann, & Gail Farr. *Archives and Manuscripts: Public Programs.* Chicago: Society of American Archivists, 1982.

Puacz, Jeanne Holba. "Bringing Archives to Life on the Web–The History of People Long Gone Finds New Life in This Library's Web-Based Archival Index." *Computers In Libraries* 20:3 (Feb. 2000).

Pugh, Mary Jo. *Providing Reference Services for Archives and Manuscripts.* Chicago: Society of American Archivists, 1992.

Rabins, Joan. "Archival Exhibits: Considerations and Caveats," In *A Modern Archives Reader: Basic Readings on Archival Theory and Practice* (Washington, D.C.: National Archives and Records Service, 1984).

Ritzenthaler, Mary Lynn. *Preserving Archives and Manuscripts.* Chicago: Society of American Archivists, 1993.

Scham, A. M. *Managing Special Collections.* New York: Neal-Schuman Publishers, Inc., 1987.

*Smithsonian Guidelines for Accessible Exhibition Design.* Office of the Provost, Smithsonian Accessibility Program. Washington, D.C.: Smithsonian Institution, 1999.

Vitale, Timothy. "Light Levels Used in Modern Flatbed Scanners." *RLG DigiNews,* Oct. 15, 1988. Available at: <http://www.rlg.org/preserv/diginews/diginews2-5.html>.

Wilstead, Thomas, & William Nolte. *Managing Archival and Manuscript Repositories.* Chicago: Society of American Archivists, 1991.

Young, Jeffrey R. "A Historian Presents the Civil War, Online and Unfiltered by Historians." *The New York Times,* June 29, 2000.

# Rare and Archival Law Materials on the World Wide Web: An Evaluation of Selected Sites

Carole Prietto

**SUMMARY.** This article outlines some of the author's criteria for good web sites (browser compatibility, stability, loading time, organization, legibility, use of plug-ins and multimedia applications, audience, and number and quality of digital surrogates), and discusses selected legal studies web sites in terms of their usefulness as public service tools. *[Article copies available for a fee from The Haworth Document Delivery Service: 1-800-342-9678. E-mail address: <getinfo@haworthpressinc.com> Website: <http://www.HaworthPress.com> © 2001 by The Haworth Press, Inc. All rights reserved.]*

What is a "good" web site? There are as many answers as there are users of Web sites. Web sites now number in the millions, with more coming online all the time. How to make sense of the mass of information now on the Internet? We can begin to get a handle on the problem by asking: good for whom, and good for what purpose? Historians and lawyers, to name two groups, have always been especially concerned

---

Carole Prietto is University Archivist, Washington University, St. Louis. She is a member of the Steering Committee of the College and University Archivists Section of the Society of American Archivists, and serves as the Section's webmaster.

[Haworth co-indexing entry note]: "Rare and Archival Law Materials on the World Wide Web: An Evaluation of Selected Sites." Prietto, Carole. Co-published simultaneously in *Legal Reference Services Quarterly* (The Haworth Information Press, an imprint of The Haworth Press, Inc.) Vol. 20, No. 1/2, 2001, pp. 67-77; and: *Public Services Issues with Rare and Archival Law Materials* (ed: Michael Widener) The Haworth Information Press, an imprint of The Haworth Press, Inc., 2001, pp. 67-77. Single or multiple copies of this article are available for a fee from The Haworth Document Delivery Service [1-800-342-9678, 9:00 a.m. - 5:00 p.m. (EST). E-mail address: getinfo@haworthpressinc.com].

© 2001 by The Haworth Press, Inc. All rights reserved.

with the quality of their sources. As librarians and archivists serving the public, we should be no less concerned with these same issues. The present paper will outline some of the author's criteria for good web sites, and discuss selected legal studies web sites in terms of their usefulness as public service tools.

## WEB SITE EVALUATION CRITERIA

Much about the quality of a web site depends on design choices made by the web designer. One of the most important aspects of web design is browser compatibility. A site should be available to the greatest number of browsers possible, with little or no variation in the user interface, and little or no difference in the level of content available to those with older browsers. In order to promote the greatest accessibility, sites should not be optimized for a particular browser or a particular resolution of monitor. Unfortunately, there is an inherent tension between browser compatibility and features which offer the greatest functionality for the user. Other web design considerations include:

*Stability.* The site should be housed on a server which is consistently available and able to handle the traffic which the site generates. Links should be checked regularly. The usefulness of any site will be hampered if the user encounters numerous "404 File not found" messages. If a site uses JavaScript, the script needs to be checked thoroughly, so that users do not encounter "Java Script error" messages and interruptions in downloading the site. Sites hosted by institutions are generally more stable than sites located on an individual's personal directory. This is especially true for sites authored by students at universities: as soon as the student graduates, the student's e-mail account and web access are terminated and any sites the student created go with it.

*Loading time.* It is difficult to make specific recommendations as to an acceptable load time because loading time is affected by many factors, including: the amount of content on a page (how much text, how many graphics and size of each graphic), the presence of Java scripts or applets, multimedia presentations such as background sounds or animated graphics, the speed of the user's connection, the speed of the user's computer, whether or not the user has enabled image loading on his/her browser, traffic on the site being accessed, and traffic on the Internet as a whole, which is affected by time of day or night.

*Organization.* Web pages, because they are read on screen rather than in print, present some special challenges for easy reading. In addition, the hypertext nature of the web means that readers do not have to start at the beginning of a document and work their way to the end, in a linear fashion. Users can start in the middle, navigate forward, navigate backward, jump to different points in a site, jump to a completely different site. This has ramifications for both writing (each individual page has to stand on its own) and organization.

*Readability on screen.* Background colors are preferable to background images. Background images can be distracting to the reader and they increase the time required for a site to download. A site has better readability on screen if dark text appears on a light background. Such pages are also easier to print. The colors used should work together to present an appealing visual picture to the user. Most experts recommend that a site contain no more than four colors, with a limit of seven throughout the site. Color alone should not be used to convey important messages; this handicaps color-deficient users who tend to see everything in shades of green and gray. It is preferable to set off important information either by size (can the information be conveyed using a header tag?) or by placement on screen. No matter what color scheme the designer chooses, there should be only *one* color scheme. Multiple color schemes within the same site can fool users into thinking they have been taken to another site entirely. Designers should not assume that users will be able to tell when they have left their site simply by looking at the URL. It is better to establish a consistent look and feel for a site and stick to it.

The text should be easy to read. Grammar and spelling should be carefully checked; instructions should be clear and concise. Paragraphs should be concise–long blocks of text are difficult to read on screen. Extensive use of decorative fonts will tire the user's eye quickly, and may not be readable for visually impaired persons. For this reason, it is best to use fonts such as Times New Roman and Arial (for Windows platforms), and Helvetica (for Macintosh platforms).

Navigational aids should appear in the same position on every page, so that the reader knows where to find them. Navigation links should be consistent, i.e., a link back to the home page on every subsidiary page; subsidiary pages can have a link to a parent directory. When graphics are used as a navigation link, they should have a consistent color and shape, they should be small, and should have a text-based alternative.

*Use of plug-ins and multimedia applications.* Required "plug-ins" or other helper applications should be clearly identified. The designer should provide a means for users to download the software should they need it. For instance, if a site contains documents in Adobe's Portable Document Format (.pdf), the site designer should include a link to the Adobe Systems home page. Similarly, sites which use multimedia tools such as Shockwave, Flash, MP3, or Real Audio, should have links to sites of the respective manufacturers, so that users can download software they need. Site designers need to provide information concerning the need for specialized tools up front, so that the users know *before they click* that they are about to see a resource which may require specialized tools for viewing.

*Audience.* Who is the site intended to serve? For a law-oriented site, possible target audiences include practicing lawyers and judges, legal scholars, law librarians, and law students. Of course, a site with law-related information could be useful to other audiences as well: historians, social scientists, and librarians and information professionals from fields outside of law. If a site is designed to appeal to a number of different audiences, the site should be organized in such a way that different user groups can get to the information they need quickly. If the content of a site is geared to a particular audience, it is helpful to provide explanatory text on the opening page which tells all users who is likely to benefit the most from the site. In this way, users can make a decision about exploring the site further. Site maps and search engines facilitate finding information in a large site.

*Number and quality of digital surrogates.* The greatest strength of the World Wide Web is its graphical nature. The full text of a given resource should, whenever possible, include digital surrogates of the resources, or selected portions of the resource. The ability to view the actual document adds to the quality of the user's experience of a site. Of course, this places a burden on the site designer, to present the graphics in a way that will not interfere with the information.

## EVALUATION OF SELECTED WEB SITES

Below are links to law-related sites which I have found to be especially noteworthy. All are sites which are represented in university collections. Some are from library special collections departments. Some are from law schools. All of these represent unique collections of material. All were selected on the strength of their design, their completeness, and their clarity of presentation. They are presented alphabetically by name of the site, and Web addresses are given.

## American Radicalism Collection, Michigan State University
*http://www.lib.msu.edu/spc/digital/radicalism/index.htm*

The American Radicalism Collection is held in the Special Collections Department at the Michigan State University Library. The web site is produced by the Digital Sources Center at Michigan State. The American Radicalism Collection holds over 17,000 items. It includes books, pamphlets, periodicals, posters, and ephemeral material covering a wide range of viewpoints on political, social, and economic issues in America. The emphasis in the collection is on materials produced by radical groups–both left and right. The collection, for example, has materials devoted to Timothy Leary, the Black Panther Party, Neo-Nazi Organizations, the Christian Right, and Steve Gaskin, founder of the commune The Farm. While the American Radicalism Collection is strongest in publications from the American Left in the twentieth century, as well as in resources for the study of American Labor History, there is considerable material from the right, most notably the Ku Klux Klan of the 1920s and 1930s. This site is relevant to historians in general, but some items will be of special interest to legal historians: items published by radical groups on the Rosenberg spy case, the Sacco-Vanzetti trial, the Scottsboro Boys, civil rights, the Ku Klux Klan, labor unions, and Japanese-American internment.

## The Avalon Project, Yale University Law School
*http://www.yale.edu/lawweb/avalon/avalon.htm*

From the site's statement of purpose: "The Avalon Project is dedicated to providing access via the World Wide Web to primary source materials in the fields of Law, History, Economics, Politics, Diplomacy and Government. We intend to add value to these primary sources by linking to other documents expressly referred to in the body of the text. We also intend to provide as many internal links within a document as are necessary to facilitate study and navigation." The site does what is sets out to do, and does so exceptionally well. The site is organized chronologically: pre-18th century, 18th century, 19th century, and 20th century. Within each time period are links to a variety of laws, treaties, and similar documents, in full text. The collection of texts includes documents dating as far back as the Code of Hammurabi and the Athenian Constitution. The 18th century collection includes, among many others, the constitutions of all thirteen American colonies. The 19th and 20th century collections include a variety of foreign treaties and inaugural addresses of presidents of the United States. Citations to source texts are provided. No commentary or secondary sources are provided; this is a place to find the legal texts themselves. The site is attractively designed; the navigation is consistent throughout–one of the best designed sites I've seen on the Web. Like the Bracton site (see below), the authors make available extensive information about how the texts were selected and how the site was constructed, and browser compatibility. Unlike the Bracton site, this information is hidden in an unexpected place: not the "author" link, which includes the names of the authors of the *primary sources,* but in the "helpdesk and frequently asked questions" link. I had to hunt for it, and I think this information needs to be presented up front–on the home page. But that is a minor point. For any student of history, law, or political science, this is a wonderful place for primary source material.

**The Bentham Project**
*http://www.ucl.ac.uk/Bentham-Project/*

From the site: "The aim of the Bentham Project is to produce a new scholarly edition of the works and correspondence of Jeremy Bentham (1748-1832), the influential jurist, philosopher, and social scientist, whom A. J. P. Taylor described as 'the most formidable reasoner who ever applied his gifts to the practical questions of administration and politics.' He was a legal philosopher of major importance, being one of the founders of the theory of legal positivism. In ethics he provided the classic exposition of the utilitarian theory which has been a major strand in moral philosophy since the eighteenth century. In political thought he was important both as a critic of established doctrines such as that of natural law, and as the originator of one of the main theoretical justifications for democracy."

The Bentham Project web site comes from University College London. The site includes biographical information on Bentham, an online newsletter, information concerning publications of Bentham's work, links to Bentham texts on the Internet, and information about access to the Bentham Papers, held at University College London.

**Bracton: De Legibus Et Consuetudinibus Angliae (On the Laws and Customs of England)**
*http://bracton.law.cornell.edu/bracton/Common/index.html*

This site is a co-production of the Ames Foundation, the Harvard Law School Library, and the Legal Information Institute at the Cornell Law School. It includes a brief biography of Henry of Bracton, versions of Bracton's *On The Laws and Customs of England* in both English and Latin, and a search engine which allows keyword searching. In addition, the authors provide a framed version which allows users to scroll through the Latin and the English simultaneously. By way of scripting, the frames version allows the user to go right to a particular page. These are advanced features which require an especially fast computer and a late-model browser. However, those with slower computers or older browsers do not lose any functionality. The home page provides access to a search engine which will be accessible for nearly all users; this search engine allows for both simple keyword searching and more complex, boolean searching. The authors also provide helpful information on technical issues encountered in putting the site together and on browser compatibility. This site is straightforward and useful for students of English legal history.

**Legal Journals on the Web**
*http://www.usc.edu/dept/law-lib/legal/journals.html*

By Wendy Nobunaga, of the Law Library at the University of Southern California. The list of online journals presented here is international in scope and covers general law reviews, subject specific law reviews, commercial law journals, foreign law journals, ABA journals and newsletters, law review locating services, and e-journal locating services. Simple codes after each link tell the user whether the online publication contains full text, abstracts, or subscription information. The site also includes a short list of general interest and computing periodicals which contains a link to *Effector,* journal of the Electronic Frontier Foundation. Sites with as many links as this one sometimes have problems with non-functioning links. This one does not, a tribute to the site's creator.

**The George Mitchell Papers Project**
*http://www.bowdoin.edu/dept/library/arch/mitchell/index.html*

From Senator Mitchell's alma mater, Bowdoin College in Brunswick, Maine. The project to catalog the Mitchell Papers, over 900 cubic feet in size, will take a number of years. However, the Bowdoin College Archives and Special Collections Department has done an admirable job putting together a great deal of information about both the collection and Senator Mitchell. The web site includes a searchable database of photographs of the Senator, photographs of selected objects from the collection, selected speeches (both excerpts and full text), a keyword-searchable index of press releases, a draft of the collection's finding aid, and a timeline of the Mitchell Papers project.

**Oyez, Oyez, Oyez**
*http://oyez.nwu.edu/*

From the Oyez Project at Northwestern University. This site bills itself on the introductory page as a "U.S. Supreme Court Multimedia Database." The site does feature a database of cases searchable by title, subject, citation, or date, including a page of "this date in Supreme Court History." The site also provides lists of Supreme Court Justices and a virtual tour of the Supreme Court building. The virtual tour requires QuickTime software. The link called "Greatest Hits" turned out to be the greatest disappointment. I was expecting audio files with oral arguments before the Court. What I got was an order form for a CD-ROM product called *The Supreme Court's Greatest Hits*. If audio clips are part of the Oyez web site, I was not able to find them. Nevertheless, this is an attractive, informative site, and the searchable database of court cases is a unique and well-designed feature.

**Lewis F. Powell, Jr. Archive**
*http://wlu.edu/~powell/*

From the Law Library at Justice Powell's alma mater, Washington and Lee University, in Richmond, Virginia. The site includes biographical information on Justice Powell and a guide to the Powell Papers. The guide, now under construction, currently contains an abstract, a biographical sketch of Justice Powell, and a summary of the collection.

**Research Guide to the Records of the Mexican American Legal Defense and Educational Fund (MALDEF) (1968-1983) at Stanford University**
*http://www-sul.stanford.edu/depts/spc/guides/m673.html*

From the Special Collections Department at the Stanford University Library. The MALDEF Records collection consists of some 1,500 linear feet of records generated by the Mexican American Legal Defense and Educational Fund as part of its efforts to define and protect the civil rights of Mexican Americans in the United States. The records contain correspondence, legal briefs, court orders, printed matter, photographs, and audiovisual materials spanning the years from the founding of the organization in 1967 to 1984. The web site for the collection is an online finding aid, in HTML format.

**Roman Law Homepage**
*http://www.jura.uni-sb.de/Rechtsgeschichte/Ius.Romanum/english.html*

Produced by the Roman Law branch of the Law-related Internet Project at the University of Saarbrücken. The introductory pages are provided in English, German, and (interestingly!) Latin. The site is not as comprehensive as its name may suggest. It consists of fragments of the Corpus Juris Civilis with the glosses of the medieval jurist Accursius, and the legal texts themselves are entirely in Latin. The need for a strong reading knowledge of Latin, particularly medieval Latin, puts this site out of reach for all but medieval historians with an interest in the evolution of law through the Middle Ages.

**Roman Law Resources**
*http://iuscivile.com*

Roman Law Resources is maintained by Professor Ernest Metzger and provided by the Centre for the Study of the Civil Law Tradition at the University of Aberdeen. This site aims to provide information on Roman law sources and literature, the teaching of Roman law, and the persons who engage in the study of Roman law. It does so very well in many respects. So much of Roman legal scholarship, both in print and online, requires a strong reading knowledge of German, which makes this site especially useful for English-speaking users. The site includes: a bulletin board for user feedback, information about the Centre for the Study of the Civil Law Tradition and a list of the Center's publications, a directory of antiquarian booksellers who carry Roman Law titles, links to primary and secondary literature (including an electronic edition of the *Palingensia of Latin Private Rescripts*), and information on ancient history conferences. A site as comprehensive as this one requires good organizational skills on the part of the web designer, and it is in this area that the site could be improved. The Centre provides a German language equivalent, a helpful feature. However, many pages in the site contain English and German versions side by side, in a multi-column layout which I found both confusing and unnecessary. Other pages, particularly the home page, can be accessed in translation by clicking on a link ("auf Deutsch" or "in English," as appropriate) which produces a page entirely in the appropriate language. The entire site should have been fashioned in this way. The English language pages and the German language pages need to be more independent of each other. Organization and layout issues aside, this is an excellent site, especially for a beginning graduate student in Roman Law.

**South Carolina Legal History Index**
*http://www.law.sc.edu/legal_history/hisindex.htm*

From the Coleman Karesh Library, School of Law, University of South Carolina. To honor that tradition and the accomplishments of some of South Carolina's most outstanding lawyers, the University of South Carolina School of Law has established the South Carolina Legal History Collection. A major portion of the Collection is devoted to eight prominent South Carolina lawyers who lived and practiced during four noteworthy periods of the state's history. The web site, more of an online exhibit at this point, highlights the careers of the lawyers represented in the collection. The site consists of images of the lawyers, all strikingly well-done, and synposes of their careers. The biographies start with John C. Calhoun and end with James F. Byrnes. To date, there are no guides to the actual collections or digitized samples of documents.

**Swarthmore College Peace Collection**
*http://www.swarthmore.edu/Library/peace/index.htm*

The Swarthmore College Peace Collection is a research archives devoted to collecting, preserving, and making accessible, materials on non-governmental efforts towards peace. The Collection now contains over 200 major manuscript collections, 2,500 smaller manuscript collections, 12,000 catalogued books and pamphlets, 400 periodicals currently received, 2,500 back titles of periodicals, 1,700 microfilm reels, 38,000 photographs, posters, graphics, buttons, bumper stickers, and other items, and thousands of audio visual items. The Peace Collection holds material on a wide variety of subjects: the history of the peace movement; pacifism; women and peace; conscientious objection; nonviolence; disarmament; internationalism; and civil disobedience. This site contains guides to the Peace Collection organized by collection and by subject, information about access to the collection (hours, staff, etc.), links to peace organizations and web sites concerned with peace studies and peace history. An online exhibits section contains exhibits on Jane Addams' Hull House, Nobel Peace Prize winner Emily Green Balch, and images of the American Peace Society. A search engine provides keyword, cross-collection searching of online finding aids. Swarthmore has provided a functional and straightforward guide to an important set of papers for any student of law or history.

# Bibliography on Rare and Archival Law Materials

Mark W. Lambert
Michael Widener

**SUMMARY.** This bibliography aims to bring together all the existing literature on the administration and use of rare law book collections and legal archives, in institutional settings. It provides a convenient finding aid to the literature for current and potential practitioners, and also serves to outline the contours of the literature, and thus point out both its strengths and gaps. *[Article copies available for a fee from The Haworth Document Delivery Service: 1-800-342-9678. E-mail address: <getinfo@haworthpressinc.com> Website: <http://www.HaworthPress.com> © 2001 by The Haworth Press, Inc. All rights reserved.]*

## *NOTE FROM THE COMPILERS*

This bibliography aims to bring together all the existing literature on the administration and use of rare law book collections and legal archives, in institutional settings. We have thus excluded works relating to the private collecting of rare law books, and those dealing with rare books and archives in general. There is some overlap with bibliographies that appear elsewhere in this volume.

The purpose of this bibliography is two-fold. It provides a convenient finding aid to the literature for current and potential practitioners. It also

---

Mark W. Lambert is Special Collections and Government Documents Librarian, South Texas College of Law Library, Houston, TX. Michael Widener is Archivist/Rare Book Librarian, Tarlton Law Library, University of Texas at Austin, and a Joseph D. Jamail Fellow in Law Librarianship.

[Haworth co-indexing entry note]: "Bibliography on Rare and Archival Law Materials." Lambert, Mark W., and Michael Widener. Co-published simultaneously in *Legal Reference Services Quarterly* (The Haworth Information Press, an imprint of The Haworth Press, Inc.) Vol. 20, No. 1/2, 2001, pp. 79-84; and: *Public Services Issues with Rare and Archival Law Materials* (ed: Michael Widener) The Haworth Information Press, an imprint of The Haworth Press, Inc., 2001, pp. 79-84. Single or multiple copies of this article are available for a fee from The Haworth Document Delivery Service [1-800-342-9678, 9:00 a.m. - 5:00 p.m. (EST). E-mail address: getinfo@haworthpressinc.com].

© 2001 by The Haworth Press, Inc. All rights reserved.

serves to outline the contours of the literature, and thus point out both its strengths and gaps.

We have used a fuller citation style for this bibliography than that used elsewhere in this volume, to make it easier for the broadest range of readers to locate the publications.

## *GENERAL*

Anglim, Christopher. *Special Collections Policies, Procedures and Guidelines: A Model Plan for the Management of Special Legal Collections.* Buffalo, NY: William S. Hein & Co., 1993.

Bander, Edward J. "Library Exhibits–Two Proposals" [in "Library Exhibits-Panel Discussion"]. *Law Library Journal* 58:1 (Feb. 1965), 15-17.

Hall, Kermit L. "Law Librarians and the New American Legal History." *Law Library Journal* 81:1 (Winter 1989), 1-11.

Hyman, Harold M. " 'No Cheers for the American Law School?' A Legal Historian's Complaint, Plea, and Modest Proposal." *Law Library Journal* 71:2 (May 1978), 227-233.

Mayo-Jefferies, Deborah. "Special Collections in Law School Libraries." *Law Library Journal* 86:3 (Summer 1994), 503-528.

Surles, Richard H. Jr. "Special Collections in Law School Libraries." *Syllabus* 17:3 (Sept. 1986), 3.

Surrency, Edwin C. (chair), Wayne C. Grover, William Jeffrey Jr., & Earl Finbar Murphy. "Legal History and Rare Books" [panel discussion]. *Law Library Journal* 59:1 (Feb. 1966), 71-92.

"Symposium: Library Administration of Historical Materials." *Law Library Journal* 69:3 (Aug. 1976), 314-28. [Part I–Acquisitions, by Myrtle A. Moody; Part II–Cataloging, by Margaret M. Moody; Part III–Exhibits, by Erika S. Chadbourne; Part IV–Microforms, by Erwin C. Surrency.]

## *RARE BOOKS*

Breem, W.W.S. "Historical Sources." In *Manual of Law Librarianship: The Use and Organization of Legal Literature* (2nd ed.; Elizabeth M. Moys ed.; Boston: G.K. Hall, 1987), 249-292.

Cohen, Morris L. "Administration of Rare Materials." In *Law Librarianship, a Handbook* (Heinz Peter Mueller & Patrick E. Kehoe eds.; Littleton, CO: by F.B. Rothman, 1983), 603-688.

Cohen, Morris L. "Bibliographic Control of Early American Law." In *Collecting and Managing Rare Law Books: Papers Presented at a*

Conference Celebrating the Dedication of the New Tarlton Law Library, the University of Texas at Austin School of Law, January 7 & 8, 1981* (Roy M. Mersky, Stanley Ferguson & Daniel Martin, eds.; Dobbs Ferry, NY: Glanville Publishers, Inc., 1981), 119-132.

Davies, Martin. "Incunabulae, Digitalization and the History of Law." In *Rare Law Books and the Language of Catalogues*: *Proceedings of the Conference at Certosa di Pontignano, Siena, 26-29 October 1997* (M. Ascheri & L. Mayali eds.; Siena: Università degli Studi di Siena, 1999), 67-79.

Diamond, Lucia. "Rare Bits and Bytes: The Use of Computers in Rare Book Librarianship." In *Rare Law Books and the Language of Catalogues*: *Proceedings of the Conference at Certosa di Pontignano, Siena, 26-29 October 1997* (M. Ascheri & L. Mayali eds.; Siena: Università degli Studi di Siena, 1999), 81-91.

Gilliam, Mary Cooper. "The Acquisition of Out-of-Print and Antiquarian Law Books." *Law Library Journal* 85:2 (Spring 1993), 385-389.

Goldberg, Jolande E. "Classification and Cataloguing in the Field of Legal History: Processing of Rare Materials in the Online Environment." In *Rare Law Books and the Language of Catalogues*: *Proceedings of the Conference at Certosa di Pontignano, Siena, 26-29 October 1997* (M. Ascheri & L. Mayali eds.; Siena: Università degli Studi di Siena, 1999), 41-65.

Heaney, Howell J. "Rare Book Librarianship and Law Librarianship." In *Collecting and Managing Rare Law Books*: *Papers Presented at a Conference Celebrating the Dedication of the New Tarlton Law Library, the University of Texas at Austin School of Law, January 7 & 8, 1981* (Roy M. Mersky, Stanley Ferguson & Daniel Martin, eds.; Dobbs Ferry, NY: Glanville Publishers, Inc., 1981), 55-69.

Hoeflich, M. H. "Legal Ephemera: A Window on Society and the Law." *Antiquarian Bookman*, Mar. 10, 1997, at 785.

Jenkins, John H. "Rare Books and the Law." In *Collecting and Managing Rare Law Books*: *Papers Presented at a Conference Celebrating the Dedication of the New Tarlton Law Library, the University of Texas at Austin School of Law, January 7 & 8, 1981* (Roy M. Mersky, Stanley Ferguson & Daniel Martin, eds.; Dobbs Ferry, NY: Glanville Publishers, Inc., 1981), 3-14.

Logan, Robert G. "The History of English Legal Bibliography Before 1900." *The Law Librarian* 10:2 (Dec. 1979), 43-46.

Luttrell, Jordan. "Antiquarian Bookselling, Bibliography, and Rare Law Books." *Legal Reference Services Quarterly* 9:1-2 (1989), 89-97.

Marke, Julius J. "Beginning a Collection of Rare Law Books." *New York Law Journal*, May 18, 1999, at 5.

Marke, Julius J. "Determining Tax Value of Gifts to Libraries." *New York Law Journal*, Jan. 20, 1998, at 5.

Marke, Julius J. "Interest Growing in Rare Law Books." *New York Law Journal*, Feb. 28, 1989, at 4.

Mersky, Roy M., Stanley Ferguson & Daniel Martin, eds. *Collecting and Managing Rare Law Books: Papers Presented at a Conference Celebrating the Dedication of the New Tarlton Law Library, the University of Texas at Austin School of Law, January 7 & 8, 1981.* Dobbs Ferry, NY: Glanville Publishers, Inc., 1981.

Mersky, Roy M. "Rare Book Collecting in a Law Library: Including a Survey of Periodical Literature of American Book Collecting." *Legal Reference Services Quarterly* 4:2 (Summer 1984), 45-50.

Modéer, Kjell A. "Why Rare Books in a Modern Law Library?" *International Journal of Legal Information* 25:1-3 (1997), 201-206.

Nissenbaum, Robert J. "Developing a Rare Book Collection Policy at Tarlton Law Library." *Legal Reference Services Quarterly* 4:2 (Summer 1984), 59-65.

Parrish, Jenni. "On the Outside Looking In: The Legal Historian's Perspective on Rare Book Collections." *Legal Reference Services Quarterly* 4:2 (Summer 1984), 51-57.

Reynolds, Thomas H. *Rare Books for Law Libraries.* New York: Glanville Publishers, 1983.

Reynolds, Thomas H. "Sharing Some Bibliographical Riches." In *Rare Law Books and the Language of Catalogues: Proceedings of the Conference at Certosa di Pontignano, Siena, 26-29 October 1997* (M. Ascheri & L. Mayali eds.; Siena: Università degli Studi di Siena, 1999), 93-102.

Reynolds, Thomas H. "Medieval Canon and Roman Law: An Introductory Bibliographical Essay." In *Collecting and Managing Rare Law Books: Papers Presented at a Conference Celebrating the Dedication of the New Tarlton Law Library, the University of Texas at Austin School of Law, January 7 & 8, 1981* (Roy M. Mersky, Stanley Ferguson & Daniel Martin, eds.; Dobbs Ferry, NY: Glanville Publishers, Inc., 1981), 317-356.

"Symposium: Bibliographic Control and Guides to Historical Sources." *Law Library Journal* 69:3 (Aug. 1976), 347-368. [Part I–American Law Library Book Catalogs, by Betty W. Taylor; Part II–Checklists of Serials, by Meira G. Pimsleur; Part III–General Monographic Bibliographies, by Balfour J. Halevy; Part IV–Legal Monographic Bibliographies, by Morris L. Cohen.]

Taylor, Betty W., & Robert J. Munro. "American Legal Bibliography 1860-1900." In *Collecting and Managing Rare Law Books: Papers Presented at a Conference Celebrating the Dedication of the New*

*Tarlton Law Library, the University of Texas at Austin School of Law, January 7 & 8, 1981* (Roy M. Mersky, Stanley Ferguson & Daniel Martin, eds.; Dobbs Ferry, NY: Glanville Publishers, Inc., 1981), 133-143.

## ARCHIVES

Beck, Karen S. "One Step at a Time: the Research Value of Law Student Notebooks." *Law Library Journal* 91:1 (Winter 1999), 29-138.

Brown, Louis M. "Lawyering Decisions: New Materials for Law Libraries to Collect." *Law Library Journal* 87:1 (Winter 1995), 7-27.

Cohen, Morris L. "Wanted for Research: The Working Papers of Lawyers." *Syllabus* 17:3 (Sept. 1986): 1, 8.

Hainsworth, Melody M. "The Role of the Law Librarian in a Legal Archives Program." *Legal Reference Services Quarterly* 10:1-2 (1990), 135-147.

Sloane, Richard. "Archives of Law Firms–A Library Function." *New York Law Journal*, Dec. 16, 1997, at 5.

Surles, Richard H. Jr. "Archives Present Special Challenges." *Syllabus* 17:3 (September 1986), 3.

"Symposium: Lawyers' Papers as a Source of Legal History." *Law Library Journal* 69:3 (Aug. 1976), 303-313. [Part I–Bridge of Words: 18th Century Lawyers and Papers, by Hiller B. Zobel; Part II–The 19th Century, by Alfred Konefsky; Part III–The 20th Century, by Jerold S. Auerbach.]

Trimble, Marsha. "Archives and Manuscripts: New Collecting Areas for Law Libraries." *Law Library Journal* 83:3 (1991), 429-450.

## PRESERVATION

AALL Special Committee on Preservation Needs of Law Libraries. "Preservation Treatment Options for Law Libraries." *Law Library Journal* 84:2 (Spring 1992), 259-279.

Cohen, Morris. "The Law Library Rare Book Room," Part of "Preservation of Law Library Materials & Disaster Planning–A Panel." *Law Library Journal* 73:4 (Fall 1980), 839-846.

Etherington, Don. "Leather Binding Maintenance Project of Rare Law Books." In *Collecting and Managing Rare Law Books: Papers Presented at a Conference Celebrating the Dedication of the New Tarlton Law Library, the University of Texas at Austin School of Law, January 7 & 8, 1981* (Roy M. Mersky, Stanley Ferguson & Daniel Martin, eds.; Dobbs Ferry, NY: Glanville Publishers, Inc., 1981), 97-115.

Marke, Julius J., et al. "Preservation of Law Library Materials & Disaster Planning–A Panel," *Law Library Journal* 73:4 (Fall 1980), 831-852.

Morrow, Carolyn. "Conservation Administration in Research Libraries," Part of "Preservation of Law Library Materials & Disaster Planning–A Panel." *Law Library Journal* 73:4 (Fall 1980), 832-839.

Vincent-Daviss, Diana. "Care and Handling of Library Materials." Part of "Preservation of Law Library Materials & Disaster Planning–A Panel." *Law Library Journal* 73:4 (Fall 1980), 846-852.

## GUIDES TO RESEARCH

Flaherty, David H. "The Use of Early American Court Records in Historical Research." *Law Library Journal* 69:3 (Aug. 1976), 342-346.

Melton, Buckner F., Jr. "Clio at the Bar: A Guide to Historical Method for Legists and Jurists." *Minnesota Law Review* 83:2 (Dec. 1998), 377-472.

Parrish, Jenni. "A Guide to American Legal History Methodology with an Example of Research in Progress." *Law Library Journal* 86:1 (Winter 1994), 105-127.

McFadden, David L. "Legal Research for Historians." *Western Legal History* 10:1-2 (1997), 3-30.

## INDIVIDUAL REPOSITORIES

Anglim, Christopher. "The Special Collections Program at the South Texas College of Law Library." *Conservation Administration News* 49 (Apr. 1992), 4-5, 25.

Hammond, Jane L. "Rare Books in the Cornell Law Library." *Cornell Law Forum* 8:3 (Feb. 1982), 8-11.

Jacob, John N. "The Lewis F. Powell, Jr. Archives and the Contemporary Researcher." *Washington and Lee Law Review* 49:1 (Winter 1992), 3-9.

Kates, Christine J.N. "The Osgoode Society: Preservation of Legal Records." *Law Society of Upper Canada Gazette* 21:1 (Mar. 1987), 58-70.

Pliguzov, Andrei I., & Barbara L. Dash. "Russian Law: 18th Century Russian Books in the Law Library of Congress." *LC Information Bulletin*, Mar. 2000, at 70.

Schaeffer, Roy. "The Law Society of Upper Canada Archives." *Law Society of Upper Canada Gazette* 21:1 (Mar. 1987), 48-57.

Shepard, Catherine, & Peter Oliver. "The Osgoode Society, the Archivist and the Writing of Legal History in Ontario." *Law Society of Upper Canada Gazette* 14:2 (June 1980), 192-202.

# RARE BOOKS

## The Role of Rare Books in Law Libraries

Joel Silver

**SUMMARY.** No other profession is so firmly rooted in historical precedent as the law. Rare law books can be used to promote a knowledge of the history of the law, the history of legal practice, the development of legal writing, the history of legal education, and the history and spread of legal printing and publishing. Since law books cover the entire spectrum of human activity, they can also be used to study any aspect of human thought or behavior that has been the subject of legislation or litigation. Contact with rare books touch the spirit in ways that the law library's other holdings cannot. *[Article copies available for a fee from The Haworth Document Delivery Service: 1-800-342-9678. E-mail address: <getinfo @haworthpressinc.com> Website: <http://www.HaworthPress.com> © 2001 by The Haworth Press, Inc. All rights reserved.]*

---

Joel Silver is Curator of Rare Books and Interim Director, Lilly Library, Indiana University, where he has been since 1983. He holds a JD from the Whittier College School of Law and an MLS from Indiana University. He has taught courses and workshops on rare book librarianship, descriptive bibliography, history of the book, and reference sources for rare books, and was a regular contributor to *AB Bookman's Weekly*.

[Haworth co-indexing entry note]: "The Role of Rare Books in Law Libraries." Silver, Joel. Co-published simultaneously in *Legal Reference Services Quarterly* (The Haworth Information Press, an imprint of The Haworth Press, Inc.) Vol. 20, No. 1/2, 2001, pp. 85-92; and: *Public Services Issues with Rare and Archival Law Materials* (ed: Michael Widener) The Haworth Information Press, an imprint of The Haworth Press, Inc., 2001, pp. 85-92. Single or multiple copies of this article are available for a fee from The Haworth Document Delivery Service [1-800-342-9678, 9:00 a.m. - 5:00 p.m. (EST). E-mail address: getinfo@haworth pressinc.com].

© 2001 by The Haworth Press, Inc. All rights reserved.

Readers of this journal don't need to be reminded of the tenuous state of the acquisitions and operating budgets of most law libraries. Law libraries, like other academic and professional libraries today, are struggling to keep up with a rapidly increasing mass of electronic information and printed material, and like other librarians, law librarians are having to make the difficult choices of what they can afford to buy and what level of service they can continue to provide. Relatively few law libraries are blessed with endowed acquisitions budgets or generous donors, and while some libraries are known for their important collections of rare legal books and manuscripts and their commitment to their continuation, many law librarians and administrators question the necessity or importance of committing even a small fraction of their strained budgets to the establishment or maintenance of such collections.

The question that these librarians ask, "Why should law libraries collect rare books?" is a good one. In the 1960s, when many institutions had a bit more money for library acquisitions than they sometimes knew how to spend, some of them established departments of special collections in their research libraries, often inspired at least in part by the existence of such departments in other peer or rival institutions. After the first flush of enthusiasm had dissipated, and in the absence of librarians knowledgeable about rare books and manuscripts and how they might be used, a number of these collections languished through indifference, active neglect, or outright hostility. Today, some of them have been dispersed, some are unloved and unused, and some are still hanging on. When faced with these examples, intelligent and politically astute law library administrators might properly decide that whatever the benefits of establishing and operating a collection of rare books might be, to do so is certainly not worth the expense and the trouble.

But to make this decision, logical though it may seem to those who are responsible for setting budgets and priorities, is to deny to the library's constituents the many tangible and intangible benefits that the presence of rare books can bring to a library. To do so also ignores the continued existence and success of the many other special collections, both older and more recently established, that are flourishing and giving their readers and visitors something that they can't get anywhere else–contact with books of the past that library users can see, read, touch, handle, and smell–which bring them closer to the worlds and thoughts of the past in ways that modern books and other artifacts cannot.

Law libraries are especially appropriate places for the existence of collections of rare books. No other profession is so firmly rooted in historical precedent as the law, and until relatively recently, this historical precedent could be found recorded only in books. Today, a great deal of legal research is conducted online, but the content of these online databases is made up almost entirely of the contents of the books of the past, and generations of lawyers and law students have studied these books to learn the law, compose documents and pleadings, prepare their cases, and think about what the law has been and is, and where it might be going. Today's readers can enter into the worlds of the lawyers and law students of the past by reading the words that their predecessors read in modern reprints or on computer screens, but today's lawyers and law students can penetrate much more deeply into the mental and physical worlds of their predecessors by reading the actual books that their predecessor did in the forms in which they read them, for there are no complete substitutes for the physical books of the past.

This concept, that a book is a physical object with a form and presence beyond the intellectual content that it contains, is an uncomfortable one for librarians who are accustomed to providing access to information rather than access to a physical object. But it is this physical object itself that contains "information" of a kind that cannot be reproduced by any other medium, no matter how high-tech or convenient. Even methods of reproduction that attempt to retain something of the physical aspect of a book or page, such as a full-sized facsimile reprint, or a digitized image, can't reproduce the original paper or binding, nor can they convey the original look of the ink as it was impressed into the surface of the paper by metal type or by a stereotype plate. These are not usually concerns of non-special collections librarians, but all librarians should be aware of the fact that the form in which something is read does have a real impact on a reader's response to it, and while reading a legal text in an original or early edition by no means guarantees that the reader will immediately be granted understanding, it does allow the reader to approach the text in a way that reading a modern edition, facsimile, or online version does not.[1]

Books are not generic objects. Even if one were to possess and study such an original or early edition, what can be learned or gained from one copy of such a book is different from what can be learned or gained from another. That this is so is due in part to the many changes and corrections that were made to books as they went through the printing and publishing process. Sheets that were found to contain errors or other undesired textual or other matter might be corrected during the printing process, but those sheets that had already been printed were not necessarily discarded, and these sheets ultimately made their way into finished books. Multiple copies of some extremely famous books, such as the First Folio of William Shakespeare, published in 1623, have been examined in detail, and the variations found in surviving copies can be astounding to those who don't know how books were produced during the period of the handpress. While such detailed study is basic to the establishment of a text, few non-literary texts have been subjected to this kind of intensive treatment, and there is a great deal of work that remains to be done before we know what the publishers really produced when they issued the first editions of Bracton, Coke, or Blackstone.

In addition to the variations caused by the many things that could happen to a work between its creation and publication, there are countless differences between different copies of a book caused by what happened after publication. Until the widespread development and use of machine-made cloth bookbindings in the nineteenth century, books were bound individually, often to the order of their original purchasers. Although it was common for some books to have been bound for publishers or booksellers, it is the owners of these books since their publication who have been responsible for many of their physical transformations. Through these books, we can study how lawyers and law libraries of the past have bound and treated their books, and we can also see what books that we consider to be separate today were bound together by their earlier owners.

By studying individual copies of books, we can also see examples of the many kinds of marks that people and institutions have made in books. No law librarian or law student is unfamiliar with the modern preference for the "highlighter" as the annotating implement of choice by those who are briefing cases, but law students and lawyers of the past also had their own preferred methods of annotation, from underlining to extensive marginal comments, some of which stray far from the legal subjects at hand. The ownership inscriptions, written notes, or half-formed thoughts of earlier owners or readers of books represent an underused resource for the study of the practice and administration of law and legal education, and for most of these books, the modern reader who studies these annotations in detail will be the first to have done so since they were first written. Often even more revealing are a succession of notations provided by generations of owners, and occasionally, a careful reader can find that the notes in a particular volume formed the basis for a later edition of the book, or for a historically important decision.

Many law libraries, through design or accident, do have volumes that are or should be designated as "rare." There is no agreement, however, in the rare book world as to the definition of the term "rare book," so law librarians should feel comfortable in designating most anything that they feel is worthy of being protected or preserved in its present form as such. Those who have attempted to define the term have written about its value or importance (intrinsic or monetary); its age; its fragility; or its historic or present rarity (i.e., number of copies that were originally produced or that have survived). Many writers have equated "rare" with "precious," and have noted that a rare book is one which for one or more of a variety of reasons, can be considered precious or important, and is worthy of being treated as such.

With this flexibility and with a little imagination, even if no rare book collection currently exists, it should not be difficult in any large law library to develop from the existing collection at least a small group of books that can be considered as rare. These books can include early English reports, statutes, or treatises; American colonial or territorial laws (which often have quite interesting printing histories); first or early editions of famous treatises or commentaries; books owned or annotated by interesting practitioners; or newly-acquired modern books that should be preserved intact, complete with the dust jackets that most libraries discard. One way or another, at least a small number of books can be set aside for special treatment and handling.

But once this is done, then what? It's not enough to simply remove these books from the general collection, designate them as non-circulating, and then think that the job is done. For a rare book collection to be effective in a law library, the intended audience needs to know that these books exist in your library, and they also need to be able to see or use them. This involves cataloging or recataloging the books, becoming aware of some of the interesting aspects of the particular copies of the rare books in the library, and devising ways to present them to the library's public, and it is this presentation that can take many forms.

My professional work in law libraries has been limited, but I have worked in a large special collections library for many years, and I know from my own experience the tremendous variety of uses that rare books, including rare law books, can have. Rare law books can be used as teaching tools in class sessions, and they can be arranged and described for viewing in exhibitions. They can be used to promote a knowledge of the history of the law, the history of legal practice, the development of legal writing, the history of legal education, and the history and spread of legal printing and publishing. Since law books cover the entire spectrum of human activity, they can also be used to study any aspect of human thought or behavior that has been the subject of legislation or litigation. As M. H. Hoeflich has written in his enjoyable and heartfelt essay, "Legal History and the History of the Book: Variations on a Theme,"

> One cannot fully understand the law and the legal profession without understanding its history. One cannot understand that history without understanding the intimate connections between law, lawyers, books, and libraries. No one can truly call themselves a legal historian without also acknowledging that they are historians of the book, of publishing, of bookselling, and of libraries. And, thus, we can say that the history of law is also the history of the law book.[2]

Legal and historical journals are filled with examples of the value of rare books in legal research, and several other articles in this special issue attest to the importance of special collections in law libraries. Despite this demonstrated importance, the establishment and maintenance of law-related special collections have never been seen as essential in most libraries, since the vast majority of users of law libraries never engage in the kind of legal or historical research that requires the use of rare law books, and in the real budgetary world, not all programs or acquisitions can be funded. So the question remains, why should law libraries collect rare books?

My own answer, which is unfashionable, since much modern literary theory views a text as a disembodied entity rather than something that is defined by or connected to its physical form, is that a rare book possesses a magnetism that has the power to exert its influence on those with whom it comes into contact. This attraction, which I have seen demonstrated time and time again when rare books are viewed or handled by young students, seasoned faculty members, or casual visitors, does not work its magic on everyone, but those who come under its spell find that their lives are forever changed. They may go on to do what scholars consider "serious" research, but they may also merely go on their way with a renewed appreciation for the books of the past and for those who read and used them.

Law students are too rarely exposed to the original volumes in which the cases that they read in their casebooks were first reported. They also too rarely see early collections of statutes, the first printings of the session laws of their state, or the treatises or form books that were used as books of practice by attorneys of centuries past. This is unfortunate, for the handling and reading of such books can shed light on the study of the complexities of property law, the development of criminal or tort law, or the formalities of trial practice. By the time these students begin practicing law, however, they are often so preoccupied with the demands of their work that there is little time for them to be introduced to the rewards to be gained from reading obsolete law books.

When I worked in the antiquarian book trade in the 1970s and early 1980s, it was a truism among booksellers that though physicians were often dedicated collectors of rare medical or scientific books, lawyers were seldom attracted to rare books in their own field. The reasons were not economic, for law books, with the exception of very early imprints or well-known high-spot law books, such as Coke and Blackstone, were sold for relatively low prices. Among the reasons advanced for this regrettable lack of interest in rare law books among members of the legal profession were that early law books were often written in Latin or Law French rather than English (though many medical books were in foreign languages as well), or that medical books often contained illustrations, which, with the exception of a table or two, law books generally did not. The situation has improved a bit since then, but law books are still far less collected than medical books, and they are still underpriced in comparison to most other rare book fields.

Law libraries have the ability to bring their students, faculty, and researchers into contact with rare law books, and they have the duty to do this as well. Contact with the sources of the legal tradition and profession should be required in a historically-based discipline such as the law, and the seeds of interest in rare books, sown early, have reaped dividends for many law libraries in the form of gifts and other support years later. Much more important than this possible future benefit to the library, however, is the good that can be done by the library for its readers today.

There are those who will never feel the attraction of rare books and who believe that law libraries have no business wasting money, space, and personnel on their acquisition, cataloging, housing, care, and service. There are also those who feel that money spent on art museums or musical programs is money that could be better spent elsewhere. But just as museums and music enrich the spirit as well as the intellect in ways that cannot be measured, so does contact with rare books touch the spirit in ways that the law library's other holdings cannot. Researching the development of a line of legal reasoning in books spanning several centuries may not make the researcher a better lawyer, but it will likely make the researcher a more humane one, as well as one with a greater appreciation for the rich heritage of the law that he or she is studying.

Rare books have a central role to play in law libraries today, but it is up to law librarians to make this possible. Appropriate rare books need to selected, described, exhibited, publicized, shown, and used, and it is the librarians who must find time among their other many duties to make these things happen. The library exists to enable its readers to find the information that they seek, but it also exists to broaden their minds and enrich their spirits. There are hundreds of thousands of other books in the library that can answer readers' questions and provide them with the citations to the letter of the law that are required, but it is the rare book collection, with its calf and sheep bindings, its handmade paper, its letterpress pages of text and commentary, and its owners' manuscript annotations, that provide their viewers with an unmatched look at the way rules of law were developed and put into practice. It is here that the spirit of the law resides.

## NOTES

1. A recent vivid reminder of the inadequacy of reformatted substitutes for original materials is given by Nicholson Baker in "Deadline: The Author's Desperate Bid to Save America's Past," *The New Yorker,* July 24, 2000, at 42.

2. M. H. Hoeflich, "Legal History and the History of the Book: Variations on a Theme," 46 *University of Kansas Law Review* 431 (1998).

# Rediscovering Rare Books in an Electronic Age

## Claire M. Germain

**SUMMARY.** Rare books provide the needed historical context to the modern study of law, and they serve as an important balance in the transition to a world dominated by computers. These treasures should be shared more widely with groups of faculty, students, staff, and alumni. They need to be preserved and shared with current and future generations of scholars and students in this new electronic information age.

When I assumed the direction of the Cornell Law Library in July, 1993, my main charge was to strengthen the foreign and international law collection and move the library further into the electronic age. But somewhere on the way to achieving those goals, I discovered and fell in love with the rare books in the library. That came as a surprise to me, because, until then, information was more important to me than the physical attributes of books. In spite of coming from a family where both my mother and sister have university degrees in history and know every-

---

Claire M. Germain is Edward Cornell Law Librarian and Professor of Law, Cornell University Law School. She has authored numerous publications on legal research and European and comparative law topics.

This article, presented here with slight modifications, originally appeared in the July 1996, Volume 23, Number 1 issue of the *Cornell Law Forum* on page 11-13. It is reprinted here with the *Cornell Law Forum's* permission.

[Haworth co-indexing entry note]: "Rediscovering Rare Books in an Electronic Age." Germain, Claire M. Co-published simultaneously in *Legal Reference Services Quarterly* (The Haworth Information Press, an imprint of The Haworth Press, Inc.) Vol. 20, No. 1/2, 2001, pp. 93-98; and: *Public Services Issues with Rare and Archival Law Materials* (ed: Michael Widener) The Haworth Information Press, an imprint of The Haworth Press, Inc., 2001, pp. 93-98.

thing about the lives of the French kings and history in general, history did not hold much interest for me, aside from its relevance to specific research projects. However, once I started discovering the treasures our library had in its midst, I quickly developed an appreciation for the beauty of the books as artifacts; I admired their rarity and the civilization they represent.

The Cornell Law Library's rare book collection, one of the finest in the United States, consists of four distinct parts: the rare books in the Edwin S. Dawson Rare Book Room (funded through a generous gift of Donato A. Evangelista '57 in honor of his father-in-law), and its centerpiece, the Samuel Thorne collection of English legal history; the endowed Bennett collection of early statutory and session laws; the Edwin Marshall collection of books on equity; and the Nathaniel Moak trials collection. What makes those collections stand apart is that each reflects the life efforts of individuals devoted to the purposeful acquisition of a collection, one book at a time. They have left us an awesome legacy.

After rediscovering the rare books that generations of scholars and librarians had patiently and actively collected over the years, I came to believe that these treasures should be shared more widely with groups of faculty, students, staff, and alumni. The question was, who would be knowledgeable enough to explain the importance and interpret the books for a diverse audience? By a stroke of good luck, my research assistant, Marshal Grant '96, introduced me to his wife, Barbara Grant. Both hold Ph.D.'s in Medieval Studies from Yale, and the library was fortunate to be able to hire Barbara as the curator of rare law books. Thanks to her background in medieval manuscripts and her paleographic and linguistic skills, she has been influential in the work we have done so far with the rare books. Her work was continued by Daniel Smith, hired as a reference librarian and curator of law rare books in 1996.

Rediscovering these treasures has helped me understand the special role of rare books in legal education and in contemporary society: rare books provide the needed historical context to the modern study of law, and they serve as an important balance in the transition to a world dominated by computers. They need to be preserved and shared with current and future generations of scholars and students in this new electronic information age.

## RARE BOOKS PROVIDE HISTORICAL CONTEXT

Rare books serve as the best exhibits in retracing legal historical milestones. They provide a historical and visual context to the study of legal developments. For instance, when I teach my introduction to French law seminar, we spend the first class session in the rare book room.

We talk about the historical development and roots of the civil law and common law systems. We go back to medieval times and discuss the revival of Roman law studies on the European continent through the rediscovery and glosses of Justinian's *Corpus juris civilis,* and the universities' role in shaping the law through the systematic exposition of legal principles.

We talk about England, which received Roman law in some fashion, as demonstrated by the great work attributed to Bracton, *De legibus et consuetudinibus Angliae,*[1] a commentary on the writs, which also expounded Roman law. We reflect on the thought that if Bracton's ideas had prevailed, Roman law might have been received more extensively into England, and the English legal system would have developed more along the lines of the continental legal systems. But Bracton was too late for England, because the royal courts had already developed a strong centralized system of writs before university law schools were founded. While European lawyers were educated in the universities and focused on substantive legal rules, rather than form and questions of procedure, the English legal system was developed on a case-by-case basis. English lawyers were trained at the Inns of Court and studied writs and pleadings. That explains the paucity of scholarly writings in England and the absence of systematic exposition of the law. It was only in the eighteenth century that Blackstone's *Commentaries*[2] was celebrated as the first comprehensive exposé of English law since Bracton.

We look at the Year Books, the first law reports of English medieval society, from about 1260 to 1535, highly subjective and written in Law French, that curious mixture of French and English that was the language of the courts from the mid-thirteenth century to the seventeenth century, developed after William the Conqueror of Normandy became the King of England in 1066. We talk about how the *Graunde Abridgment* by Anthony Fitzherbert and the one by Sir Robert Brooke were the sixteenth-century predecessors to the West digest system. We discuss the controversial proposition that on-line searching is now fundamentally altering the way we find legal information, and perhaps even the notion of "the law."[3]

We study Dyer's *Reports,* written by the well-known judge and court reporter, Sir James Dyer, and compare it with the manuscript by the same reporter, circa 1560, written in cursive secretary's hand. It is touching to imagine the person writing the annotations with a typical sixteenth-century script. We talk about the Napoleonic Code, which was used as a model for many nations of the civil law tradition. The law library's edition of 1809 has a fine engraving of the emperor that gives a feel for the person.

The students appreciate the atmosphere and beauty of the room. They linger after class and ask questions. They enjoy seeing and touching the books. They are also intrigued to find out that they, as modern-day law students, speak Law French without realizing it, since so many common words of the modern legal language, used in courts and even in TV shows, came through the French: "voir dire," "grand jury" and "petit jury," "plaintiff," and "trespass" are but a few examples.[4] Also, the habit of using paired words, "act and deed," "breaking and entering," "to pardon and forgive," "to devise and bequeath," and so on, comes from the hesitation to use the French alone, and the desire for clarification or emphasis.[5]

Every student should have the opportunity to touch the books that have contributed to shaping the common law and that form the basis of the Anglo-American legal system, and to see the early statutes of the state they come from, even back to colonial times. It is through the contact with rare books that students can gain a true sense of the evolution of law.

## *RARE BOOKS ARE TREASURES TO BE PRESERVED FOR THE FUTURE*

Rare books are part of our international heritage and bear witness to our civilization. They reflect a distinctively human enterprise and need to be preserved for future generations. The library collection is considerable. Amazingly, it holds the originals of most of the works cited in the standard texts on English legal history.[6] It possesses the original editions of books that scholars have devoted their lives to studying.[7] Reproductions exist, and are used when usage warrants it,[8] but to hold the original book in one's hand is to touch a part of human history. One needs the physical contact with the artifact to realize the importance of the book in the dissemination of information and the communication of knowledge.

Rare books have been admired for a long time and have always been important to scholars. What is different today is that rare books offer great comfort and a pleasant respite from the rigors of modern life. At a time when most of us are bound to sit for hours and strain our eyes before a terminal, spending time in the rare book room with one of these marvelous books is like sitting in a beautiful gothic cathedral and finding a quiet place to reflect on the best the human mind has produced. In this age of tumultuous changes in every facet of life, rare books offer calm, peace, and a sense of security. They also force us to slow down. Rare books cannot be speed-read. Deciphering the annotations written in old cursive handwriting or the mysterious Law French takes time.

Rare books are not just old books. They come alive through the skill of those who know how to put the book into the proper historical context and impart knowledge about it. Books should be treated not as museum pieces but as usable objects, accessible to all. They present a great potential for continuing use over time. For rare books in law, the added value is that they are needed for research.

The collection is vulnerable, however, and the library needs help to preserve the collection for future generations. Unlike many rare collections that passed from private collectors to rare book libraries, much of the Cornell law collection was in active use by the law school community or in the private libraries of lawyers. As the collection now stands, more than half of the volumes are too fragile to be handled without risk of further damage. Preservation treatment may consist of complete rebinding and deacidifying and repair of paper, as well as restoration of original binding fragments. Archival linen boxes can also be custom-made for each book to protect the original bindings. Although the costs of preservation are high, once the books are stabilized, they will need no further treatment for perhaps a hundred years. This is a one-time expenditure.[9]

The Cornell Law Library is resolutely embracing the future and building a vast digital library by providing access to worldwide electronic information sources from the many computer stations in the law school and through its own web site, accessible from any point in the world.[10] The distinction of the library, however, now and even more so in the future, comes from its possessing an extensive print collection, including over two thousand rare books. We encourage alumni and friends to come and look at the books and appreciate them. By discovering or rediscovering these treasures of the past, one can savor their beauty, be inspired by the human spirit they attest to, and acquire new perspectives in approaching legal problems.

## NOTES

1. Written circa 1250-1260, with the first printed edition published by Richard Tottell in 1569.
2. We have the first edition, published in 1765-69.
3. See David Post, "The Law Is Where You Find It," 18 *American Lawyer* 98 (1996); Robert Berring, "Legal Research and Legal Concepts: Where Form Molds Substance," 75 *California Law Review* 15 (1987).
4. David Mellinkoff's *The Language of the Law* 15-16 (1963) has many such examples and represents an admirable work on the subject.
5. *Id.*, at 121.
6. E.g., J.H. Baker's *An Introduction to Legal History* (3rd ed. 1990). John Baker actively used the collection for his research.
7. E.g., Boersma's *An Introduction to Fitzherbert's Abridgment* (1981). Samuel Thorne translated and wrote the definitive work on Bracton, *On the Laws and Customs of England*, 1968-77, using the first printed edition that the library now holds.
8. For instance, Blackstone's *Commentaries*.
9. A preservation report, prepared by Barbara Grant, highlighting the needs and costs of preserving the collection, is available from the author.
10. The URL for the library web site is <http://www.law.cornell.edu/library>. The Cornell Law Library is also participating with other libraries in efforts to preserve rare books through digital technologies. Digitization of rare materials serves two purposes. One goal is to preserve and save information printed on brittle paper, acidic since the beginning of the industrial revolution. That will help preserve our collection of nineteenth-century trials. The second goal is to make the information available to a larger group of people by producing digital facsimiles. The Cornell University library system is joining the efforts of the Library of Congress's National Digital Library program, which aims to make available five million items, including photographs and rare materials. The Library of Congress web site can be accessed at <http://www.loc.gov/>.

# Roman and Canon Law Research

Lucia Diamond

**SUMMARY.** Historians interested in law and lawyers interested in history all find something of interest in both the civil law of classical Rome, the Corpus Juris Civilis, and the canon law of the Church of Rome, the Corpus Juris Canonici. This article describes the types of researchers who consult Roman and canon law sources, discusses the research needs of these researchers, and explains the varying citation formats that have been used for these works. *[Article copies available for a fee from The Haworth Document Delivery Service: 1-800-342-9678. E-mail address: <getinfo@haworth pressinc.com> Website: <http://www.HaworthPress.com> © 2001 by The Haworth Press, Inc. All rights reserved.]*

## I. INTRODUCTION

This article will take a look at the reference needs of those who use a special collection of historical sources of canon and Roman law. This article will also provide an introduction to the sometimes-cryptic citations handed to the reference staff. At the Robbins Collection we are fortunate to have excellent collections, scholars, and other reference tools at hand to answer our reference questions. I hope that this introductory discussion of our researchers and of some useful resources in

---

Lucia Diamond is Librarian of the Robbins Collection, University of California at Berkeley, School of Law. She received her JD cum laude from the University of California, Hastings College of the Law and her MLS from the University of California at Berkeley. She is a member of Beta Phi Mu.

[Haworth co-indexing entry note]: "Roman and Canon Law Research." Diamond, Lucia. Co-published simultaneously in *Legal Reference Services Quarterly* (The Haworth Information Press, an imprint of The Haworth Press, Inc.) Vol. 20, No. 1/2, 2001, pp. 99-112; and: *Public Services Issues with Rare and Archival Law Materials* (ed: Michael Widener) The Haworth Information Press, an imprint of The Haworth Press, Inc., 2001, pp. 99-112. Single or multiple copies of this article are available for a fee from The Haworth Document Delivery Service [1-800-342-9678, 9:00 a.m. - 5:00 p.m. (EST). E-mail address: getinfo@haworthpress inc.com].

Roman law and in the canon law of Western Christendom will assist those who get only the occasional researcher in these fields.

### A. The Robbins Collection Patrons

The researchers who use the reading room of the Robbins Collection come with a variety of interests. Most are academicians, professors or graduate students, or researchers, either sponsored by an institute or privately funded. A few are attorneys, and fewer still are pro se litigants.

Some may be working on historical issues for their own sake or may be using historical studies to enlighten modern issues. Some are looking at the historical roots of modern decisions or concepts. Some may be hoping to use ancient wisdom to guide modern judges or legislators. Some of the ecclesiastical courts have existed for several centuries, and a researcher may be studying extremely old decisions in order to write a study of some body of law or period of the court's history, or in order to conduct a rather extensive case history. Although most of the resources of the Collection are devoted to legal history, the Collection does include some modern religious law, both substantive and procedural. Canon lawyers and pro se litigants with current cases in secular or ecclesiastical courts, therefore, find some useful material in our collection, but we also refer them to other libraries that collect more of the modern ecclesiastical court decisions and legislative or pontifical updates.

### B. The Robbins Collection

The founder of The Robbins Collection, Lloyd M. Robbins, was a San Francisco lawyer and Chancellor of the Episcopal Diocese of Northern California. In his position as Chancellor, he gave legal advice to the Diocese and developed an interest in ecclesiastical law. His first major donation to the library was William of Lyndwood's *Super constituciones provinciales laus deo* (Oxford: Theodoricus Rood, 1483), the foundation of English canon law. As an attorney, in a tax case that eventually went to the United States Supreme Court, Mr. Robbins used his knowledge of the historical development of California law to trace the definition of a wife's community property interest back through the Spanish civil law that was enforced in California until 1849. These two interests of Mr. Robbins, in religious law and in European civil law, now form the core of The Robbins Collection, although it has much expanded from these origins.

The Robbins Collection now includes material that physically dates back more than a millennium and covers legal cultures that date back more than six millennia. Our religious law collections include the canon law of the Roman and Greek churches, the law of the Protestant churches, and Jewish, Buddhist, and Islamic law. Our secular law collections include ancient law, classical Roman law, medieval jurisprudence, the *ius commune* tradition, European legal history in general, and modern comparative, international, and foreign law. Much of the subject matter of the historical material is timeless: marriage, divorce, taxes, interest-bearing loans, bankruptcy, wills and testaments. Our collection of legal materials complements the general collections of the University of California at Berkeley (UCB) as well as the theological collections of the library of the Graduate Theological Union (GTU) next to the Berkeley campus.

In addition to what is available at hand in the Collection, we have access through computers in the reading room to the digital collections of the University of California at Berkeley and to the California Digital Library. Patrons and staff can also use these computers to search the Internet for relevant material. Foreign language dictionaries, lists of Latin place names, publishers' catalogs, as well as full-text substantive databases of primary and secondary texts (some freely available and some not), have all been helpful to us. Although specific sites come and go, and that is one reason why the mega search engines are useful, there are other approaches one can take. The home pages of the classics departments or medieval studies departments of many universities have relevant material and links to other useful sites. Similarly, the rare books and manuscripts or legal history sections of library or law-related professional associations may provide links to substantive sites or e-mail discussion lists. If working with materials from a modern institution, whether the Vatican or the Monumenta Germaniae Historica, a look for a web address for that organization may be worthwhile.

Researchers can prepare in advance for a visit by looking at our online catalogs. Our documents, manuscripts and microfilm are listed only in printed finding aids at present, but most of our microfiche, CD-ROMs, and printed book holdings are included in the online catalog of the law library at Boalt Hall. To reach the Boalt Law Library Catalog, telnet <lawcat.law.berkeley.edu> and type "library" at the login prompt, or direct your browser to <http://lawcat.berkeley.edu/search>. The LAWCAT contains the most up-to-date records, but most of our holdings can also be accessed in the University of California systemwide online catalog, MELVYL. We often use a local search limit (at UCB) to bring up holdings at all libraries on the Berkeley campus, including GTU and The Robbins Collection, allowing easy access by researchers to all local resources. To reach MELVYL, telnet <melvyl.ucop.edu> or direct your browser to <http://www.dbs.cdlib.org> and then choose the database MELVYL Catalog. Although I have used only our catalog as an example, many major collections and institutes have online catalogs and finding aids available to the public.

## *II. REFERENCE PATRONS*

This section discusses the law reference needs of those inside and outside the legal profession. Attorneys may be modern practitioners representing individual or institutional clients on religious matters or looking at historical roots or other fields of law for comparative purposes. Practitioners and academics often write to influence a decision-making body, whether a court, a legislative body, or an influential organization such as The American Law Institute. Some law professors may work mainly in modern fields, but may also use the historical materials to add weight or authority to their argument. Other law professors may be primarily legal historians, writing as historians or as comparativists. Non-law professors and graduate students who use the law collections may come from any field, but are often historians who find in the ordinances, legal documents, and reports of court cases much detail of life and culture of a particular period. Theologians often use our materials as theology, ethics, and law often overlap, and in some religions the distinction between law and theology is an artificial construct imposed by outsiders.

Attorneys (and pro se individuals) use the modern collections to represent individual clients in a legal matter. The major religions have established ecclesiastical tribunals in which issues governed by the religion, for example the authenticity of a marriage or divorce, may be raised. The religious issue might also be part of a case being heard in a secular court, in criminal as well as civil matters. Other attorneys may be advising a religious organization on a legal matter, perhaps for example, a matter involving property owned by the organization. Although using the modern collections, these attorneys or individuals may find they need to go back into the older cases and materials for support for their position. Many organizations and tribunals are continuing from earlier times. The decisions of the Sacred Roman Rota (a tribunal of the Roman Catholic Church) and its predecessor have had explicit authority since a decretal, the *Ratio Juris,* issued by Pope John XXII in 1331. A regular cite-checking process can go back quite a ways. Of course, as well as providing long-standing support on a point of law, an analysis of the roots of modern law may also assist an argument for a change in direction of current law.

Law professors and historians may use the historic materials strictly for straightforward legal history research. They may use rare materials to illustrate and explain oddities of modern legal language that hang on from early times. It is especially interesting for property or contracts classes to see some examples of old contracts transferring ownership, to have archaic words explained in context, or to actually see a seal on a document. Theological historians may also work on straightforward historical themes or may be writing on subjects that they regard as a continuum. General historians often use legal resources to gather information for a society and culture type of study. So much of life is and was covered by rules and regulations that a non-lawyer can learn much about daily life from legal documents and law texts of a particular time. The lawyer, too, should not overlook other fields of historical research. For example, some knowledge of Roman political history is essential to understand Roman law in its context.

Academic or other writers may look to influence modern legislators, judges, or advisory bodies by reference to historic sources of modern law or by reference to an historic model or methodology. Roman law, for example, started about two and a half millennia ago as the rules of a relatively small group of people in a village that we call Rome, but that body of law grew to influence and shape legal thinking right up to our time. The history of Roman law, its structure and the adaptations of later wide-ranging jurisdictions now provide a framework or methodology for the modern European Union and others trying to harmonize diverse local laws into a coordinated, cooperative body of law. The study of the history of Roman law, its distortion through the Dark Ages, its academic revival in the medieval universities, and resulting practical adaptations is an interesting study in itself. Roman law also can provide insights into our modern law, as very few, if any, Western jurisdictions have not been touched in some way by Roman law, and it has had its influence in the East as well. This is true of common law as well as civil law jurisdictions. Furthermore, from a legal methods standpoint, the development of Roman law was a sophisticated cultural achievement and the law represents a model of rational legal analysis. Its study is an excellent way to learn to think as a lawyer.

## III. SOURCES

First, *caveat lector*. Some knowledge of other languages, ancient and modern, and especially of Latin, classical, medieval, or ecclesiastical, is useful to a study of Roman or canon law. A few years ago, a rough survey of the Roman law titles in the Robbins Collection showed that out of about 4,500 titles, less than 500 were in English. Occasionally, even the English language books will casually use a Latin or other foreign phrase without translation. Assisting the reader in finding a translation of these phrases has often proved to be among our most difficult of reference questions, especially when the writer does not give an entire rule or saying, but starts in the vein: "that well-known rule that begins 'it is better . . .'." Sometimes the full-text databases are useful to find such a phrase in its original or common context and then the meaning can be determined.

Furthermore, the subject matter speaks for itself as regards the need for some multilingual facility. All primary sources of Roman law and early canon law are not in English. Some have been translated to English, but the study of law involves close attention to the words used and their context, express or implied. Translations, necessary as they are, are always imperfect at doing this. Many scholars prefer those translations that have the original text and the translation on facing pages. This format is especially useful to those with some reading knowledge of the other language, if not easy fluency. It also can provide useful clues to those with little or no reading knowledge of the other language. Fortunately, for the reference librarians who may not be multilingual, most of the primary and secondary source materials in Roman and canon law use alphabets that look much like our own. Librarians are sophisticated enough in library skills to find a requested title in the catalog or on the shelf or in a volume of collected works, even if we haven't a clue to the exact subject matter of the text. Although at The Robbins Collection we require multilingual reading knowledge of our employees, we each have to work from time to time with unknown languages and even, though admittedly with great difficulty, with unfamiliar alphabets. Probably too, we all had to learn Roman numerals in grade school or sometime, as even our English books often have pages that are numbered with the little "i"s, and "v"s, and "x"s. Thus, with a little initial assistance, even those who consider themselves monolingual can pick out the right section, rule, or question in a citation to hand the correct volume to a patron. An introduction to the variety of Roman and canon law citations that may be offered to the reference staff is given below. Some actual examples of the modern style of citation can be found in the *Uniform System of Citation: The Bluebook* by the Harvard Law Review staff.

### A. Roman Law Sources

There is relatively little primary source material available for the study of Roman law. We see Roman law, for the most part, not from original sources, but from a successor to the Roman law, a codification of the writings of earlier Roman legal jurists ordered by the Byzantine emperor Justinian I in the early 6th century. Justinian, in his decree, the *Constitutio Deo auctore,* authorizing the compilation of the writings of the Roman jurists, wrote that the state of the law was so confused that no one could comprehend it. He ordered the collection of all existing legislation, the elimination of all obsolete and repetitious matter and the compilation of one clear code. This work came to be known in the Middle Ages as the Corpus Juris Civilis, the body of civil law, to distinguish it from the body of church law, the Corpus Juris Canonici. Researchers will find that both Corpus Juris Civilis and Corpus Juris Canonici are used as uniform titles in library catalogs.

The Corpus Juris Civilis comprises four parts: the Institutes, the Digest, the Code, and the Novels. The Institutes is an introduction to Roman law. The Digest is a collection of fragments and texts of the best of prior Roman legal writing, and is the most influential part of the Corpus on the civil law tradition. As nearly all of the source materials for the Digest have been lost, we have only the word of Justinian's compilers on the quality of their selections and we see only what they chose for us from the content of earlier Roman law. The Code is a collection of imperial constitutions, and the Novels are a collection of imperial legislation enacted after the Code and Digest. The Code and Digest were meant to be the Restatement of Roman Law something like The American Law Institute's Restatements of Torts, Property and other American law subjects.

The Institutes, the introductory text for students, was originally written in the classical period of Roman law as a legal textbook by the jurist Gaius. Justinian had this work revised and officially approved this revised version of the Institutes as a guide for beginning law students to the basic principles of Roman law. The Institutes is made up of four books, divided into titles that are subdivided into fragments that are further subdivided into an introduction followed by numbered paragraphs. Older citations used abbreviations of the title of an institute and the first words of the relevant fragment within that title. Modern citations will start either with "J. Inst." (Institutes of Justinian) or "G. Inst." (Institutes of Gaius) followed by the numbers of the relevant book, title, fragment, and paragraph. The introduction of a fragment does not have a number but is called in Latin the *principium.* Thus "pr." is used in a citation to the introduction.

The Digest, the excerpts from the writings of jurists of the Roman Republic and the early Roman Empire, contains 50 books that, similar to the Institutes, are divided into titles that are subdivided into fragments that are usually further subdivided into an introduction followed by numbered paragraphs. Thus modern citations to the Digest (Dig.) follow a similar form to those of the Institutes described above. Sometimes a citation will start merely with the letter "D." rather than "Dig." Do not confuse this for a citation to the Decretum of canon law. In general, the Roman law citation will follow the "D." only with a string of numbers representing the books, titles, fragments and other subparts of the Digest. The canon law citation, however, will include additional letters that refer to the different subparts of the Decretum (for example, the *causa*).

The books of the Digest were divided by scholars of the Middle Ages into three parts. The first group, from Book 1, Title 1 to Book 24, Title 2 was called the old Digest, the *Digestum vetus,* often abbreviated "Dig. vet." The second group, from Book 24, Title 3 to Book 38, Title 17 was called the *Infortiatum,* abbreviated "Infort." The third group, from Book 39, Title 1 to Book 50, Title 17 was the *Digestum novum,* abbreviated "Dig. nov." Older citations use abbreviations of the names of these parts followed by abbreviations of the text of the relevant title or fragment. In addition, the Digest was also known as the *Pandecta,* a latinization of a Greek word, and thus the Digest was cited by medieval writers with the letters "ff", meant to symbolize the Greek letter pi.

The Code, the systematic compilation of imperial law, contains 12 books, divided into titles that are subdivided into individual laws that may be further subdivided into numbered sections. The laws are cited by the abbreviation "Code Just.", "Code J.", "Cod. J.", or "C.J." (for Code of Justinian) followed by the numbers representing the book, title, law, and subsection. The citation may also include the relevant emperor and date in parentheses at the end of the citation. If the citation drops the

"Just." or "J." and only uses a "C.", the citation could be confused for a citation to a *causa* of the Decretum of canon law. Usually, the canon law citation, however, will include a reference to a smaller subsection, such as a "q." for *quaestio*. Older citations do use just the capital "C", but follow it with the words, or abbreviations of the words, of the titles and laws.

Medieval jurists usually studied only Books 1 through 9 as the Code. Books 10 through 12 were referred to as the *Tres libri* (three books) and studied separately. These three books and the Institutes were often bound together in a work called the *Volumen* (the volume), which work also included the *Liber authenticorum* (a book of the Novels) and the *Libri feudorum* (a compilation of feudal customary law). Be aware that references to the *Tres libri* or the *Volumen* are references to the last three books of the Code.

The Novels are the new laws enacted after the promulgation of the Code (*Novellae Constitutiones Post Codicem* or New Constitutions after the Code). Novels is abbreviated "Nov." in a modern citation, followed by the numbers representing the number and subparts (usually, the *prefatio,* numbered paragraphs, and the *epilogum*) of the law. The date of promulgation of the law in parentheses ends the citation. The publishing history of the Novels makes for some difficulty in locating citations and requires use of indices. Originally, most of the Novels were written in Greek and a collection of them circulated primarily in the East. The Western medieval writers used a Latin translation of the Novels known as the *Authenticum* or *Liber authenticorum.* The common version of the *Authenticum* grouped the laws into nine *collationes* that were then subdivided into the titles and fragments (made up of the *prefatio,* numbered paragraphs and *epilogum*). Medieval writers usually cited these by reference to the words of the title, the fragment or other subpart of the fragment, followed by the number of the *collatio.* Modern writers will cite the *collatio* (Auth. coll.) followed by the numbers of the *collatio,* the title, and the fragment or subpart. In addition to these collections of the Novels, medieval writers also incorporated *authenticae,* summaries of the Novels, into relevant sections of the Code. The *Corpus authenticorum,* the body of the summaries, was cited by reference to the words of the relevant title of the Code followed by those of the summary. Modern writers will cite the number of the subpart of the novel followed by the number of the code section in which the summary appears.

Following the fall of the Western Roman Empire, Roman law underwent a few centuries of neglect and distortion. Then, at the end of the

11th century and the beginning of the 12th century, Irnerius, an apparently inspiring teacher who attracted many students to listen to him, began to lecture on the Corpus Juris Civilis in Bologna. There has been some controversy on the subject, but it seems settled that Irnerius was an influential figure in the revival of Roman law, and Bologna certainly was the place to study law at the time. Students came from all over Italy and later Germany and other parts of Europe to study law in Bologna. The Corpus was then glossed and commented upon throughout the Middle Ages. Glosses were notes on the meaning of the text often written in the margins of the manuscripts. Another professor from Bologna, Accursius, in the 13th century compiled the glosses of his predecessors. Accursius's definitive work is called the *glossa ordinaria* (ordinary gloss) to the Corpus Juris Civilis. The *glossa ordinaria* was written or printed around the margin of virtually every edition of the Corpus Juris Civilis until the mid-17th century. Accursius and his predecessors are usually called glossators; later jurists are called commentators. The commentators, who included such luminaries as Cino da Pistoia, Bartolo of Sassoferrato, and Baldo degli Ubaldi, did not confine themselves to an explanation of the text of Justinian's compilations, as the glossators did, but also integrated an interpretation of Roman law with a study of laws of other sources of their time.

### B. Canon Law Sources

Most religious groups of a certain size find at some point that they wish to set forth rules to govern relationships among their followers, whether rules of monastic life or rules of marriage. As they become established within larger communities and acquire property, they develop rules governing the acquisition and management of property. Numerous compilations of canon laws were made over the years, but it was the text written by Gratian around 1130 to 1140 that became part of that body of canon law that the 15th century labeled the Corpus Juris Canonici. The other significant parts of the Corpus Juris Canonici are the collections of later Church law, including mainly the decretals, which were letters written by popes in response to particular issues brought to them.

Gratian composed his systematic study of canon law drawing upon papal bulls, writings of the Church fathers, and legislation of church councils. He called his work *Concordia discordantium canonum,* which title speaks to his purpose of harmonizing the discordant contradictions of canon texts, but others came to call his work simply the Decretum of Gratian. The Decretum is made up of three parts.

Part 1 (Pars I) contains 101 *Distinctiones* (distinctions) subdivided into *capitula* (the canons) and *dicta* (comments by Gratian). Each *Distinctio* covers one subject or group of closely-related topics on such areas of law as the sources of law, the status of clerics, the status of prelates, and the power of pontifical legates. Part 2 (Pars II) contains 36 *Causae* (cases). Each *Causa* sets forth a situation and then asks one or more *Quaestiones* (questions) about the case, subdivided into *capitula* and often followed by *dicta* by Gratian. Question 3 of case 33, unlike the rest of Part 2, is subdivided into distinctions (following the same pattern as in Part 1). This question 3 is also known as the *Tractatus de penitentia* (treatise on penance). Part 3 (Pars III) is a treatise on liturgical law, the *Tractatus de consecratione*. Part 3 is divided into five distinctions, each subdivided into *capitula*. Unlike Parts 1 and 2 there are no *dicta* by Gratian in this third part. Part 3 is sometimes also cited as *Causa* 37.

Citations do not refer to the particular collection used, nor to the particular Part of the Decretum, but the format of each citation differs from part to part. Formerly, the canons of the Decretum were referred to by giving the number of the distinction or cause in Roman numerals followed by the opening words of the canon or of the topic. Later, as citations tended to use the numbers more and the words less, they tended to start with the *dicta* or *capitula* followed by the number of the distinction. Modern citations use Arabic numerals. Citations to Part 1 refer to the individual *Distinctio*, abbreviated "D.", followed by its number. This is followed by the numbers of the individual *capitula*, abbreviated "c.", and *dicta*, abbreviated "d." Citations to Part 2 refer to the number of the *Causa*, abbreviated "C.", followed by the numbers of the *quaestio*, abbreviated "q.", and the *capitula*, abbreviated "c." Part 3, being the *Tractatus de consecratione*, is cited "De Cons.", followed by the individual *Distinctio*, abbreviated "D.", and the *capitula*, abbreviated "c."

The Decretum of Gratian was never an official compilation, but it was widely studied and commented upon throughout the Middle Ages, just as were the texts of the Roman law. The canonists, or canon law scholars, who commented on the Decretum, are known as decretists. Decretists must be distinguished from decretalists, those canonists who commented on the decretals of the popes.

Decretals are papal decisions in a particular matter, often including the rationale for the decision. In the past, some decretals might have been filed in the papal correspondence files, but others might only have been sent to the parties. Early collections were nothing more than copies of whatever decretals the compiler happened to have. Eventually, the collections were organized by subject and date, and the best known of these were five called the *Quinque compilationes antiquae* (the five ancient compilations), individually the *prima* (first), *secunda* (second), *tertia* (third), *quarta* (fourth), and *quinta* (fifth). Each compilation was divided into five books, *libri,* that each dealt with a particular subject.

Pope Gregory IX ordered an official compilation of all law since Gratian, along the lines of the Code of Justinian. Raymond of Peñafort put together a large collection for the Pope of close to 2,000 decretals arranged by subject matter into five books. Much of this was based upon earlier collections, especially those known as the five ancient compilations. The collection, entitled the Decretals of Gregory IX, is usually referred to as the *Liber Extra.* When the Pope promulgated the Decretals of Gregory IX in 1234, he ordered the universities of Bologna and Paris to teach it as the official law of the Roman Catholic Church. This remained part of the official law of the Church until the first modern code was enacted in 1917.

Later popes added their own compilations of decretals. Pope Boniface VIII promulgated a collection of the decretals of himself and his predecessors (from Gregory IX to himself) known as the *Sexte* (the sixth book or *Liber sextus*). The *Liber sextus* is also made up of five books. Pope Clement V added the Constitutions of Clement V (*Constitutiones Clementinae* or just Clementines). This collection was actually promulgated by Pope John XXII, because Pope Clement V died before the work was perfected. Although Pope John XXII called it the seventh book of decretals, the work is still known as the Clementines. The decretals of Pope John XXII, himself, were published as the *Extravagantes.* These and a final collection of well-known but unpublished decretals of popes from Boniface VIII to Sixtus IV, the *Extravagantes communes* (common extravagants), formed the Corpus Juris Canonici as it was known at the end of the 15th century.

Old compilations of decretals were cited by medieval authors as "ex." or "extra", based on the fact that they appeared outside the Decretum of Gratian, and gave an abbreviated form of the title and chapter. Sometimes the number of the book also appeared. Later the abbreviation "Comp." for compilation was used; the citation would begin with the chapter, abbreviated "c.", followed by "Comp." and the number of the compilation, with the book and title numbers appearing in parentheses at the end. The modern form puts the number of the compilation first, followed by the abbreviation "Comp.", followed by numbers representing the book, title and chapter.

Citations to later compilations followed a similar pattern of first using words or abbreviated words of the chapter. Later, a number for the chapter was given, followed by an abbreviated name of the collection, and numbers representing the book and title being cited. The modern style is to give an abbreviated title of the compilation followed by Arabic numerals for the book, title and chapter. The Decretals of Gregory IX, or the *Liber Extra,* is abbreviated to "X". The Decretals of Boniface VIII, or the *Liber Sextus,* is abbreviated to "VI". The Clementines is abbreviated "Clem." The Extravagants of John XXII is abbreviated "Extrav. Jo." The Common Extravagants is abbreviated "Extrav. Com."

By the 20th century, the same issues of size, complexity and confusion that faced the Emperor Justinian, Gratian, and Pope Gregory IX, forced the Catholic Church to publish a modern Code of Canon Law. The first Codex Juris Canonici was promulgated in 1917. The current Codex was first promulgated in 1983. Both codes are made up of canons and sections and are cited as either the 1917 Code or 1983 Code, followed by reference to the canon, abbreviated "c.", and its number and the section, using the section symbol, followed by the section number.

## IV. CONCLUSION

Scholars of the Middle Ages developed two major areas of study in law. Those who studied texts of Roman law are known as civilians. The glossators largely studied and explained the Institutes, Digest, Code and Novels promulgated by the Emperor Justinian I, and referred to these works as the Corpus Juris Civilis, the body of civil law. Later commentators also wrote on these subjects, but added new analyses based upon changes in the economic and political situation of their time and included other sources of law in their studies.

Those scholars who studied the law of the Church are known as canonists. The canonists are divided into two sub-groups: the decretists, who commented upon the Decretum of Gratian, and the decretalists, who commented upon the decretals of the popes. Both the Decretum and the decretals form the Corpus Juris Canonici, the body of canon law.

Early citations by these scholars normally used opening words or abbreviated words to describe the particular part to which they were referring. Later, often as numbering came to be standardized, numbers, usually Roman numerals, rather than words were used in citations. The numbering commonly started with the smallest part being cited, followed by the name of the work and the larger parts leading down to the smallest. The modern form commonly starts with an abbreviation of the work followed by the largest down to the smallest part being cited.

Modern scholars, especially those who can manage medieval or ecclesiastical Latin, find a wealth of law and commentary in the manuscripts and early printed books of the medieval scholars, who form a bridge to us of timeless themes. We find there analysis of personal relationships, of control of property, of the power of a prince or a pope, and ultimately, of the nature of justice.

# ARCHIVES

## Lawyers, Archivists and Librarians: United or Divided in the Pursuit of Justice?

Menzi L. Behrnd-Klodt

**SUMMARY.** Although attorneys operate within a system foreign to the world of archivists and librarians, they may become consumers of reference services. This article discusses the fundamentals of the American court system and litigation, and the ways in which information professionals and attorneys work. The author suggests a number of ways to smooth the interactions between the professions. *[Article copies available for a fee from The Haworth Document Delivery Service: 1-800-342-9678. E-mail address: <getinfo@haworthpressinc.com> Website: <http://www.HaworthPress.com> © 2001 by The Haworth Press, Inc. All rights reserved.]*

Menzi L. Behrnd-Klodt is Counsel for Pleasant Company, a subsidiary of Mattel, Inc., and is also responsible for Corporate and Product Archives and Records Management. She also has an archival consulting firm, Klodt & Associates, which works with organizations, museums, historical societies, universities, and corporations. She was previously Archivist with the State Historical Society of Wisconsin, CUNA Mutual Insurance Group, and Circus World Museum, and an attorney with the Axley Brynelson law firm. Ms. Behrnd-Klodt has presented many papers, workshops, and seminars on legal issues for archivists, and on administration of archival programs. She holds a JD and Master's Degrees in History and Library Science, all from the University of Wisconsin.

[Haworth co-indexing entry note]: "Lawyers, Archivists and Librarians: United or Divided in the Pursuit of Justice?" Behrnd-Klodt, Menzi L. Co-published simultaneously in *Legal Reference Services Quarterly* (The Haworth Information Press, an imprint of The Haworth Press, Inc.) Vol. 20, No. 1/2, 2001, pp. 113-133; and: *Public Services Issues with Rare and Archival Law Materials* (ed: Michael Widener) The Haworth Information Press, an imprint of The Haworth Press, Inc., 2001, pp. 113-133. Single or multiple copies of this article are available for a fee from The Haworth Document Delivery Service [1-800-342-9678, 9:00 a.m. - 5:00 p.m. (EST). E-mail address: getinfo@haworthpressinc.com].

© 2001 by The Haworth Press, Inc. All rights reserved.

Lawyers require information to serve their litigation clients. They investigate claims, research legal issues, and gather facts and evidence to prove or defend their clients' legal cases. When lawyers become consumers of information and reference services, archivists, records managers, and special librarians can benefit by understanding more about the American civil litigation process, how lawyers operate in the judicial system, and how to provide good reference services to the legal community. This article explores the litigation process and the nature of legal claims, the ways in which archivists, librarians, and attorneys work, and their professional interactions.

## THE AMERICAN COURT SYSTEM

The American court system is multi-layered. Each state has three levels of courts. *Courts of inferior jurisdiction* hear small claims and traffic cases and minor municipal matters. *Trial courts of general jurisdiction* decide civil and criminal cases and appeals from administrative proceedings such as workers compensation hearings. In addition to these general "courts of record," specialized courts may handle probate, juvenile, and divorce. *Appellate courts,* which may include the *supreme courts,* are the highest levels of state courts. A parallel series of federal courts includes district courts, courts of appeal, and the U.S. Supreme Court, and courts of limited jurisdiction (e.g., tax courts).

## THE CIVIL LITIGATION PROCESS

The judicial process decides controversies among private individuals, organizations, businesses, and public entities, all of which are called *parties.* Although many controversies are resolved informally through negotiation, mediation, arbitration, or other alternative dispute resolution, some aggrieved parties rely on the law to furnish relief through litigation. Litigation that is not disposed of via out-of-court settlement or negotiation between the parties will be decided in court.

The American judicial system is by nature adversarial. The parties to a controversy are responsible for initiating a lawsuit, shaping the issues by investigating claims and contentions, uncovering evidence, and presenting the facts in court through witnesses and testimony. The judge takes very little part in the proceedings other than as an umpire who exercises limited management and control over the proceedings. Theorists reason that through such a contest between the interested parties, a truer decision is reached.[1]

The process begins when an injured or aggrieved party (the plaintiff) files with the court a written *complaint or statement of claim* against a defendant. The complaint frames the issues, outlines the plaintiff's claims against the defendant, and seeks a remedy such as monetary compensation. A *summons* is issued and served on the defendant to provide the required formal notice of the commencement of the action. Filing these written documents or "pleadings" with the court triggers a series of critical litigation deadlines.[2]

Within a defined period of time, the defendant must file and serve on the plaintiff a written *answer* to the complaint setting forth any defenses or counterclaims, and naming any other parties to the lawsuit. The defendant may attack the plaintiff on procedural grounds, for example, whether the plaintiff is legally competent to sue and whether the complaint states a proper claim, names the proper defendant, is filed in the appropriate court, and was properly served.

From these initial pleadings, the lawyers develop a preliminary theory of the case outlining the claims or defenses and plan how to prove them in court. Both parties to the lawsuit may file motions or requests for court orders to narrow and clarify issues and seek dismissal of claims. In order to frame effective motions, the attorney must understand and analyze all of the facts and issues quite early in the process.

Prior to trial, both parties need to obtain information. The *pre-trial discovery* period begins as soon as the defendant files an answer, and enables the parties to find information relevant to the case. Discovery permits parties to investigate the strength of their claims, gather evidence, preserve relevant information for trial, and plan litigation strategies. They interview witnesses, take oral depositions,[3] serve each other with written interrogatories,[4] request and gather documents,[5] and request admissions.[6] Each party is required to share its facts, witnesses, and evidence with the other well in advance of trial. Using what is learned during discovery, a case may be settled out of court or thoroughly prepared for trial. By the time trial begins, each side knows the other's case and can anticipate what the courtroom testimony will be.

Gone are the days of dramatic Perry Mason-style courtroom revelations!

The subpoena is a powerful litigation tool during discovery and at trial. A subpoena compels appearances at a specific time and place for a specific purpose with serious legal consequences for non-compliance. Any litigation party may serve an archivist or librarian with a subpoena to appear at a deposition or trial, and may demand production of books, papers, documents, or tangible things within the archivist's or librarian's possession, custody, or control. The actual ownership of the subpoenaed items is irrelevant.

A subpoena must comply with certain procedural formalities, however. It must be written and sufficiently definite to indicate what is demanded, issued by a proper person, party or court[7] as part of an ongoing legal action, signed by the proper person, and served personally,[8] and allow reasonable time for compliance.[9] Any demand for immediate possession of documents should be brought to the attention of counsel at once.

Yet even a valid subpoena received by an archivist or librarian may be challenged if it:

- Is unreasonable and oppressive (e.g., seeking masses of documents merely to search through them).
- Is overly broad or so vague or indefinite that responsive documents cannot be identified.
- Seeks all or a substantial part of a witness's records.
- Seeks documents the disclosure of which would cause annoyance, embarrassment, or undue burden or expense.
- Seeks documents that can be obtained from a party to the lawsuit (e.g., a donor) rather than from a non-party (e.g., the repository).
- Seeks records that are or may be confidential or restricted by law (e.g., medical records, certain court or student records).
- Seeks documents that are not relevant to the litigation.
- Violates a right of privacy that outweighs a party's need for information.

The attorney for the individual or authorized representative of an organization named in the subpoena can negotiate with opposing counsel to limit the demand, eliminate unnecessary and extraneous documents, or obtain additional time to comply with an objectionable subpoena. If necessary, counsel can apply to the court for relief.

A formal challenge to an overreaching subpoena is made by filing with the issuing court timely written objections, a motion to quash or modify the subpoena, or a motion for a protective order. Such motions seek to limit, narrow, overturn, or postpone the effect of the subpoena. Until the court decides whether to limit, terminate, or direct the scope of discovery or to order production of documents, compliance with the subpoena is not required.[10] While the court usually will not thwart discovery entirely, it may encourage the parties to compromise on a set of documents that can be disclosed or agree to seal, edit, or control access to documents or information sought to be produced.

Prior to the actual release of any documents, the archivist or librarian under subpoena should review each item with counsel who will help prevent unnecessary and harmful disclosures. Any documents to be produced should be organized and labeled to correspond with the categories in the request and separated from all other files. A duplicate set should be kept as a record of the disclosed items. The attorney can arrange for copies to be sent to opposing counsel or for an on-site viewing with access to a photocopier. Lawyers discourage deponents from taking documents to a deposition unless cleared by counsel to do so.

After the parties have gathered enough evidence to understand the positions thoroughly, it may be discovered that the claims are weak and the lawsuit may be settled between the parties. If it is discovered that there is no real factual dispute, the lawsuit may be terminated through the courts. However, if there remain any unresolved issues, they are decided in a *trial* to a judge or jury at which both parties present evidence through testimony and documents. The plaintiff bears the burden of proving its case by "clear and convincing evidence" or "a preponderance of the evidence" or "the greater weight of the evidence." The defendant attempts to refute the plaintiff's claims with valid defenses and counterclaims. The jury or judge determines the facts, applies the law to the facts, and issues a judgment, ending the lawsuit.

## THE PROFESSIONAL ROLES OF ARCHIVISTS AND LIBRARIANS

As the roles and responsibilities of archivists and librarians are well-known, a brief description here will suffice. Librarians and archivists acquire, preserve, manage, and facilitate widespread access to significant sources of information. Archivists strive to understand and respect the provenance and original order of the historical records they collect, reflecting the unique structures and systems of the organizations documented.

Information specialists operate within statutory parameters, institutional policies and guidelines, and professional standards and ethics. Both groups of professionals value equal and open access to information while recognizing the delicate balance often required between access, scholarly research needs, freedom of information and right-to-know concepts, contractual obligations to donors, privacy rights and statutory protections, and other rights and concerns. The protection of the interests of the corporate parent generally requires that corporate archivists and special librarians must help safeguard intellectual properties,[11] corporate trade secrets, research and development data, and proprietary information of businesses and organizations, which is an exception to the general tenet of promoting equal and open access.

Both professions strive to provide quality reference service to researchers. Records that are available to one researcher are generally available to all. Regardless of the research topic or the patron's point of view, the role of the archivist or librarian is to facilitate research objectively without injecting personal opinions or biases.

## THE ROLE OF THE ATTORNEY: HOW ATTORNEYS WORK

Lawyers traditionally are gatekeepers to the legal system. Lawyers offer services that clients need and that are presumed to be in the clients' best interests. As possessors of specialized knowledge and skills in working with and managing the legal system, lawyers are viewed as experts upon whom clients depend for direction, advice, and rational but achievable solutions to the client's problems, often on an urgent basis.

The attorney's primary professional and ethical duty is to "zealously advocate" on behalf of the client yet to be accountable to the legal system. "Zealous advocacy" requires that the lawyer carefully analyze and completely understand the facts of the case and the applicable law. Paradoxically, the client is best served by open communication and cooperation with the lawyer, yet good lawyers do not accept a client's story at face value. They test its strength and know its weaknesses to achieve the best possible result for the client under the circumstances. Lawyers investigate facts and gather background information and documentation to understand all of the issues as they prepare to prove all claims and defend against all counterclaims. Notwithstanding the scope of their information, the attorney does not pretend to be developing an objective treatment of the case. The lawyer searches for evidence to support the client's legal position and information to discredit or discount the opponent's case.

The concepts of objective treatment and historical and scholarly research are worthless and meaningless to the lawyer who must advocate a particular position. While the litigation lawyer may care little for the historical significance of archival records, it may be critical to understand the content and context of files and documents, their chain of custody and provenance, ownership, access, and overall security of resources. Knowing whether a document exists may be as important as its content.

Yet despite their adversarial stances in litigation, lawyers must maintain long-term relationships with other lawyers, agencies, and courts. Their reputations for integrity, fairness, firmness, and aggressiveness are important, as is their compliance with professional standards, ethical codes, and local court rules. Lawyers cannot alienate those they will work with or appear before next month, or those on whom they must rely for future fair dealings. Nor are lawyer-client interactions isolated. Lawyers and clients may have on-going professional relationships to be preserved and nurtured, particularly in institutional settings.

Unlike most archivists and librarians, lawyers are not accustomed to collegial environments. They are accustomed to competitive arenas where the primary goal is to succeed. Attorneys generally do not enjoy surprises, which can be costly to both client and lawyer. Often the litigation attorney has more to lose than do most archivists or librarians, as the lawyer's failure can result in unhappy clients, fewer fees, lost business, litigation defeats, or even complaints to the bar and malpractice suits.

## *WHAT ATTORNEYS NEED TO SUCCEED*

To prepare thoroughly, the expert litigation lawyer needs ALL documents and information relevant to the claims and the litigants. To find all relevant items, the lawyer must review and analyze reams of documents. A document that is missing or undiscovered can affect the viability of the client's claims or defenses and the result of the litigation. A significant document that is discovered only late in the proceedings might completely alter the attorney's theory of the case, wasting not only time and money, but rendering worthless the evidence already accumulated. Lawyers want to see everything there is to see about the case and they need accurate and probative facts and evidence.

A significant part of litigation occurs early in the process during the compressed time frame of discovery and investigation. Much of what attorneys do is time-sensitive. Absolute statutory and court-decreed deadlines directly affect the client, to say nothing of stress levels. A missed deadline can determine whether a case will be won or lost. Lawyers generally need information and evidence NOW!

After the discovery period ends, however, months of painstaking work lie ahead. By the time the trial date arrives, the attorneys on both sides of the case will know every fact, document, and legal precedent that could possibly be involved. They will know their own client's case and that of the opponent, and will be able to anticipate every move and countermove of both sides. However, to get to that point the lawyer must carefully and extensively analyze and evaluate the documents and items produced. Extensive legal research and additional investigation may be required. Documents may be retained and pored over for months or years until the case is settled or tried in court. Lawyers need to know and understand everything there is to know about the case. They need to have documents and information safely within their possession, available for review and preserved for trial.

For each item actually produced as evidence in court, there may have been hundreds of relevant pages that were potential proof and labeled as exhibits, which in turn were selected from the dozens of cartons of documents, objects, and items gathered for research and investigation. However, lawyers want to be those who do the sifting and weighing of the evidence to corroborate the client's claims or demolish the opponent's assertions. Eventually, when the proof is needed for court, lawyers will want to have the best available proof. They then will want original documents or authenticated copies. They would be delighted if recordskeepers thoughtfully preserved their records with the lawyer and client in mind, kept them in a useful order (useful to the attorney, that is), made records and information readily accessible (at least to the attorney), and kept attachments with documents, so that the lawyers could see the original document order and relationships.

The truth is that often the immediacy and demands of the litigation process leave no time for the attorney to consider issues, goals, needs, or positions other than those that help the client. As many law clerks and support staff will attest, lawyers are unable to appreciate the time frames and workloads of others, including those in other professions. Busy and focused lawyers may not be sympathetic to the concerns and needs of others.

## ACCESS AND CONFIDENTIALITY

Two areas affecting records and litigation can occasionally be a sore subject between attorneys, archivists, and librarians: access and confidentiality. Access and confidentiality issues arise most frequently in the context of how attorneys and archivists operate differently. They are most visible in corporate and organizational archives, records management programs, and libraries, but bear on relationships between attorneys and information specialists in any private or public repository.

*Access*

Access can be a complex issue when an attorney seeks access to records that are restricted by law, institutional policy, or donor agreement. The archivist or special librarian legally and ethically must deny access to records closed or restricted to all researchers by statute or policy. The donor agreement requiring the archives to restrict records necessitates compliance with and enforcement of the donor's wishes. Like any fervent researcher, the lawyer may try to persuade the archivist or librarian to grant access or even may take the issue to court or to the archives' governing body, but the archivist or librarian legally and ethically may not grant selective access nor access in violation of statute, policy, or donor agreement.

Access may be difficult when records are not physically available or are inaccessible because they are too fragile, not arranged, lost, in use by others, or in a format which can no longer be accessed. When records are inaccessible because of physical condition (e.g., fragile or unprocessed records or inaccessible format), the archivist should determine whether the expressed need of the attorney (or any researcher), warrants taking extraordinary or unplanned measures such as scanning, reformatting, dubbing, transcribing, or microfilming to make the records or information accessible. Sometimes the attorney may be willing to pay for such special services, which may ease the financial burden on the repository.

Access issues can be a problem when attorneys want to take records away from the repository. The archivist or librarian in a public repository must retain custody and control over records by rejecting selective access or preferential removal by private individuals. Simple measures may prove efficacious, such as generous free reference assistance, referrals to experienced searchers to do research work on-site for a fee, and providing legible, accurate photocopies of documents.

If needed, the archivist or librarian can provide the investigating attorney with an affidavit attesting to facts about the records that are within the archivist's or librarian's knowledge. The archivist or librarian cannot verify the truth of the information in the records, but can attest to facts about the provenance, donation, arrangement, and location of the archival records to help the attorney establish the credibility and context of the evidence. The archivist or librarian can also attest to the accuracy of photocopies, so that a court may feel comfortable in accepting photocopies instead of original documents. If the archivist must testify about the location and provenance of the documents or the accuracy of photocopies, the ability to trace routine steps and standard procedures taken to locate and copy documents and summarize how records are filed and maintained, lends credibility to the archivist and the records.

Corporate archivists may feel pressure to permit removal of records by in-house counsel for the good of the company. Similar tensions may be felt in other settings where pressure can be brought to bear through supervisors, directors, fiscal or development officers who fear loss of funding, or through other ways. In such instances, the archivist may have to defend archival procedures and standards, or perhaps even the archives' right to exist and to hold or collect and administer its records.

*Confidentiality*

Attorneys are always deeply concerned about confidentiality and disclosure of records and information, both within their offices and in general settings. Within their own professional spheres, attorneys are bound by ethical obligations to preserve the special relationship between attorney and client. Once an attorney-client relationship is established (usually at the time the lawyer is engaged to represent the client), professional legal ethics require the lawyer to maintain the client's communications in confidence. This principle encourages full and frank communication between attorney and client in the broader interest in the administration of justice. The privilege governs all lawyers and their clients.

The attorney-client privilege protects documents, oral advice, and items that are created by the client or lawyer and supplied to the lawyer as part of the legal consultation. Although the attorney-client privilege has certain limits and exceptions, its protections reach beyond the confines of the law office and may extend into the archives. Records of an attorney or law firm that may be donated to an archives, generally remain subject to the obligations created by the attorney-client privilege. While the attorney-client privilege does not prevent disclosure of privileged information through other means or disclosure of facts underlying the privileged communication, it is well-settled that the lawyer may not ethically reveal the client's secrets or breach the attorney-client privilege. Depositing legal records in an archives does not remove the attorney-client privilege nor make the records available for general perusal.

Only the client may give up or waive his or her privilege and open his or her records. Although the client may deliberately, voluntarily, or accidentally make this waiver, it is incumbent on the repository to ensure that privileged records are not inadvertently disclosed. The repository should document the client's express intent to disclose confidential information and if there is no waiver, take reasonable documented precautions to prevent disclosure of privileged or confidential records.

There are several practical guidelines that are helpful in maintaining the confidentiality of documentation protected by the attorney-client privilege. Any pending or anticipated litigation should be noted in the minutes of the governing body of the organization or corporation, the retainer agreement with the lawyer, and in the documentation itself. Management or administration should advise staff to maintain strict confidentiality. Employees should not take notes of discussions with lawyers or for discussions with lawyers. Protected documents should be clearly labeled "privileged and confidential, attorney-client privilege, attorney-work product prepared in anticipation of litigation." Distribution of documentation should be limited only to those who need to be included. Copies should be numbered, signed out, and returned to the attorney. The lawyer should clearly label and keep separate those items protected under the work product doctrine. Both client and lawyer should be careful not to disclose or refer to confidential materials.

If privileged documents are inadvertently disclosed, the lawyer must try to protect the privilege on behalf of the client. A demand for return of disclosed documents should be followed with a motion for a protective order, seeking return of the documents and all copies and notes, and prohibiting any disclosure, use, or reference to the documents.

Materials developed by an attorney for use in litigation also may be protected from discovery under the work product doctrine, intended to prevent unwarranted inquiries into the lawyer's files and mental impressions, and recognizing the need for some privacy to plan and formulate legal strategy. This doctrine protects the lawyer's research, analysis, legal theories, notes, and memoranda, prepared in anticipation of litigation or for trial.

## EXAMPLES FROM PRACTITIONERS[12]

It is a seeming paradox that lawyers appear both to need to gather as many records as possible yet desperately want to avoid locating or discovering damaging information. Perhaps this is better understood by remembering that the threat of harm to the client's position is a powerful motivating force. Corporate attorneys may fear retention of certain records in the corporate archives or records department. They may more forcefully advocate destruction of potentially harmful records under their control, while plaintiffs' attorneys may equally fervently seek those documents to prove claims and connections.

Corporations that have faced complex and huge product liability class action lawsuits involving years of litigation and enormous awards against them would argue strongly against retention of the "wrong" records. The tobacco, Johns Manville/asbestos, and A. H. Robbins/Dalkon Shield cases and others turned on the discovery of critical documents retained too long in corporate files and used against a defendant. Perhaps the plaintiffs would not have succeeded or viable defenses would have been raised if such damning documents had been destroyed in the ordinary course of business. While plaintiffs' lawyers undoubtedly cheered the presence of so many records, the corporate attorneys did not.

Consumer products companies may be concerned about product liability claims. In some industries, products which were safe at the time of marketing according to then-current scientific or medical results have become vulnerable to litigation over injuries or reactions, or to claims based on later-enacted and stricter safety regulations. While such claims may be successfully defended, juries are not always sympathetic and the adverse publicity can be particularly damaging.

Food products companies may be particularly vulnerable to such claims and may fear the risk that an injured party could successfully prosecute liability claims if documents are retained rather than shredded. In a particular instance, after much pre-emptive internal negotiation and file-level review, the archivists and corporate attorneys agreed that the archives had to yield to the legitimate legal department requests to institute records management with systematic and scheduled destruction of certain older records deemed too sensitive to be retained. The policy decisions in this instance were professional and appropriate, even if the results may not be cheered by many plaintiffs attorneys.

In both of the instances cited above, plaintiffs and their attorneys benefited from the retention and production of as many records as possible, while defendants and their lawyers did not. However, discussion with principled practicing defense lawyers shows a strong concern that too *few* records are retained in general and that those that are retained are not sufficiently accessible. To these defense attorneys who work with personal injury or money issues, abundant and available documentation always assisted in the evaluation of *both sides of the case* and allowed for the best possible result for the client. The optimal result may be an early settlement without the costs and delays of litigation, paying full insurance policy proceeds, or paying a judgment after trial. To achieve such results, the lawyers' preference is to review the documents, understand all of the facts and issues, evaluate the client's position, and if necessary, cut the client's losses while doing the right thing for both client and injured party.

Among the many types of documentation that are useful to both parties in litigation are contracts and agreements; formal corporate policy documents and written procedures; records of debts, obligations, payments, and other financial transactions; and personal and business letters, memos, and notes. Individuals who are involved in litigation may find their past lives and personal credibility at issue. The attorneys who represent such litigants will seek personal letters, medical bills and records, records of employment and earnings, records of moving violations, bank documents, and personnel files and evaluations to support or destroy the claims and rationalizations of clients and adversaries.

Certainly the informational content of the documents described above can be extremely important in litigation. In addition, many of these types of records also provide evidence of a particular individual action or an organizational or corporate function, policy, activity, or event. Both the informational content and the evidential value of records can be valuable proof of actions, intentions, and policies. Even the presence or absence of documents can lead to adverse inferences and judgments about the parties that have control and access over them.

A corporate archivist for a large firm was asked to search the archives for documents to support management's position in a grievance with an employee union. Management and labor differed over whether a traditional annual Christmas payment to employees was a "bonus" that had become part of the company's payment structure and employee work rules or a one-time "gift" that was specially decreed and approved each year. If the payment was a bonus, it could not be withdrawn or reduced except through collective bargaining; if it was a gift, it could be paid or terminated at management's discretion. As the financial stakes were high, management hoped the records would support its position that the payment was an annual "gift." Corporate counsel was wary about the archives, but both sides knew it held the only available proof. As might be expected, the corporate board minutes were the primary documents illustrating the board's intent when approving the payment each year. The language of the board minutes was consistent in labeling the payment a "gift." What was surprising, however, was the discovery of internal memos and ephemeral Christmas cards from the directors to each employee issued decades ago to enclose the payment. Some of the memos and cards labeled the payment a "gift," while others called it a "bonus." Perhaps management was wise to fear the contents of the archives in this instance, because the union won and the "bonus" remained until the next round of collective bargaining.

Employment records and employee handbooks and policy manuals provide both good and bad evidence for lawyers and their clients. Obviously employment records can be used to prove eligibility for individual Social Security and pension benefits. However, in discrimination litigation, wrongful termination cases, and workers' compensation and employee health and safety issues, employee handbooks or internal memoranda and other records can also establish wrongful past employment practices and an unflattering or illegal course of dealings between employer and employee, generally to the detriment of the employer.

Insurance policies, whether expired or in force, are important tools in litigation to determine the amount of any potential recovery of the injured party and the liability of the non-injured party. When policies are unavailable, the legal tactics must shift from rationally determining damages incurred and policy limits available to be paid out. Similar thinking can occur when there is no written contract to reveal the intentions and actual agreement of the parties. Instead, the parties' positions become fixed as polar opposites, often along the general lines of "the insurance/contract/document never existed so I'm completely off the hook" versus "the insurance/contract/document did too exist, and what bad activity are you as a bad person trying to hide by denying or destroying it?" Clearly this change in strategy and posture can alter completely the tenor and course of the litigation, to say nothing of the outcome.

A complete run of records over a period of time is often useful in litigation. In a particular instance, a company needed to prove the continuous use and "fame" of its foremost brand name and trademark in order to defeat a foreign trademark "pirate" who had appropriated the brand name for its own use. Establishing the worldwide "fame" of the brand required locating records of use of the brand name in advertising, promotion, and sales of products. The attorneys who originally hoped to find a few advertisements showing brand name use were astonished to learn that the corporate archives also held year after year of sales and revenue figures, comprehensive marketing and business plans, marketing pieces, press releases, newspaper articles, and product packaging and labels. The corporate intent to make the brand "famous" from its inception was clearly demonstrated, as was the company's consistent use and protection of the trademark. In this instance the archivist was able to "feed" the attorneys documents they did not dream still existed.

Draft documents and letters, financial work sheets, and internal memoranda also may provide lawyers with pertinent information about the parties' intentions, particularly if final documents do not exist, or exist in a very different form. Such documents also may serve as evidence of changes in procedures or requirements over time. For example, in a case about exposure to chemicals, the issue was the exact wording on the product label at the time of exposure, and whether the product was properly labeled in accordance with regulations then in effect. Only the current and a few prior product labels existed. Had the complete run of labels been available, both the facts and the thought processes behind the development of the labels would have been clear, and the questions about the legality and appropriateness of the warnings would have been resolved more easily.

Many companies maintain different versions of minutes of meetings, often with no evil or deceptive intent. Handwritten minutes may be edited and corrected to improve the expressions of speakers or delete irrelevant details. Some companies may tape record and prepare verbatim minutes where every hiccup is transcribed. An edited, sometimes sanitized and shortened version may be prepared to detail the important decisions made without retaining the unimportant maunderings of the participants. However, an attorney who is interested in investigating the background of a business decision would be delighted to locate in the archives the unedited audio recordings, handwritten notes, and verbatim minutes of the meeting. The different versions may be helpful, harmful, or merely illustrative, but the attorney would prefer to review them to make the determination rather than guessing.

Destroying or altering damaging documents indeed may do more harm than good. When documentation is expected to be present and is missing through other than accidental means, its absence is noted. Skilled lawyers and judges usually can determine what records once existed or should have existed. Lawyers and judges understand the functions performed by local governments or agencies, events documented by business practices and retained in the archives, or actions described by other witnesses, or through a series of documents with noticeable gaps. Forensic document analysts and handwriting experts are skilled at unmasking forgeries and alterations and attorneys are quick to find such experts when needed. When all such discrepancies in the record of "the ordinary and usual course of business," "course of dealing," or "past practices" are revealed, it fuels speculation or creates uncertainty about the motives of those with access to the documents. It is indeed difficult to cover up intentional or deliberate records destruction, just as it is perilous to try to conceal or alter the facts by destroying or altering documents. Adverse inferences drawn from a missing document or bad actions may be quite damaging to the perpetrator. Good lawyers will know the documents once existed and will use that fact to damage the opponent.

In a particular instance, a defense attorney who knew his case intimately realized that the client had not produced all of the documents and information that should have existed. The facts indicated that more information was available. Despite the client's denials, evidence of the missing document eventually surfaced through other means. But by its very absence from the client's records, the lawyer was able to infer that his client had indeed considered the pertinent issue and that the client had probably destroyed the document. The lawyer understood that the client's case was weakened and his credibility destroyed. He was able to persuade the client to accept the realities of his action and situation and agree to a settlement, which as it happened was very favorable. Had the client instead gone to trial on the evidence, the client would have lost.

Sometimes missing documents may make it difficult to determine whether a client is actually the proper party to the action. While it may be tempting on the client's part to destroy an offending paper, it may not deliver the desired outcome. In another case, the difficulty was determining whether the client had manufactured a doorstep with an inherently dangerous design flaw. The client's first design drawing for the doorstep could not be found. The earliest drawing found was a revision. Without the first drawing, it was impossible to determine whether the client actually manufactured the defective doorstep. But instead of exonerating the client, the gap in the records destroyed the client's credibility and its chances of prevailing at trial. The litigation settled because the client's case was weak. Nonetheless, the lawyer lamented that even a run of damaging records would have been helpful because it would have caused an earlier settlement, fewer costs and attorneys fees incurred, and would have given the injured party its full and accurate due.

As archivists and special librarians know, records management responsibilities and the lack of sufficient resources may overwhelm many organizations, companies, and government agencies. In such cases, mismanagement or lack of management of records can be as detrimental as deceptive practices. As a result, lawyers may be hampered by access to too few records caused by the ad hoc nature of records practices. In one such instance, a local government had inadequate records management retention and disposition procedures, compounded by high staff turnover and a concomitant lack of institutional memory. A long-term consequence of this, as related by a lawyer who represented the local government, was that local government officials often treated individuals differently because records of past actions on similar topics were missing or inaccessible. Without any records or institutional memory, government officials could not determine what prior action had been taken in similar circumstances, resulting in disparate treatment of citizens. The availability of complete records might eliminate or reduce discrepancies in treatment and differences in institutional responses.

## *HOW CAN THE ARCHIVIST OR LIBRARIAN CONTRIBUTE TO THE LITIGATION PROCESS?*

To best serve the client, the lawyer seeking evidence or information during discovery or investigation may appeal for assistance from a number of sources. In civil litigation cases, the most obvious and widely used sources of records and information are governmental agencies, vital records bureaus, hospitals and physicians, businesses, financial institutions, utility and insurance companies, automobile repair shops, and the like. Both corporate counsel and attorneys for plaintiffs suing companies may look toward the office of the corporate secretary, the corporate records manager, and the corporate archives for information. In some cases, the needed documentation will be found in local government records, the records of businesses and organizations, or the papers of individuals which have been donated to an archives, special collections, or library. Then, the attorney may need the assistance of the archivist or librarian who has custody of relevant documents.

As discussed in depth above, the actual records may be evidence of activities and intentions, or tools to support or debunk theories or to prove or refute a claim. Assuming the archivist or librarian to be a neutral party rather than a litigant or adversary, the following general good public service tips are especially relevant in dealing with attorneys who visit the archives or library:

- Always keep your own legal counsel fully apprised of any requests for records, subpoena, or known visits by litigation attorneys, and seek advice on how to proceed.
- If the records sought have been donated by a private individual, organization, or business, discuss with the archives' counsel whether and when to inform and involve the donor. The donor may be a party to the lawsuit and may wish to have its own counsel on hand, or may wish to try to take whatever legal steps are available to it, if any, to restrict or withdraw its records.
- When dealing with lawyers, be professional and very patient. Lawyers may be demanding and abrasive and they are sure to be short of time.
- Good communication is essential. Make sure the attorney hears and understands what you are saying and knows the repository's ground rules and policies.
- Use the reference interview to learn what the lawyer seeks and to give and obtain meaningful feedback. Lawyers constrained by attorney-client privilege may not communicate their information needs openly to the archivist or librarian. Paralegals, law clerks, and clerical staff who may be sent to gather information from the archives may not perfectly know what evidence is needed. Explore the kinds of records the lawyer *ideally* would like to find, then translate that into what actually exists.
- If they don't ask, tell, or at least inform. Lawyers and legal staff may not know about what librarians and archivists do when preserving and processing records, nor will they understand all that they may need to know about access, security, and donor relationships. Perhaps they do not even know what they need to ask. Be proactive. Communicate. Educate them so they can help you do your job and vice versa.
- Lawyers often prefer documents as they are kept in the usual course of business or filing. Provide any available information about provenance and original order. Encourage the use of copies until originals are required for production in court.
- Understand and communicate issues that may bear on the request or the evidence, for example, records lost, destroyed or unavailable, and restricted materials. Documents that may be protected by attorney-client privilege or privacy laws, or contain trade secrets and proprietary information should be shown to the repository's counsel before disclosure to litigation counsel. Any records under subpoena for deposition or trial or the subject of a request for production of documents should be segre-

gated to avoid disruption of their arrangement, but not be destroyed or transferred.
- Original documents or certified copies may be requested. Understand the chain of custody of originals and discuss with repository counsel procedures for certifying copies and providing affidavits attesting to various aspects of custody and ownership.
- Maintain confidentiality and abide by professional standards and ethical codes concerning equal access and the non-disclosure of research topics and research resources to others. Instruct staff and volunteers in these matters to ensure their compliance.
- If the key to winning or losing a case is in the archives, both parties to the litigation may visit the reading room for assistance. Objectivity, neutrality, and fairness are critical components to the information professional's success.

Many attorneys may view with suspicion both collections and collectors of records. Most lawyers probably know little about archives or records management, while to many, the existence of archival records may be a real or perceived threat to the client's claims. A little education may help the process. The archivist or librarian must advocate for the repository and its policies, the collections and the archival process, and professional standards and ethics. Describe the archives' philosophy or mission and services and offer an overview of the collections. Explain what archivists or special collections librarians do and why. Concepts of provenance, original order, and series may need explanation. If appropriate, offer a brief tour–it can be a revelation and provides an opportunity to educate and communicate. If a long-term relationship with the lawyer is essential to maintain, consider sharing professional codes of ethics. The result may be an attorney who views the archival or library programs with more trust and cooperation.

## *CONCLUSION*

Lawyers need information to serve their clients' needs in litigation. Although they operate within a system foreign to the world of archivists and librarians, they may become consumers of reference services. This article has discussed the fundamentals of the American court system and litigation process, the ways in which information professionals and attorneys work, and suggested a number of ways to smooth the interactions between the professions. Attorneys, despite their adversarial posture, workload, and world view, rely on others to provide them with information and services. Archivists and librarians preserve and disseminate information, value equal and open access, and provide excellent reference service. The trick in making the interaction work. But by demonstrating and communicating professionalism and sound and standard archival and library procedures, the archivist or librarian can go a very long way toward creating a favorable impression about access, security, confidentiality, and by extension, the trustworthiness of the information specialist and the information.

## NOTES

1. Mermin, Samuel, *Law and the Legal System,* Boston, Little, Brown and Co., 1982, pp. 214-215; Cound, John J., et al., *Civil Procedure,* St. Paul, MN, West Publishing, 1985, p. 2.

2. Do not ignore a Summons and Complaint, Notice of Deposition, Interrogatories, Subpoena, or any legal document requiring a response. Consult your repository's lawyer at once, and if needed, your personal attorney. Most legal documents have a deadline for an action or response, often 20 or 30 days after mailing or service. If you miss a deadline, you might lose your case or ability to enforce your claim, or reduce your opportunity to preserve your legal rights. Courts do not readily excuse missed deadlines.

3. Depositions are generally oral proceedings where attorneys for all parties take turns asking questions of the deponent who answers them under oath. A court reporter or stenographer records the proceedings, collects and copies any documents produced, and prepares transcripts for all parties. Any person with pertinent information or evidence to offer, including those who are and are not parties to the lawsuit, may be summoned or subpoenaed to provide sworn oral testimony at a deposition.

4. Interrogatories are written relevant questions served on an opposing party who must answer them under oath. There is no formal proceeding and no court reporter or other officer present. The party prepares answers, writes them down, signs under oath, and forwards copies to the court and the other parties within the time specified. Interrogatories may *not* be sent to non-party witnesses.

5. A request for production and inspection of documents and other items permits the other party to inspect, photograph, or copy any relevant materials or property that is in the possession of another party to the lawsuit.

6. A request for admissions is a formal request to admit or deny under oath specific facts in controversy or to admit that certain documents are genuine. This is a method of narrowing, focusing, and resolving issues before trial.

7. A court cannot compel the appearance of a witness who is outside of its jurisdiction, and federal district courts may enforce subpoenas only within 100 miles of the hearing site.

8. Personal service requires in-hand delivery to the named person or an authorized representative of a repository. Service of a document to a minor or an unauthorized representative, or a document that is slipped under the door during the night, is procedurally improper in all cases and should be challenged.

9. A minimally reasonable time for compliance is generally 7-10 days, although it may be longer and certainly can be lengthened by agreement of the parties.

10. In reviewing the motion to limit or modify the effect of a subpoena, the court will consider the relevance to the litigation of the materials sought, the requesting party's need for the materials, the breadth of the request, the particularity with which the materials are described, and the burden which compliance would impose on the person to whom the subpoena is directed. The court will balance the potential hardship caused by compliance against the hardship that non-compliance causes to the party seeking the documents.

11. "Intellectual property" includes patents, trademarks, copyrights, trade secrets, proprietary information, and other confidential information owned by companies and individuals.

12. All examples cited in this section were drawn from many interviews and conversations with practicing attorneys willing to share concerns without revealing personally-identifiable client information, and from personal experiences. The author respects the wishes of all who prefer to remain anonymous.

# Using the Tom Clark Papers for a Seminar: A Faculty Member's Perspective

Michael J. Churgin

**SUMMARY.** Professor Churgin describes a legal history seminar he teaches, in which he requires students to make use of the papers of U.S. Supreme Court Justice Tom C. Clark at the Tarlton Law Library, University of Texas at Austin. He describes the typical contents of Justice Clark's Supreme Court case files, how he prepares the students for their research projects, and the challenges that the students typically face in conducting archival research. *[Article copies available for a fee from The Haworth Document Delivery Service: 1-800-342-9678. E-mail address: <getinfo@haworthpressinc.com> Website: <http://www.HaworthPress.com> © 2001 by The Haworth Press, Inc. All rights reserved.]*

The University of Texas School of Law is the depository for the papers of Justice Tom C. Clark, who served on the United States Supreme Court from 1949 to 1967. While not one of the well-known justices during this period, Clark did maintain a complete set of case files that were delivered to the University of Texas upon his death. Professor Dennis Hutchinson, a biographer of Justice Byron White and a researcher in the various collections of justices of the Supreme Court, describes the Clark

---

Michael J. Churgin is Raybourne Thompson Centennial Professor in Law, The University of Texas at Austin. A member of the faculty at Texas since 1975, Professor Churgin received his JD from Yale University in 1973. His major areas of interest include immigration, criminal procedure, mental health and the law, and legal history.

[Haworth co-indexing entry note]: "Using the Tom Clark Papers for a Seminar: A Faculty Member's Perspective." Churgin, Michael J. Co-published simultaneously in *Legal Reference Services Quarterly* (The Haworth Information Press, an imprint of The Haworth Press, Inc.) Vol. 20, No. 1/2, 2001, pp. 135-138; and: *Public Services Issues with Rare and Archival Law Materials* (ed: Michael Widener) The Haworth Information Press, an imprint of The Haworth Press, Inc., 2001, pp. 135-138. Single or multiple copies of this article are available for a fee from The Haworth Document Delivery Service [1-800-342-9678, 9:00 a.m. - 5:00 p.m. (EST). E-mail address: getinfo@haworthpressinc.com].

papers as complete and without any evidence of an effort to polish the image of the justice.[1]

From time to time, I have taught a legal history seminar and have required all the law students to make use of the Clark collection for their seminar papers. For students used to reading appellate decisions, the use of the actual drafts of opinions and an individual justice's case files provides a unique opportunity. Many students find the assignment intimidating, and have difficulty both selecting a topic and undertaking the research. As an initial matter, the archivist and rare book librarian of the Tarlton Law Library, Mike Widener, provides the students with an orientation to the collection and a lecture on the various finding aids. Students are assigned to read portions of a University of Texas government department Ph.D. dissertation concerning Justice Clark to give them a perspective on the individual justice and those with whom he served on the Supreme Court.[2]

As would be expected, the case files are uneven in terms of bulk and substantive information. For example, some files will contain a few printed drafts of the opinion ultimately issued by the Court. Others, particularly those cases for which Justice Clark wrote the opinion of the Court or a dissent, will contain rich information about the decision-making process of the Supreme Court, including memoranda from various justices. In addition to the case files, for several years there are notes taken at the weekly conferences of the justices concerning pending matters, docket sheets indicating the votes of the justices on whether to grant certiorari to hear the case, and the initial and any subsequent vote on the merits of the cases. Finally, there are memoranda prepared by law clerks for Justice Clark's use in deciding whether to grant certiorari, or perhaps a memo on a particular issue in a case when the justice was writing an opinion.

Generally, when Justice Clark was preparing an opinion for the Court or a dissent, he wrote a first draft using a yellow legal pad. The secretary would type the second draft, and the Court printer would handle all subsequent drafts. The printed drafts would be distributed to the other members of the Court. Occasionally, justices would write a memorandum suggesting changes to the opinion, or note agreement or an intent to write a concurrence or a dissent. In other situations, justices would mark up the draft printed opinion and send it back to Justice Clark for consideration of revisions. Some files contained numerous draft opinions, some containing only stylistic revisions and others showing evidence of significant, substantive changes.

The librarian and I suggest particularly rich cases to the students for consideration of paper topics, and the goal is for each individual to develop a topic within a few weeks of the beginning of the semester. Since the Rare Books & Special Collections reading room is available for researchers during 8 a.m. to 5 p.m., and since the students frequently have jobs outside the law school in addition to their classes, it is imperative that the research be begun in the early part of the semester. The librarian has been very accommodating and occasionally will extend the hours of the collection for the use of the students.

Topic selection varies considerably. Some pick a general area in which Justice Clark had been particularly active. For example, he wrote opinions in conscientious objector cases for both the Korean War and the Vietnam War.[3] Students sometimes focus on particularly informative case files, such as the school prayer cases. Others will treat a particular area over a period of time–e.g., obscenity cases. A student with a military background chose to use the series of cases in the mid-1950s concerning the use of military courts without juries to try civilian spouses of military personnel serving overseas.[4]

While topic selection is ongoing, I often use the school desegregation cases as a way to illustrate some of the strengths of the collection. Dennis Hutchinson has written about Justice Clark's key memorandum in the case involving The University of Texas School of Law, *Sweatt v. Painter*.[5] In addition, there are interesting memoranda in many of the other desegregation cases, which illustrate the richness of some of the files, and the processes by which the justices reach their decisions.

Some disagreements among the justices are documented through internal letters concerning a block of cases involving prosecutions of communist party officials and the perception of some, including Justice Clark, that the Court was delaying reaching a decision in the cases. The series of orders by the Supreme Court, often vacating and asking lower courts to reconsider issues or granting rehearing, particularly vexed Justice Clark, and he was strong in his denunciation of these tactics.

> Much has been said of late of the law's delay, and criticism has been heaped on the courts for it. This case affords a likely Exhibit A. It looks as if Scales' case, like Jarndyce v. Jarndyce, [of Charles Dickens' *Bleak House*] will go on forever, only for the petitioner to reach his remedy, as did Richard Carstone there, through disposition by the Lord.[6]

Students initially often find it difficult to put the material together and develop a thesis for a research paper. The organizing principle varies dramatically depending on the approach. For example, Justice Clark wrote the decision in several cases involving the question of fair trial and free press, particularly undue publicity affecting a verdict and the use of television cameras in the courtroom. One approach is to focus on the attitude of the Court in successive draft opinions concerning the fear that television can fundamentally alter the fair trial rights of the defendant. Justice Clark was a frequent dissenter in cases in which the majority struck down statutes concerned with pornography. One student prepared a paper based on these dissents and some of the material in the files from magazines and other sources indicating the danger of pornography for the populace. Other criminal cases of particular interest involve the Fourth Amendment. Justice Clark wrote the decision for the Court in *Mapp v. Ohio*,[7] indicating that the exclusionary rule would apply to the states. This particular file is replete with notes from other justices, some of his fellow conservative justices expressing surprise at the breadth of his opinion in the case, while the liberals are fulsome in their praise.

Law students today increasingly are accustomed to doing research on-line. Using original papers is often a new experience and occasionally frustrating. The Clark collection has not been scanned electronically, and researchers must work page by page. I have found it necessary to schedule numerous individual conferences, both to suggest approaches to the material and to prod the students along. First drafts are due a month before the semester ends, and students assist one another in the critique process. In addition, each author makes a presentation to the class during the closing weeks of the seminar. Because of the nature of the source material, I usually set a due date of the first week of the following semester for the final paper.

## NOTES

1. Dennis J. Hutchinson, "A Scholar's View of the Tom C. Clark Papers," in *A Symposium on the Tom C. Clark Papers, March 19, 1985* (Austin, Tex.: Tarlton Law Library, University of Texas School of Law, 1987).

2. Mary P. Beeman, *New Deal Justice: Tom Clark and the Warren Court, 1953-1967*, Ph.D. dissertation 1993, The University of Texas at Austin.

3. See, e.g., *United States v. Seeger*, 380 U.S. 163 (1965) and *Sicurella v. United States*, 438 U.S. 285 (1955).

4. *Reid v. Covert*, 354 U.S. 1 (1957) on rehearing from 351 U.S. (1956).

5. 339 U.S. 629 (1950); Dennis J. Hutchinson, "Unanimity and Desegregation: Decisionmaking in the Supreme Court, 1948-1958," 68 *Georgetown Law Journal* 1, Appendix A (1979).

6. *Scales v. United States*, 360 U.S. 924, 926 (1959).

7. 367 U.S. 643 (1961).

# Access to the Working Papers of State Supreme Court Justices: A Case Study from Texas

Michael Widener

**SUMMARY.** Two former Texas Supreme Court justices recently offered to donate their personal court files to the Tarlton Law Library, University of Texas at Austin. These offers forced the Law Library, the Texas Supreme Court, and the State Archives to confront several issues. Should such files ever be made public? If so, what would be an appropriate waiting period? What research value, if any, do such papers have? These working files would be valued not only by legal historians, but also by litigants, voters, and political opponents, raising some sticky access issues. *[Article copies available for a fee from The Haworth Document Delivery Service: 1-800-342-9678. E-mail address: <getinfo@haworthpressinc.com> Website: <http://www.HaworthPress.com> © 2001 by The Haworth Press, Inc. All rights reserved.]*

---

Michael Widener is Archivist/Rare Books Librarian, Tarlton Law Library, University of Texas at Austin, and a Joseph D. Jamail Fellow in Law Librarianship. Earlier versions of this paper were presented at the annual meetings of the Society of Southwest Archivists (Galveston, TX, May 30, 1997), the Texas State Historical Association (Austin, TX, Mar. 5, 1998), and the Society of American Archivists (Pittsburgh, PA, Aug. 26, 1999). An unpublished version of this paper was cited by Joseph L. Sax in *Playing Darts with a Rembrandt: Public and Private Rights in Cultural Treasures* (Ann Arbor: University of Michigan Press, 1999).

[Haworth co-indexing entry note]: "Access to the Working Papers of State Supreme Court Justices: A Case Study from Texas." Widener, Michael. Co-published simultaneously in *Legal Reference Services Quarterly* (The Haworth Information Press, an imprint of The Haworth Press, Inc.) Vol. 20, No. 1/2, 2001, pp. 139-149; and: *Public Services Issues with Rare and Archival Law Materials* (ed: Michael Widener) The Haworth Information Press, an imprint of The Haworth Press, Inc., 2001, pp. 139-149. Single or multiple copies of this article are available for a fee from The Haworth Document Delivery Service [1-800-342-9678, 9:00 a.m. - 5:00 p.m. (EST). E-mail address: getinfo@haworthpressinc.com].

© 2001 by The Haworth Press, Inc. All rights reserved.

In the past several years, two former Texas Supreme Court justices have offered to donate their working papers to the Tarlton Law Library at The University of Texas at Austin. These offers have caused the law library, the Texas State Archives, and the court itself to confront a wide range of issues involving the preservation of these materials for future research. The issues include the definition of state records; the confidentiality of the Texas Supreme Court's deliberations; the potential uses and abuses of the materials by legal historians, litigants, and political campaigns; and the obligations of archivists in dealing with sensitive materials.

A judge's "working papers" are defined as: "All the papers generated in the course of rendering decisions, including conference notes, notes exchanged between judges or justices, bench notes, draft opinions, research notes, law clerks' memoranda, docket books, notes of conversations, and certiorari memoranda."[1] They are also known as "chambers papers," especially in reference to papers of federal judges. In essence, they constitute a paper trail of the court's decision-making process.

The decision-making process in Texas is similar to that in the U.S. Supreme Court and other state appellate courts. It typically begins when a case is appealed from an intermediate appeals court; civil cases go to the Texas Supreme Court and criminal ones to the Court of Criminal Appeals. One of the nine justices is assigned to write a memorandum on the appeal, which summarizes the facts of the case, discusses the arguments for each side, and recommends whether to accept the case for review. A vote is then taken; at least four justices must vote to review the case. Most cases are denied a review at this point. For those cases which are accepted, a justice will be assigned to draft an opinion. Opinions can go through several drafts. The justices may also exchange memoranda on the case, hear oral arguments, and meet once or more in conference to discuss the case before a final vote is taken. The court's decision will then be announced and published, sometimes accompanied by dissenting opinions, concurring opinions, or combinations of the two. Throughout this process, the secrecy of the deliberations are carefully guarded.

It's also important to note that state and federal appellate courts are considered "courts of record," and as such, common-law practice requires that certain documents be retained as the record of the court's official acts. Such a clearly defined official record may have discouraged the preservation of unofficial working materials, says one author.[2]

It's curious that in a judicial system so laden with rules, there seem to be so few laws or regulations, state or federal, which require appellate judges to maintain the confidentiality of their conferences. Standard texts on judicial ethics do not mention judicial confidentiality.[3] Nevertheless, the tradition of judicial secrecy is widespread and has a long tradition in Anglo-American common law. Leaks are rare. In Texas, Canon 3(B)(11) of the Code of Judicial Conduct addresses this issue. It states, in part:

> The discussions, votes, positions taken, and writings of appellate judges and court personnel about causes are confidences of the court and shall be revealed only through a court's judgment, a written opinion or in accordance with Supreme Court guidelines for a court approved history project.[4]

It should be noted that Texas' Code of Judicial Conduct applies only to sitting judges, not those who have retired from the bench.

The long-standing practice of the Texas Supreme Court has been to deny outsiders access to working papers in the court's custody. Only briefing attorneys and other court officials are allowed to attend its conferences on appellate cases. The U.S. Supreme Court is even stricter; no one but the justices themselves are allowed in the conference room.

State law grants Texas courts extensive control of their own files. Judicial records are specifically exempted from the Texas Open Records Act,[5] with the exception of "final opinions, including concurring and dissenting opinions, and orders issued in the adjudication of cases," which are designated as public information.[6] The *1995 Texas Open Records Handbook* explains that, "The judiciary exception . . . is important to safeguard judicial proceedings and maintain the independence of the judicial branch of government, preserving statutory and case law already governing access to judicial records."[7] In addition, both Texas and federal case law recognize a court's power to control access to its records to prevent their improper use or interference in the administration of justice.[8]

Legal disputes involving access to judicial records in Texas have generally involved administrative records. Attorney General Dan Morales challenged the exemption for judicial records in July 1997, when he issued an open records decision declaring that the Texas Supreme Court's telephone records were subject to the Open Records Act.[9] The court took only four weeks to issue a stinging rebuke in a unanimous, unsigned decision, stating that "The exclusion of the judiciary simply could not be plainer," as confirmed by every Attorney

General in the 24-year history of the Open Records Act, including Morales himself.[10]

There are a number of rationales for maintaining the secrecy of judicial deliberations: protecting the free exchange of ideas among the judges, ensuring judicial independence in the face of popular pressure, guarding against interference in the administration of justice, and protecting the rights of the litigants.[11] Some would add another reason: the desire of judges to maintain an aura of mystique and authority about their work and their role in society.[12]

The threat to fairness posed by premature disclosure of judicial deliberations is real. Former Chief Justice Jack Pope told of an occasion when the Texas Supreme Court was close to rendering a decision in a case about a business transaction involving a huge sum of money. The New York Stock Exchange contacted the court's clerk and asked for 15 minutes advance notice of the time when the court would announce its decision—not *what* the court would decide but simply *when* it would decide—in order to withdraw the company's stock from trading. An advance leak of the decision itself, or of the court's discussions, could have resulted in unfair windfalls for some and financial disaster for others.

An example of how judicial deliberations can become political fodder comes from California. In 1978, Chief Justice Rose Bird of the California Supreme Court faced vigorous and well-financed opposition in a retention election. On election day a newspaper reported that Bird had helped postpone two controversial decisions until after the retention election. Much of the resulting investigation by the California Commission on Judicial Performance was televised. One critic of the proceedings, Justice James Duke Cameron of the Arizona Supreme Court, later wrote that "personal opinions, habits and prejudices of the members of the supreme court were revealed and explored . . . the public entertained and titillated, and the California Supreme Court extensively damaged."[13]

Some scholars, while acknowledging the clear need for judicial secrecy, believe that "ultimate exposure at the bar of history," after an appropriate waiting period, can do much to balance the risks of corruption and impropriety when power is exercised unseen.[14] Many 20th-century U.S. Supreme Court justices have shown that they agree by making their working papers available for research. These collections have been invaluable in documenting the lives and legal thought of leading jurists, and in understanding the dynamics of the judicial process, in ways that the published opinions alone do not permit.

The federal judiciary, with the support of the National Archives, has taken the lead nationally in promoting the preservation of judicial working papers. These efforts provide a useful model in dealing with state judicial papers. While the Library of Congress and the Harvard Law Library were actively collecting the papers of U.S. Supreme Court justices by the mid-20th century, the real catalyst was the 1977 report of the National Study Commission on Records and Documents of Federal Officials, an outgrowth of the Watergate scandal. The Commission heard from numerous scholars who stressed the importance of judicial working papers for understanding the judiciary and the law,[15] and its report lamented that "these papers usually stay in family custody to be gradually scattered and lost, or are destroyed."[16] A 1992 report by the National Archives, *Records Management in Federal Courts,* encouraged voluntary efforts to preserve judicial papers, and also acknowledged the tradition that "the files accumulated by Federal judges are regarded as the judge's personal papers and are not subject to the laws and regulations governing the disposition of Federal records."[17] The National Archives does not accept these files.

Since that 1977 report, the Federal Judicial History Office of the Federal Judicial Center has developed guidelines for preserving the papers of federal judges and has recently published an excellent booklet, *A Guide to the Preservation of Federal Judges' Papers,*[18] which explains the historical significance of judicial working papers, how to identify and manage them, selecting a repository, and access issues.

For state appellate judges, the situation is much less clear. The Tarlton Law Library's experience with state judicial papers serves as a good illustration.

In the summer of 1992, former Texas Supreme Court Justice William Kilgarlin contacted the Tarlton Law Library about donating 36 linear feet of working papers from his tenure on the court (1983-1988). I recognized this collection as a valuable resource for studying the Texas Supreme Court, because of its completeness and because of the information it provided which was unavailable in published sources. Justice Kilgarlin also recognized the collection's value, as well as the sensitivity of the information it contained. He wished the collection to remain closed until 1999, in deference to his former colleagues on the bench.

The Law Library's first concern was that the documents which Justice Kilgarlin was offering could be state records. A review of relevant statutes suggested to me that they were "state records" under the Texas Government Code, "document[s] . . . made or received by a state department or institution according to law or in connection with the transaction of official state business,"[19] and "government records" under the

Texas Penal Code: "anything belonging to, received by, or kept by government for information."[20] So, I contacted the State Archives.

Chris LaPlante, the State Archivist, took the time to make a detailed reply, in which he agreed that the judge's working papers appeared to be state records, although he added that the court's justices might not agree. LaPlante recognized their research value for supplementing the "official" court records, and he stated his preference that the papers go to the State Archives, rather than to the Tarlton Law Library via a loan agreement.[21] When I explained this to Justice Kilgarlin, he agreed to transfer his working papers to the State Archives, where they were closed to research until 1999 as per the deed of gift.

I thought we had settled this issue once and for all, and said as much to a second former Texas Supreme Court justice, Oscar Mauzy, who contacted the Tarlton Law Library in the summer of 1996 with a similar offer. However, Mauzy urged us to pose the question anew to the State Archives, which we did (without identifying him).

After lengthy research and conversations with myself and Supreme Court personnel, LaPlante wrote a new letter to the Tarlton Law Library, Chief Justice Tom Phillips, and the court's Executive Assistant, Bill Willis. In this letter, I learned for the first time of a record series entitled "Justices' Working Files" on the court's retention schedule, which was marked "confidential" and for long-term retention. This series is the designated record copy of the internal memoranda that circulate among the justices in the course of deciding cases. LaPlante stated that any copies of these memoranda retained by individual justices (in essence, the same materials being offered to the Law Library) would be considered "convenience copies," not required to be listed on the court's records schedule.[22] There are some important differences between the two sets: the court's record copies can be reliably assumed to be complete, unlike the sets kept by individual justices, but they will not bear the annotations that will often be found on the "convenience copies," which give a fuller picture of the development of an opinion.

In any event, LaPlante implied that the Tarlton Law Library was now free to accept these "convenience copies" as donations of personal papers by former justices, since "state record," as defined in the Texas Government Code, "does not include . . . an extra copy of a document preserved only for convenience of reference."[23]

So, although my library was apparently able to accept working papers, some new and difficult access issues arose. These documents were copies of confidential state records. For how long should we restrict access to them? We did not want to compromise the court's deliberations by providing premature access. Our hope was that if the court would set a closure period on its "Justices' Working Files", the Tarlton Law Library could use this as a guideline for access restrictions on the working papers of individual judges. We posed these issues in a letter to Chief Justice Tom Phillips. We pointed out that the confidentiality of the court's working papers was potentially being circumvented, not so much by having copies of the papers available in archival repositories, but by the mere fact that it had allowed retiring justices to take these papers with them in the first place. We appealed to the court to strike a balance between protecting its deliberations and serving the needs of history.[24]

Chief Justice Phillips named Justice Rose Spector to present the issue to the court. Justice Spector later told me that their conclusion was that the "convenience copies" are the personal property of the individual justices, and that there was little the court can do to control access to these papers, apart from requesting that archives restrict access at least until the cases are closed. The opinion of Justice Spector and several attorneys with experience in Supreme Court litigation was that five years from the date of the case file would be an adequate closure period, although ten years might be preferable. On some occasions a case will go up and down the appellate ladder several times as the courts rule on separate issues.

In light of this, the Tarlton Law Library accepted Justice Mauzy's gift of his Texas Supreme Court working papers, with the stipulation that files from a given court term will be opened ten years after the end of that term. The ten-year period provides reasonable assurance that files pertaining to still-active cases will not be opened, and will also keep the files closed until most, if not all, the justices involved in the discussions have left the court. Turnover on the Texas Supreme Court has been relatively high in recent years, and court observers expect this trend to continue.

The court has not resolved the issue of when, if ever, to allow access to its record copies of the working papers. Justice Spector reported that, although the court discussed the matter on several occasions, it was unable to form a consensus around a single option. Justice Spector made it clear that she understands the value of these records for legal history and supports opening them for research at an appropriate time.

Comments by former Chief Justice Jack Pope and some court observers who requested anonymity indicate that the court was divided between those who supported opening the files and others who felt they should remain permanently closed. Justice Pope, who stressed he is not trying to give advice to the present court, is strongly opposed to opening the files. I should note that he is a strong supporter of historical research. He has given the Tarlton Law Library a valuable collection of judicial photographs, and is preparing his own papers (without any working files from his Texas Supreme Court service) for donation to his undergraduate alma mater, Abilene Christian University. He told me the clear understanding had always been that in conference there was complete freedom to discuss the cases, but that the door was closed when the justices walked out and that they were never to talk about what he called "the blood on the floor." "A judge speaks through solemn judgment, and then silence," is almost a motto to Justice Pope. He said the court will rue the day it lowers the wall of secrecy around its deliberations, because of the detrimental effect it will have on both the justices and the litigants.[25]

A less formidable barrier is that some judges still do not realize why anyone would be interested in looking through these papers. A large number of federal judges reported this attitude in a 1976 survey by the National Study Commission on Records and Documents of Federal Officials.[26] Bill Willis, the Texas Supreme Court's administrator, told me he'd always been skeptical that their files contain anything worth researching, other than for someone truly desperate for a dissertation topic. While I don't agree with Mr. Willis on this point, he has good reason for thinking this way. John Phillip Reid, one of the few legal historians who has specialized in state courts, has pointed out that if the state judiciary has been passed over by legal historians in favor of the U.S. Supreme Court, it's not because of any fundamental unimportance. Rather, the legal issues that state courts most often deal in are more technical in nature and less glamorous in academic circles than constitutional law, and many historians are simply not equipped to understand their significance. The burning issue of tort reform is an excellent example for Texas; many of the really significant efforts at tort reform have taken place not in the state legislature but in the decisions of the Texas Supreme Court. Another reason given by Reid is especially significant in our context: *source material for the U.S. Supreme Court is much more abundant.*[27]

This gap is beginning to be remedied here in Texas. Justice Oscar Mauzy's case files are now at the Tarlton Law Library, and the files from his first years on the court will be available as soon as they are processed. The William Kilgarlin Papers at the State Archives were scheduled to be opened to research as early as 1999. The papers of former Justice Charles Barrow at Baylor University include 26 folders of conference memoranda spanning 1977-1984, with no restrictions on access.[28] Two years ago the Sam Houston Regional Library & Research Center received the judicial files of Texas governor Price Daniel, who served on the Texas Supreme Court in the 1970s. Robert Schaadt of the Center tells me that the papers will be processed "on demand," and that confidential materials such as conference memoranda will be flagged and not provided to researchers. In the Tarlton Law Library, the papers of Justice Graham Smedley, known as "the great little dissenter" when he served on the Texas Supreme Court during 1945-1954, contain a scattering of conference memoranda and annotations on typescript opinion drafts. His correspondence also includes discussions of the court's work. The Smedley Papers are unrestricted.

In 1997 former Justice James P. Wallace, who served on the court from 1981 to 1988, managed to get all of his Supreme Court files scanned and stored on CD-ROMs, and placed a CD-ROM copy at the Daniel Center for Legal History, State Bar of Texas.

The Texas Supreme Court's administrative records, such as those phone records that Attorney General Morales unsuccessfully tried to open up, are also receiving renewed attention. In 1998 one candidate for the court attacked its open records policy in his campaign.[29] The Texas Judicial Council appointed a Committee on Court Records charged with examining how the Open Records Act applies to the judiciary.[30]

There is evidence of a ground swell of interest in preserving and documenting the history of the Texas Supreme Court. The Texas Supreme Court Historical Society is sponsoring a two-volume history of the Texas Supreme Court, and the State Bar of Texas has an active Committee on History and Traditions. My experience convinces me that it is not only possible but necessary to form a fuller documentary record of the Texas Supreme Court, and that this can be done without compromising the confidentiality of the court's deliberations. Secrecy need not be eternal to serve its purpose.

## NOTES

1. Alexandra K. Wigdor, *The Personal Papers of Supreme Court Justices: A Descriptive Guide* 3 (1986).

2. Wigdor, *supra* note 1, at 4.

3. For instance, see the American Bar Association's *Compendium of Professional Responsibility Rules and Standards* (1999) and Jeffrey M. Shaman, Steven Lubet & James J. Alfini, *Judicial Conduct and Ethics* (2000).

4. Tex. Code Jud. Conduct, Canon 3(B)(11), *reprinted in* Tex. Gov't Code Ann., tit. 2, subtit. G app. B (Vernon 1998).
5. Tex. Gov't Code Ann. § 552.003(1)(b) (Vernon 1994).
6. Tex. Gov't Code Ann. § 552.022(12) (Vernon 1994).
7. *1995 Texas Open Records Act Handbook: Including Updates From the Seventy-fourth Legislature* (1995).
8. See the following cases: *Ashpole v. Millard*, 778 S.W.2d 169, 170 (Tex. App.–Houston 1989, no writ); *Nixon v. Warner Communications, Inc.*, 435 U.S. 589 (U.S. Supreme Court 1978); *In re Four Search Warrants*, 945 F.Supp. 1563 (U.S. District Court, N. Dist. Georgia 1996).
9. Op.Atty.Gen.1997, No. ORD-657 (July 24, 1997).
10. Decision No. 97-9141 (Supreme Court of Texas, Aug. 21, 1997).
11. See generally Wigdor, *supra* note 1, at 15-20. See also James Duke Cameron, "The California Supreme Court Hearings–A Tragedy That Should and Could Have Been Avoided," 8 *Hastings Constitutional Law Quarterly* 11 (1980).
12. See David A. Anderson, "Democracy and the Demystification of Courts: An Essay," 14 *Review of Litigation* 627 (1995).
13. Cameron, *supra* note 11m at 18.
14. J. Woodford Howard, "Comment on Secrecy and the Supreme Court," 22 *Buffalo Law Review* 837 (1973); quoted in Wigdor, *supra* note 1, at 17-19.
15. Wigdor, *supra* note 1, at 15.
16. National Archives and Records Administration, *Records Management in Federal Courts: A NARA Evaluation* 42 (1992).
17. *Id.* at 41.
18. Federal Judicial Center, *A Guide to the Preservation of Federal Judges' Papers* (1996). Archivists who are negotiating with judicial donors, or who are working with judicial collections for the first time, will find this publication very useful for arrangement, description, and access issues. The publication is available on the Federal Judicial History Office's website, in PDF format, at <http://air.fjc.gov/history/publications_frm.html>.
19. Tex. Gov't Code Ann. § 441.031 (Vernon Supp. 2000).
20. Tex. Pen. Code Ann. § 37.01(1)(A) (Vernon 1994). This statute was amended in 1997 to include a definition of "court record" as "a decree, judgment, order, subpoena, warrant, minutes, or other document issued by a court . . . "; see § 37.01(1) (Vernon Supp. 2000).
21. Chris LaPlante to Mike Widener, 20 Aug. 1992, on file in Holding Records–Transferred Collections: Kilgarlin Papers, Rare Books & Special Collections, Tarlton Law Library, University of Texas at Austin.
22. Chris LaPlante to William L. Willis, 12 July 1996; copy on file with author.
23. Tex. Gov't Code Ann. § 441.031 (Vernon Supp. 2000).
24. Roy M. Mersky to the Hon. Thomas R. Phillips, 30 July 1996; copy on file with author.
25. Telephone conversation with Justice Jack Pope, May 1997.
26. Wigdor, *supra* note 1, at 4.
27. John Phillip Reid, "Commentary: Beneath the Titans," 70 *New York University Law Review* 653 (1995).
28. Thanks to Ben Rogers, archivist of the Baylor Collections of Political Materials, for providing this information.

29. "Hopwood Attorney Runs for Texas Supreme Court," *Daily Texan,* Jan. 26, 1998, at 6, quoting Republican candidate Steve Smith: "We should release records that do not impinge on judicial power . . . How officials spend their money, and to whom, are basic public confidences."

30. The committee's final report, "Public Access to Judicial Records," is available on the Web at < http://www.courts.state.tx.us/jcouncil/97-98charges.htm >. The committee's recommendations became Rule 12 of the Texas Rules of Judicial Administration.

# Providing Access to Lawyers' Papers: The Perils... and The Rewards

Akiba J. Covitz

**SUMMARY.** Professor Covitz provides an overview of the collection of issues that is traditionally referred to as "attorney-client privilege," specifically as it relates to providing access to the papers of lawyers in law libraries and other settings. He also relates how he and his colleagues at Yale University addressed this matter of lawyers' papers when it came to Yale's extensive legal manuscript holdings. The guidelines that resulted from this process are included as an appendix. While there are perceived obstacles to collecting materials in this area and making them available to patrons, these obstacles are not necessarily insurmountable, and the rewards for those willing to understand this issue are potentially great. *[Article copies available for a fee from The Haworth Document Delivery Service: 1-800-342-9678. E-mail address: <getinfo@haworthpressinc.com> Website: <http://www.HaworthPress.com> © 2001 by The Haworth Press, Inc. All rights reserved.]*

---

Akiba J. Covitz teaches constitutional law, American politics and government, civil rights law, and legal history at the University of Richmond (E-mail: acovitz@richmond.edu). He received his PhD from the University of Pennsylvania, his MSL from Yale Law School, and his BA from St. John's College. He was previously Senior Research Associate at Yale Law School, and Archivist at Sterling Memorial Library, Yale University, for the papers of U.S. Supreme Court Justices Abe Fortas and Potter Stewart.

This article is a revised and extended version of his presentation for the panel, "The Paper Chase: The Old Perils and the New Rewards of Collecting the Papers of Lawyers and Judges," at the 1999 Annual Meeting of the Society of American Archivists in Pittsburgh, PA.

[Haworth co-indexing entry note]: "Providing Access to Lawyers' Papers: The Perils . . . and The Rewards." Covitz, Akiba J. Co-published simultaneously in *Legal Reference Services Quarterly* (The Haworth Information Press, an imprint of The Haworth Press, Inc.) Vol. 20, No. 1/2, 2001, pp. 151-179; and: *Public Services Issues with Rare and Archival Law Materials* (ed: Michael Widener) The Haworth Information Press, an imprint of The Haworth Press, Inc., 2001, pp. 151-179. Single or multiple copies of this article are available for a fee from The Haworth Document Delivery Service [1-800-342-9678, 9:00 a.m. - 5:00 p.m. (EST). E-mail address: getinfo@haworthpressinc.com].

## I. A BRIEF CASE STUDY

I came to this question of the papers of lawyers in manuscript collections, because, not surprisingly, attorney-client files were found in one of the manuscript collections at Yale University. Like many law schools and universities,[1] Yale and its various component libraries had accumulated many collections containing manuscript materials over its history. The papers in question were those of Kenneth Farrand Simpson. Simpson was a Yale College and Harvard Law School graduate. He was also a high-ranking official in the New York Republican Party in the 1920s and 1930s, helping to rebuild the party during a key transitional phase in state politics. In this role as party insider, Simpson had extensive dealings with such people as Thomas E. Dewey, Fiorello H. LaGuardia, Alfred M. Landon, and Wendell L. Willkie. In 1940, Simpson was elected to Congress, although he died soon after taking his seat at the age of forty-five. His papers were originally accepted by Yale because he had played such a prominent role in politics and had played that role in a state that was vital to the national political scene at the time. Simpson was also friends with and often corresponded with such luminaries as Alexander Fyodorovich Kerensky, Pierre Matisse, and Gertrude Stein. Additionally, Simpson was, somewhat unfortunately for us at Yale, a practicing lawyer.

Simpson's daughter, many years after the first accession of her father's papers, came across some additional boxes of papers filled with client files. The senior archivist directing work on these papers, Diane E. Kaplan, noted that it was clear from her knowledge of Simpson that this was only a selection from a far larger number of cases that Simpson handled as an attorney. Why these client files had been saved by Simpson, and other files had not, was not immediately evident. Perhaps these files were of particular interest to Simpson because of personal connections to the clients. Perhaps other files that he retained had been (purposefully? or accidentally?) discarded at some point since Simpson's death in 1940. There was little possibility of getting answers to these important questions.

What was clear was that most of these files seemed to be of little or no conceivable historical interest at this point in time. These files largely dealt with minor real estate and insurance matters. However, there were also a few client files with potentially considerable historical value. There were files relating to some of New York City's artistic and political elite, such as the conductor Leopold Stokowski, as well as people like Kerensky and Matisse mentioned above. These files and others contained not simply legal documents, but also personal correspondence. This correspondence often illustrated the depth of Simpson's political power, and how he brought those political relationships to bear in the service of his personal dealings with friends and clients. A few files in particular caught the attention of Kaplan. These files documented Simpson's handling of a real estate transaction for the husband and wife American literary giants, Mary McCarthy and Edmund Wilson. There was also a file on the divorce proceedings between Wilson and his earlier wife, Mary Blair Wilson. Of course, McCarthy, Wilson's third wife, was the famed author of such works as *The Group, The Oasis,* and *Venice Observed,* as well as the long-time drama critic for the *Partisan Review*. Wilson was one of the leading literary and social critics of his era, and author of dozens of works of fiction and non-fiction.

Again, please note that these files labeled with McCarthy's and Wilson's names did not simply contain papers that were entirely of a legal nature. There were detailed, personal letters that passed between this lawyer and his clients that spoke to McCarthy's and Wilson's influential fiction and non-fiction writings. Without any other information to go on, we could only speculate that Simpson did not differentiate between personal letters between himself and his clients, on the one hand, and purely legal correspondence that would constitute what might be called attorney-client "work product," on the other. Were these entire, historically valuable letters and these whole files forever confidential because of "attorney-client privilege"? If so, would it simply make sense to shred these materials? Could we seal them for some specific period of time and then ethically open these materials to researchers? The latest date on any file was 1939, so some sixty years had passed since any of these files were active legal matters. Should we make a determination that the blander files, not potentially embarrassing to anyone, could be opened, but those dealing with more personal matters such as divorce or estates, should be closed forever or shredded?

I was asked to lead our department's work toward answering these questions, for the particular case of the Simpson Papers, and more generally for Yale's currently held attorney-client materials, and for future collecting in this area. Given the prevalence of lawyers in American society, and Yale College and the Yale Law School's often leading role in producing America's leaders at the bar and beyond, it was no surprise that there were attorney-client materials in many other collections held by Yale. In addition to the Simpson Papers, there was, for instance, also the particular question of what to do with the attorney-client files in the Harry Weinberger Papers. Weinberger's clients included many political activists and prominent artists, such as Emma Goldman and Eugene O'Neill. Weinberger's papers had long been in Yale's collections and had long been open to researchers without restriction. Many researchers over the years had poured over Weinberger's files, including those relating to Goldman, a leading figure in the American anarchist movement. In the process, researchers learned as much about Goldman, an undeniably important historical figure, and about many other of Weinberger's clients than perhaps from any other single source. Should these files be closed forever or, if never to be made accessible to researchers, simply destroyed? These were the questions that I and my colleagues at Yale faced.

## II. LIMITS AND SCOPE

Given the strong feelings often engendered by the subject matter of this article, please allow me to begin the formal discussion of these complex issues I have just raised with a few words on what this article will *not* attempt to do. What follows will not be an exhaustive history of the rules and codes that govern the attorney-client relationship. Many others have set this as their task in the past; the literature is extensive and quite good, and the two leading articles on the subject are directed specifically toward law librarians.[2] I do not wish to repeat nor critique the work of those who have written previously on this subject. What we will in fact need in order to assess the importance of lawyers' papers to the work of law librarians and other legal information professionals is a basic sense of what lawyers, law librarians, and other information professionals who deal with legal materials can ethically do in the realm of lawyers' papers, with the ultimate goal of better serving their respective clients and patrons.

Let me say clearly that this article is *not* an attempt to call into question the importance of the attorney-client privilege. That privilege, as the United States Supreme Court demonstrated recently in the case known as the Vincent Foster case,[3] is a fortress built around an attorney's "work product," and six justices of that court have determined that forced access to that work product survives the death of the client.[4] Lawyers should not be compelled to disclose information about their clients, except under the conditions given in the laws of evidence,[5] and in lawyers' ethics codes and the rules of conduct that specifically relate to lawyers and that we will discuss below.

The virtual citadel that is attorney-client privilege need not be assaulted in order for law librarians and their colleagues, under very specific and strict conditions, to collect and provide access to the old, inactive client files of lawyers. A lawyer (or a lawyer's heir), fully appraised of her or his ethical duties and with the sense of public responsibility that the American Law Institute (ALI), The Law Governing Lawyers, says that a lawyer should have in relation to her or his role in society, "may cooperate with reasonable efforts to obtain information about clients and law practice for public purposes, such as historical research. . . . "[6] If that fully-informed and ethical lawyer (or a lawyer's heir) willingly seeks to allow researchers to have access to the lawyer's long-inactive, historically valuable personal and professional files, then law librarians should reasonably be able to respond.[7]

I hope now it is clear what this article does not intend to accomplish. It is in fact the purpose of this article to provide the basis for action for legal information professionals such as law librarians in academic or law firm settings, special collections librarians, archivists for legal materials, and others similarly charged, should such a scenario occur involving the papers of lawyers. At Yale University, our work on this subject allowed us to provide access to valuable, existing materials in Yale's collections that shed light on historical figures and eras, as well as on the lawyering process. Moreover, Yale was ready when approached by one of America's oldest and most prestigious law firms then looking for a place that had thought carefully about attorney-client issues, that could accept that law firm's historical materials, and that could provide professional access to them. Our work in this area also allowed Yale to move forward with a new, pro-active collection development policy in the area of legal materials beyond the standard emphasis on materials solely related to appellate court opinions and analysis.[8]

Louis M. Brown, distinguished professor and attorney, has ably argued that the practice of law is certainly not limited to the analysis of the decisions of appellate courts.[9] Why, then, should legal education, and the libraries and other repositories devoted to facilitating that education, emphasize appellate litigation above all else? Practicing lawyers know that a great deal of what they do has little or nothing to do with formal court practice, particularly courts of appeal. I argue that our law libraries should reflect the world of law into which law students are about to enter and in which lawyers already exist.[10] That world is one in which what Brown calls "lawyering decisions," not necessarily appellate court opinions, are paramount.[11] These real-life lawyering experiences are made evident through the study of actual lawyers' files.[12] A number of prominent law firms have helped in the broader understanding of the lawyering life by allowing limited access to their files to historians writing firm histories or general books on legal practice.[13] This article will help legal information professionals determine whether seeking to develop their collections in the direction of reflecting the real-life practice of the law is what is right for their institutions.

## III. DEFINITIONS AND NOMENCLATURE

We next must get our language clearer. I am afraid that I have already bandied around too many terms which have complex, specialized meanings. Let me begin by providing working definitions of the most controversial of these terms. The attorney-client "privilege" relates to the law of evidence.[14] This privilege was extended under the common law, beginning at least in the sixteenth century, to lawyers appearing before courts or before other official proceedings.[15] It allows a lawyer, in specific circumstances, to avoid revealing information about a client.[16] Anyone else not part of an attorney-client relationship, asked to reveal information that was produced as a result of that relationship, would have to provide that information if ordered to by a court or other official tribunal. Lawyers are afforded this privilege of refusing to divulge such information.[17]

The attorney-client privilege is in many ways defined by how it works and what it covers. The materials that might fall under attorney-client privilege are more limited in scope than many would assume. According to Judge John T. Noonan, Jr. and Professor Richard W. Painter,

> The privilege is limited, and only certain communications fall within its reach. An initial requirement for a communication to be privileged is that it must be relevant to a legal problem about which a client seeks a lawyer's advice. Furthermore, although protected communications may include advice given by the lawyer to the client, or disclosures made by the client to the lawyer, facts that are objectively discoverable are not protected. For example, documents that pre-exist an attorney-client relationship are no more protected after they are handed over to the lawyer than they were before the transfer of possession.[18]

Thus, if a law librarian dealing with client case files comes across, for instance, a personal document that belonged to the client prior to the establishment of the attorney-client relationship in one of those case files, it could not be assumed that such a document is subject to this privilege. More generally, it seems that materials contained within client files that are unrelated to the specific legal problem that led to the creation of the attorney-client relationship are not clearly covered by this privilege. Additionally, a document that would normally fall under the privilege, but is also made available to someone outside the attorney-client relationship, is not considered privileged.[19]

What constitutes an attorney's "work product" also relates to this matter of attorney-client privilege. A document that is considered an attorney's work product is one that is produced by an attorney while preparing for litigation.[20] This doctrine mainly exists in order to protect materials produced by the lawyer in the process of representing the client from the discovery reach of opposing counsel, except in extreme instances.[21]

Before we get too caught up in the fascinating details of this lawyerly evidentiary privilege, two things must be kept in mind. The first is that the privilege is a matter of essentially settled law in the United States. The attorney-client privilege was debated in a very public manner–at least public as compared to most other abstruse legal matters–in the case discussed above involving the notes of the lawyer representing Deputy White House Counsel Vincent W. Foster, Jr. that were sought by Independent Counsel Kenneth W. Starr. Because of its presidential connection, the United States Supreme Court's decision in that case was carried as a lead story around the nation and the world.[22] The majority opinion cites dozens of judicial and scholarly opinions that have held that the privilege allowing lawyers to avoid releasing attorney-client communications, specifically in cases such as this one, survives the death of the client and the lawyer.[23] Beyond its definition, there is no question that this privilege serves the valuable social purpose of encouraging frank communication between client and lawyer. The American Bar Association's (ABA) Model Rules of Professional Conduct (Model Rules) states that the client's presumption that what is communicated to the lawyer is privileged encourages the client "to communicate fully and frankly with the lawyer even as to embarrassing or legally damaging subject matter."[24] I certainly have no serious qualms with Chief Justice Rehnquist's excellent majority opinion, which reversed the decision by the Court of Appeals for the District of Columbia Circuit, and nothing you read here will attempt to call that opinion into question.[25]

The second thing to keep in mind is that we as legal information professionals interested in access to useful resources (such as lawyers' papers) for our patrons should not, in the end, be all that concerned with this privilege. No one, particularly me, is talking about law librarians forming something like reference assault groups, barging into law offices, and demanding the papers of practicing lawyers. The Swidler & Berlin and Hamilton opinion involved the attempt by Judge Starr to forcibly take admittedly protected materials from Vincent Foster's lawyer in the name of "truth seeking" and criminal justice.[26] The record clearly stated that Foster had explicitly requested and been explicitly assured that everything that he said in his lawyer's office that constituted attorney-client communications would be privileged.[27] The attorney-client privilege is, as Chief Justice Rehnquist states, "intended to encourage 'full and frank communication between attorneys and their clients and thereby promote broader public interests in the observance of law and the administration of justice.'"[28] No attorney should be compelled, in the name of legal history or any other noble or mundane cause (such as Judge Starr's attempt to seek the truth when it came to Hillary Rodham Clinton's role in the White House Travel Office firings), to divulge the secrets and confidences developed within the attorney-client relationship.

Ultimately, the issue of attorney-client privilege is only tangentially relevant to this question of access to attorneys' papers. Because it is what first comes to mind when people hear that one is talking about access to attorney-client files, it is necessary to understand it in order to set it largely aside. Thus, matters of privilege and the law of evidence more or less behind us,[29] there remains the vexing ethical question of confidentiality. Are not all attorney-client communications utterly and forever confidential?

Before we get to that (rhetorical) question as to perpetuity and confidentiality, what constitutes those "attorney-client communications" to which confidentiality is to apply? I turned to the primary and secondary literature on this subject to provide an answer to this latter definitional question. Based on that research and in close collaboration with my legal and archival colleagues at Yale and elsewhere, I developed the following working definition for attorney-client communications that may be subject to confidentiality restrictions: (1) any form of communication between attorney and client directly related to the client's representation; or (2) any form of communication to or from the lawyer directly related to the client's representation; or (3) any internal document created by the lawyer directly related to the client's representation. At the same time, it is important to note what is not included within the definition of materials that constitute attorney-client communications and what is not, therefore, subject to privilege or confidentiality restrictions. As I read the various codes, rules, and commentaries (to which we will return more specifically in a moment), attorney-client communications do not include such things as official, published legal documents. By this I mean to include court opinions, pleadings, and the like, which are matters of public record and not subject to confidentiality restrictions. Thus, even if such materials are found within files that would otherwise be deemed confidential, these particular documents would not, in my view, fall under that restriction. However, preliminary, internal drafts of such public, official documents, as well as those that are annotated by the lawyer, are likely subject to confidentiality restrictions.

What I had at this point in the process of developing guidelines for dealing with attorney-client materials in legal manuscript collections were some basic, working definitions of the key terms: privilege, work product, and attorney-client communications. What was then needed was a broader sense of the context within which these terms are used.

Attorney-client privilege is part of the law of evidence. A lawyer served with a court order and called upon to testify in some fashion against a client may and should withhold information that is subsumed by the specifics of that privilege. Before the ABA's Model Rules were promulgated, the guiding document in this realm of legal practice was the ABA's Model Code of Professional Responsibility (Model Code).[30] While the attorney-client privilege is a matter of law, a lawyer's duty to protect what the Model Code calls the "secrets" and "confidences" of a client contained within these attorney-client communications, is not, strictly speaking, a matter of law, but one of sometimes conflicting professional ethics for a lawyer.[31] Of course, as I have argued above, in the interests of making a client feel secure and ensuring that a client is completely forthcoming, a lawyer should also protect a client's secrets against their forced revelation. This is particularly the case if that revelation would lead to harm of any kind to the client. But what of the case of a lawyer who wishes to leave her or his professional papers to a law library or its affiliated special collections department or archives for use at some future date? Or what if a lawyer wants to allow legal researchers access to her or his files, with the understanding that no names or characteristic information is revealed in the process?[32] In the ALI's view as reproduced above, a lawyer "may cooperate with reasonable efforts to obtain information about clients and law practice for public purposes, such as historical research. . . ."[33] How is it that a lawyer should carry out this socially and historically important role?

First, we must understand the flexibility and limits inherent in lawyers' ethics codes and rules. Even the strict Disciplinary Rules found within the ABA's Model Code that define these "secrets" and "confidences" limit the scope of this lawyer-client confidentiality. The Model Code seems to link the need to maintain absolute confidentiality to instances in which the client requested that the information in question be "held inviolate, or the disclosure of which would be embarrassing, or would likely be detrimental to the client."[34] Moreover, as Geoffrey C. Hazard, Jr., Director of the ALI for some fifteen years beginning in 1984,[35] points out in his "Foreword" to the ALI's The Law Governing Lawyers, the ABA's "lawyer codes" and the state rules based on those codes are indeed vital and guiding, but nonetheless, even by these codes' own admission, they are limited in legal effect.[36] At the same time, there is no denying the clear tenor of all the elements of the ethical strictures to which lawyers are told they must adhere. For instance, the ALI's Restatement of the Law (Third), The Law Governing Lawyers, clearly states that:

> The duty of confidentiality continues so long as the lawyer possesses confidential client information. It extends beyond the end of the representation and beyond the death of the client. Accordingly, a lawyer must take reasonable steps for the future safekeeping of client files, including files in closed matters. . . .[37]

Obviously, the simplest, safest path for a lawyer would be to close her or his client files forever, or perhaps even to shred them to ensure safekeeping. The question remains whether this is the only path open to lawyers, especially ones who see their practice in a larger social context. We will return to a more exhaustive review of these ethical questions in a moment.

I hope that I have now whetted your appetites with a taste of the issues involved in access to lawyers' papers. Before I get to the inevitable section of this presentation that goes step-by-step through the relevant case law, codes, rules, and the like, let me put a somewhat finer point on what is at stake in this debate. I will do this through the standard but generally unfair device of an unfair hypothetical example.

### IV. BOOTH, J.W.

A second year law student gets her dream position as a summer associate at an established, prestigious Washington, D.C. firm. She wants to be a litigator and has dreams of sitting in on important pre-trial strategy sessions. The reality of her situation quickly becomes apparent. She indeed meets many of the legendary senior partners, some of whom are former, high-ranking government officials. She is also enjoying her two-hour lunches and evening cruises on the Potomac, but her first work assignment is a bit less high-powered than she imagined.

She made the mistake of emphasizing in her interview that she took her undergraduate degree with highest honors in American history, and has continued to take courses at law school in legal history. She is assigned to an associate who in turn has been assigned by a senior partner to "deal with" the firm's outdated and inactive "historical" client files that are taking up valuable on-site storage space. She spends her first day on this task in the storeroom on the firm's top floor. She methodically goes through box after box, looking through each file for she's not entirely sure what, removing duplicate filings, and coding the files either for shipment to the firm's warehouse (if, as she was told, the file may actually be of some interest to the firm's current business, say, documenting the firm's work in a few particular practice areas), or, in most cases, coding the files to be sent out for shredding.

In her half stupor, nearing the end of her second day in the storeroom, she finally finishes with the "A" files, and has made her way through most of the "B"s. She comes to a file marked "Booth, J.W." Nonplussed, she opens the file as she has all the previous files, and finds a few pages of hand-written notes taken by a member of one of the earliest, two-person, parent versions of the now 200-plus lawyer firm. The notes are dated 15 April 1865. A fellow named Booth had, it seems, seen a lawyer's shingle, knocked on the door, and woken the lawyer up in the early morning hours. In a fevered interview, Booth had told his lawyer everything; how he had planned and killed President Lincoln; the names of all those who helped him carry out the assassination; whether Mary Surratt was involved; the political statement he was trying to make by shooting the president, etc. The entire untold story is right there in the file.

The young summer associate catches her breath. She runs to the office of the beleaguered associate who is supervising her. He is only two years from making partner and does not need this controversial kind of thing right now, but he manages to calm himself down, and walks with the excited law student to the office of the managing partner of the firm. After the managing partner consults with some of his senior firm colleagues, it is decided to seek out the advice of various legal ethicists.

A decade ago, a lawyer/journalist and the director of the National Archives and Records Administration's Legislative Archives Division, jointly created something closely resembling this Lincoln/Booth hypothetical.[38] They used it as a test question to try to determine where various members of the legal community stood on the issue of attorney-client confidentiality. Predictably, the experts split. Some, including Professor Stephen Gillers of the New York University School of Law, argued that even if the notes taken by Henry VIII's lawyer were found, and "there were a successor firm . . . and it still had records that the client expected to be confidential . . . the firm would be bound."[39] Others, including Lawrence M. Friedman of Stanford Law School, considered such open-ended statements as to the endlessness of confidentiality restrictions to be "absolutely absurd."[40]

Professor Geoffrey Hazard is, of course, one of the country's leading legal minds and one of the experts on legal ethics.[41] Hazard is also one of the primary architects of the ABA's relevant ethics code, serving as Reporter for the ABA's Model Rules of Professional Conduct. Hazard, as Director of the American Law Institute, then went on to guide the writing of the ALI's ethics guidelines. Hazard functionally takes the middle ground, often arguing for a somewhat flexible approach, including the possibility of a specific time limitation on confidentiality. When I contacted Professor Hazard and told him about Yale's quest for guidelines to help us deal with attorney-client materials in our collections, he wrote to me as follows:

> I still adhere to the view that the attorney-client privilege should terminate at the end of 25 years or the death of the client involved, whichever is later, except for material that would be embarrassing to the memory of the client. For the latter case, I would think 50 years . . .[42]

A parallel approach and a similar stance had already been taken by a joint committee from the American Society of Legal History and the Organization of American Historians (OAH).[43] This committee devoted itself to the subject of access to lawyers' papers.[44] This joint committee built upon previous conclusions and recommendations reached by an Ad Hoc Committee on Access to Lawyers' Files appointed by the OAH's Executive Board and chaired by Professor Kermit L. Hall.[45] Each of these groups hoped to find a specific number of years or some other procedure which could be implemented to provide reasonable, ethical access to lawyers' papers. The key to their deliberations is that the ethics codes were written to protect the financial and reputational interests of clients. If enough time has passed, and a lawyer makes the determination that allowing access to files at some point in the future will not cause harm to her or his clients, then access should be allowed and perhaps even encouraged.

As you will see in the guidelines that I developed to deal with this admittedly complex and difficult issue (see the Appendix following this article), I adopt Hazard's stricter rule of fifty years as a guidepost. Although instead of using the death of the client (which is often time-consuming and nearly impossible to determine as a matter of practice) as the key, I use the last date on the legal materials in question. This date can nearly always be determined directly from the papers in question. What we need as legal information professionals are clear, enforceable guidelines that tell us what to do and how to do it. I have developed such guidelines, and presented them to lawyers, law professors, and a specific sub-group of information professionals, namely archivists. Each group has had fairly predictable responses. What remains for me to do now is formally to promulgate these guidelines to legal information professionals in particular. They often have the unique perspective of trained lawyer and equally well-trained librarian. We can now move to a more careful analysis of the so-called "lawyer codes."

## V. A BRIEF OVERVIEW OF THE "LAWYER CODES"

There is no way around the fact that the United States is a country of law and of lawyers. There have been lawyers at many of the most significant—and the most mundane—moments in American life.[46] The presence of lawyers in the worlds of business, politics, academia, and in nearly every other realm and aspect of American life, means that the materials contained in their personal and professional files are vital to understanding that American life. The ABA's ethical codes and rules seem, at least on the surface, to be rather clear, and the prospects for access somewhat bleak. But was the issue as straightforward as it seemed? I and my colleagues at Yale and elsewhere were determined to find out.

The first thing I discovered was, thankfully, that others, long before I came on the scene, had attempted to answer these questions surrounding the issue of access to the papers of lawyers. One person in particular, my esteemed colleague at the Yale Law School, Professor and Law Librarian Morris L. Cohen (along with University of Southern California Law School Professor Louis M. Brown and then Yale Law School Deputy Dean Edward A. Dauer), had written a bold proposal in 1984 to begin the process of collecting lawyers' papers around the country.[47] This proposal, while greeted with significant enthusiasm and support in the legal history community, failed to develop the necessary groundswell of support from the library community. As a result, the Cohen proposal failed to receive financial support from interested funding organizations. It was still good to know that a trio as thoughtful and careful as Cohen, Brown, and Dauer had attempted to move in the same direction as we were beginning to move at Yale.

I then turned to the text of the ABA codes and the ALI restatement.[48] The first two key texts in determining the ethical responsibilities of a lawyer in regard to her or his professional papers are, as I have discussed above, the ABA's Model Code of Professional Responsibility and its Model Rules of Professional Conduct. Canon 4 of the ABA's Model Code states rather simply that "A lawyer should preserve the confidences and secrets of his client."[49] As I have previously noted, Disciplinary Rule 4-101 (DR 4-101) of the Model Code defines these difficult words, "confidences" and "secrets," as follows:

> (A) "Confidence" refers to information protected by the attorney-client privilege under applicable law, and "secret" refers to other information gained in the professional relationship that the client requested be held inviolate, or the disclosure of which would be embarrassing, or would likely be detrimental to the client.[50]

Here, in the Model Code, we have what appear to be rather clear definitions. However, note that the meanings of the words "confidence" and "secret" are predicated on an explicit request made by the client that the information in question be kept secret, or on the potential harm that would result from disclosing that information held in confidence. For example, the fact pattern in the Vincent Foster case clearly applies to this aspect of the Model Code. As I have noted above, Foster asked his lawyer, Swidler & Berlin's James Hamilton, whether what he was saying was privileged. He was assured that what he was saying could not be used against him or his associates in the White House. Needless to say, any lawyer who is asked by a client if what is being discussed is confidential, should certainly think very carefully before allowing anyone outside that attorney-client relationship access to her or his work product in any form. My advice to that lawyer would be that no one ever should have access to those materials. I do not debate the prevailing, closed and secretive spirit of this rule, but it should be clear that DR

4-101 is by no means stated as an absolute. The rule seeks a certain outcome, and it seeks that outcome for a purpose, not as a means in itself.

Continuing with the relevant portions of DR 4-101 of the Model Code, we see laid out the exceptions to this blanket ethical prohibition against revealing client confidences and secrets.

> (C) A lawyer may reveal:
>
> (1) Confidences or secrets with the consent of the client or clients affected, but only after a full disclosure to them.
> (2) Confidences or secrets when permitted under Disciplinary Rules or required by law or court order.[51]

Of course, the ideal situation for any legal information professional would be if the lawyer in question contacted each and every client and received that client's explicit permission to disclose what may be deemed their secrets and confidences. In the case of attorney-client privilege, the law is quite settled that it is solely in the power of the client entirely to waive that privilege that we discussed above.[52] However, most of those with whom I have discussed this issue have agreed that this process of contacting each client of a lawyer would be far too time-consuming, either for the lawyer (or the lawyer's heirs), or for the legal information professional. Imagine if we were to have decided to go in this direction with the papers of Congressman Kenneth Simpson. The most recent case among the client files that Yale holds was decided in 1939, with some cases dating back to the early 1920s. One case involves a matter for a client whose last name is Brown, and who has a common first name. How would we at Yale go about tracking down such a client's heirs, if any exist, even with the extraordinary genealogical resources of the Internet age?

Beyond the ABA's Model Code, we must also examine the ABA's Model Rules. The Rules are somewhat more expansive and provide more guidance than the Model Code. The Model Rules seem, at least at first glance, to leave open even less of a window for access to lawyers' papers. According to Rule 1.6 of the Model Rules, "A lawyer shall not reveal information relating to representation of a client unless the client consents after consultation, except for disclosures that are impliedly authorized in order to carry out the representation. . . . "[53] Again, the key according to the ABA is consultation with, and explicit consent from, each and every client.

The Library of Congress (LC) agreed to implement a modified version of such a system of client permission in the case of the papers of Joseph L. Rauh, Jr. Rauh was one of the leading voices of liberal Democrats for nearly half a century, helping to found Americans for Democratic Action in 1947, and gaining national prominence for his defense of celebrities such as Lillian Hellman and Arthur Miller before the House Un-American Activities Committee.[54] He was approached by LC in 1987 about donating his historically valuable papers documenting his life and legal practice. Rauh was reportedly somewhat shocked when it turned out that LC did not have a policy in place to deal with attorney-client communications.[55] Undaunted, Rauh resourcefully came up with a policy of his own, and the archivists at LC agreed. The policy as implemented shifts the burden completely to the researcher.[56] The relevant portions of the policy on access to the Rauh Papers are as follows:

> Access to the Joseph L. Rauh, Jr., papers is not restricted. However, users of the Rauh papers are advised that many of the legal files in the Rauh papers contain privileged communication between client and attorney. There is to be no use of privileged communication between client and attorney without permission of the client, or, if the client is deceased, the executor of the client's estate. It is the users' responsibility to obtain consent or to make reasonable effort to contact the client or executor.[57]

As is clear, Rauh chose not to undertake the arduous task of locating each client, consulting with that client, and then securing that client's permission. In the case of the Rauh Papers, researchers must sign a form acknowledging that they have read and will abide by the stated policy. To my knowledge, the staff at LC does not keep track of whether researchers are actually seeking out clients or their heirs. It is my understanding that LC sees this burden-shifting from both the lawyer and the information professional to the client, as being similar to informing patrons of relevant copyright laws and then not attempting to enforce those laws.

We rejected this approach at Manuscripts & Archives at Yale. If a lawyer (or a lawyer's heir) has determined that her or his files will not cause any form of harm to clients, and an archives offers to apply a significant closure time to those files, then, in our view, the lawyer and the archives have done their part and made a clear, good faith, ethical effort. This is the view that is held by the many American repositories that hold attorney-client files. Asking researchers to do what we know they will likely not, in actuality, do (i.e., take the time to track down a client or that client's executors from a case closed perhaps five decades earlier) is not something that we as an archives had contemplated doing in other situations, and could not conceive of doing here. The stated purpose of the lawyer codes and rules are to protect the client. Fifty years after a file has ceased to be active in any way whatsoever, what, beyond a better understanding of various moments, figures, and places in history, can be impacted by opening up these files?

In the case of Joseph Rauh, he was obviously still alive when these arrangements were made. What of the case when non-lawyer heirs or executors seek to understand their options when it comes to the status of the deceased lawyer's papers? At least one state bar association has determined that simply because ethics codes and rules apply to lawyers does not mean that those codes and rules therefore apply to a lawyer's heirs.[58] The ethics codes and rules governing lawyers, in my view, certainly do not apply to law librarians and legal archivists in their entirely non-lawyerly roles as librarians and legal information professionals.[59] However, in opposition to the historic-minded bar association that looked positively on the donation of a lawyer's papers to an academic archives, a number of other bar associations have ruled otherwise.[60] Of course, state bar associations, often battling public image problems for lawyers, benefit from handing down advisory opinions that portray lawyers as forever protecting the secrets of their clients at all costs. This helps explain why the law firm that represented Lizzie Borden in 1892 continues to refuse to allow access to the files on that famed case involving multiple ax whacks. Certainly, no lawyer should be compelled to open their client files, except under the provisions stipulated by law and ethics codes, but I do not personally understand how keeping such files closed protects anyone or anything. In defending his firm's decision, Jeffrey F. McCormick stated that protecting the secrets of clients such as Lizzie Borden, who died in 1927 without any heirs, is "one of the principles in our culture that is sacrosanct."[61] The perceived sacredness of this principle of secrecy is undoubtedly true. However, simply because a lawyer has this option of protecting these old files does not mean that those lawyers seeking to play a broader socially and historically useful role cannot in good faith and conscience allow reasonable access to old client files closed more than fifty years in the past. I believe that law librarians and archivists can also reasonably and ethically continue to provide access to such files, and seek to expand their collections in this area. It is important to point out in this regard that many major American law libraries and other repositories containing legal materials allow access to attorney-client communications in their collections.[62] To my informed knowledge, not a single institution or law librarian or archivist has ever been sued or troubled in any other way for allowing reasonable access to their files. I think the key to this outcome has been that these legal information professionals have always demonstrated a clear sense of good faith in their dealings with lawyers and patrons. The Restatement (Second) of Contracts' resonant statement that "good faith and fair dealing" should infuse all our contractual relationships[63] is an important professional tone to keep in mind. My guidelines do everything possible to keep all relevant parties completely informed of their options and opportunities. This should always be our goal, particularly when it comes to sensitive matters like broadly held views on attorney-client materials.

## VI. OPTIONS

When I was first asked to begin thinking about this question of access to the client files that were found in the papers of Kenneth Farrand Simpson at Yale, I and my colleagues considered a wide variety of access options. The first and simplest option was to discard these files. Yes, there were clearly some historically valuable materials in those client files, but perhaps the issues involved in making them available to researchers were just too complex for the possible benefit. We rejected this option, for a number of reasons, most importantly because such a solution would mean discarding many attorney-client materials in other collections, some of which had long been open without concern or incident, and with great benefit to our patrons and the scholarly community at large.

We also considered the option of removing the personal correspondence in the client files and shredding the remainder of the more clearly "work product" materials. The best materials from a research standpoint were perhaps the personal correspondence. But Simpson was a lawyer. It was as a practicing lawyer in the 1920s and 1930s that he rose to political prominence and power in the first place. If we shredded these "lawyering materials," as Louis Brown called them above, the context of and purpose for which these personal materials were created would be destroyed. In addition, if the concern that would lead us to the drastic step of shredding the vast majority of materials in these files was to protect the privacy interests of clients, then perhaps we would still have to take the time to black out the names in these personal letters. We rejected this option because it would simply require too much staff time to leaf through each file to identify the correspondence, and then read through each letter to black out the identifying names, addresses, personal references, and the like. We also considered the Library of Congress/Rauh option of shifting the burden to the researcher, but rejected it as not consistent with our standing policies on the role of the information professional in relation to the researcher/patron.

There are, of course, additional options. One solution focuses on pre-emptive actions that can be taken by a historically-minded lawyer or law firm. A recent popular article in *The American Lawyer* on this subject of access to lawyers' papers discusses the Rauh approach and then raises the possibility that historically-minded clients might be willing to sign access agreements when first hiring a lawyer.[64] These agreements would state that at a given point in the future, client files may be open to researchers.[65] Otherwise, clients would be guaranteed eternal confidentiality.[66] This option is still being actively considered by committees and others at a variety of legal and historical organizations. Of course, many, if not most, lawyers would hesitate to approach clients with such a possibility. Ultimately the purpose of developing a client base is not to further the work of historians or even to enhance the often lackluster image of lawyers in the public mind. The ultimate purpose of lawyering is to make money for the lawyer and law firm. If requesting that lawyers and clients consider the historical import of what is, in the end, their business transaction, leads to the outcome or perception that some clients will go elsewhere for legal services, then this option seems less than ideal.

There is also the option of making arrangements with lawyers or law firms of having, for instance, every twentieth of their long-inactive client files donated to a law library. This would serve the purpose of randomly demonstrating the nature of the work in that firm or office, and would advance legal educational goals. But this option may still well require the labor-intensive step of going through materials document by document to remove identifying characteristics. There are surely other options that escaped our analysis.

## VII. CONCLUSION

After I and my colleagues at Yale discussed this issue many times, and after we had carefully reviewed all the relevant legal and archival materials, including the case law, the state bar association advisory opinions, the arrangements that had been created at other repositories, and the myriad secondary sources relating to lawyers, legal information professionals, and ethics, I devised a series of guidelines for dealing with attorney-client communications in existing collections and in possible future acquisitions. I then circulated a draft of these guidelines to many of the interested parties, including a number of the leading minds in their respective fields. In designing these guidelines, I rely in part on the fact that the ABA's codes and rules predicate their confidentiality restrictions on potential harm caused to clients. Unlike Morris Cohen's earlier plan for a comprehensive approach to collecting the papers of lawyers, I am more focused on collecting the papers of a few, prominent lawyers, who have also led fairly public lives. Each of our communities has such people. Oftentimes, the cases that such people are involved with are matters of public record, and attorney-client confidentiality, as I have argued above, is generally considered to be vitiated if the information is otherwise released, such as has been the case with Abraham Lincoln's legal papers.[67]

It is, ultimately, the lawyer who can determine whether opening up a given file could conceivably cause potential harm to a client. If the lawyer does not believe that to be the case, then the predicate for the confidentiality restriction, in my view, is gone. This does not mean that I recommend in any way opening such client files immediately. I settled on the number of fifty years after the file became inactive based on the reactions of many who read the guidelines. The Family Education Rights and Privacy Act, known as the Buckley Amendment, put a seventy-five year restriction on releasing the grades of students to third parties.[68] President Clinton's April 1995 Executive Order 12958 mandates that even documents that are deemed "Top Secret" by the government of the United States, unless an agency makes a strong case otherwise, are presumably declassified after twenty-five years.[69] Fifty years splits the difference between these two legally specified time periods for restriction of sensitive materials. When we considered a one hundred-year restriction, many of those information professionals with whom we consulted simply said that they would not be willing to store materials for that long before making them available to researchers. A number of the lawyers and law professors with whom we consulted also felt that practicing lawyers who had a sense of their own historical importance would be less intrigued by the possibility of donation of their papers if, when the papers were opened, their names may well have faded into obscurity. Fifty years also has the advantage of going beyond the average working life of most individuals, thus removing at least one element of possible professional financial harm to clients.

This collegial and open development process resulted in specific default rules that determine what we at Yale decided to do when faced with the variety of scenarios that many have previously faced and continue to face at institutions around the country. Many of the people I contacted simply assumed, without having done any investigation, that collecting and providing access to lawyers' papers was simply impossible. What was needed was a clear set of rules that determine a course of action in the three basic situations confronted by most of those charged with caring for legal manuscripts: (1) attorney-client materials already in collections with a living donor; (2) such materials in the case of an existing collection with no living donor; and (3) future collecting in this area. Again, as you can see, these scenarios are all based on a fifty-year closure period, but allow the attorney or attorney's heirs to choose to open materials at a time of their choosing. Again, it must be kept in mind that the scenarios with which we are dealing are friendly ones in which a lawyer has decided that some of what he or she has done has permanent historical value. Perhaps this realization has come about because he or she sits on your board of directors, is a graduate of your educational institution, has seen an exhibit that you have put up, has read about your institution in the local paper, or has heard from you or read elsewhere about another lawyer taking such a step. I am also not talking about accepting or opening any files that may be reasonably deemed to cause financial or reputational harm. Again, a lawyer's ethics code strictly forbids such actions.

Attorney-client privilege arises when a court demands that a lawyer produce documents. Being assertive is an important trait in a legal information professional, but I am certainly not recommending that anyone demand that a lawyer donate his or her papers, regardless of the strictures of privilege. What can, and in my view, should, be done, as an ethical and pro-active information professional, is to examine this issue and be prepared should an opportunity present itself.

I hope that I have shown, at very least, that the case against collecting lawyers' papers is not closed. All laws and ethics codes exist within a given context and are written to serve given purposes. Once those purposes are examined in the case of confidentiality restrictions for lawyers' papers, new vistas and opportunities open. What we are left with is a rich resource that relates to nearly every aspect and facet of our undeniably legally-driven American culture. This resource is currently being neglected, and valuable historical materials are being destroyed. This is not a matter of little or specialized importance. Every community has lawyers and is shaped by those lawyers. Unless a more concrete argument than tradition or a general feeling of discomfort can be made for why these papers should not continue to be collected and by an ever-wider group of institutions, then it is time to welcome the papers of lawyers and judges into our repositories.

Obviously, there are some who have found and will continue to find what I have said here to be questionable. Any and all the options listed above, in addition to some I have not considered, should be evaluated by legal information professionals attempting to consider what role access to attorney-client materials should play in the life of their institutions. Through the study of such materials, law schools and allied institutions can realize their fullest potential as centers for the training of lawyers and the study of law.

## AUTHOR NOTE

The author is grateful for the generous assistance of the following individuals: Morris L. Cohen of the Yale Law School; Geoffrey C. Hazard, Jr. of the Yale Law School, the American Law Institute, and the University of Pennsylvania Law School; Nancy F. Lyon, Christine Weideman, Diane Kaplan, Tom Hyry, and Richard Szary of the Yale University Library; Michael Churgin of the University of Texas at Austin School of Law; Marsha Trimble of the University of Virginia School of Law; Menzi Behrnd-Klodt of the Pleasant Company; and the author's fellow panel members, particularly Rayman L. Solomon, and audience members at conferences of the Association of American Law Schools, Society of American Archivists, Mid-Western Archives Conference, and the New England Archivists. Special thanks go to Mike Widener for accepting the author's invitation to speak on the panel for which his presentation-turned-article originated, and for then inviting the author to contribute to this remarkable volume. Final and paramount thanks go to Miriam B. Spectre, Special Collections Librarian at Bryn Mawr College, for her guiding thoughts. The author retains sole and exclusive rights to and responsibilities for errors in this article.

## NOTES

1. *See* Marsha Trimble, "Archives and Manuscripts: New Collecting Areas for Law Libraries," 83 *Law Library Journal* 429 (1991) at 429 and 447. According to Trimble, nearly a third of all law libraries she surveyed in 1992 responded that they had "law-related manuscript collections." See also "Survey of the Use of Archival Materials by Legal Historians" (1987) (unpublished, available from Yale Law Library).

2. *See* Trimble, *supra* note 1; Louis M. Brown, "Lawyering Decisions: New Materials for Law Libraries to Collect," 87 *Law Library Journal* 7 (1995); Bonnie Hobbs, Note, "Lawyers' Papers: Confidentiality Versus the Claims of History," 49 *Washington & Lee Law Review* 179 (1992); Jon Gertner, "The Lex Files, What's To Be Done With Lawyers' Private Papers After Their Death?," *American Lawyer* (June 1998) 76;

Hiller Zobel, Alfred Konefsky, & Jerold Auerbach, "Lawyers Papers as a Source of Legal History," 69 *Law Library Journal* 303-28 (1976).

3. *Swidler & Berlin and James Hamilton v. U.S.*, 524 U.S. 399 (1998) [hereinafter *Swidler & Berlin*].

4. *See also* Brian R. Hood, "The Attorney-Client Privilege and a Revised Rule 1.6: Permitting Limited Disclosures After the Death of the Client," 7 *Georgetown Journal of Legal Ethics* 741 (1994).

5. In the case of certain types of criminal conduct by the client known to the lawyer and in what the Supreme Court describes as instances where "the interest of justice was compelling," a lawyer is sometimes ethically obligated to make his knowledge of that activity or prospective activity known to the proper authorities. See *Swidler & Berlin, supra* note 3, at 404. See also *Model Code of Professional Responsibility* Canon 4, DR 4-101(C)(3)-4-101(C)(4) (1969) [hereinafter *Model Code*]; *Model Rules of Professional Conduct* Rule 1.6(b)(1)-1.6(b)(2) (1983) [hereinafter *Model Rules*]; and *Restatement (Third) of The Law Governing Lawyers* (Proposed Final Draft, No. 1, 1996), Chapter 5, Topic 1, Title B., § 115, "Using or Disclosing Client Information When Required by Law," at 304-307 [hereinafter *Law Governing Lawyers*].

6. *Law Governing Lawyers, supra* note 5, Section 112, "Lawyer's Duty to Safeguard Confidential Client Information," at 282.

7. Again, the articles by Trimble, Brown, and Hobbs on this subject are the best, most authoritative, and most accessible pieces written on this matter of law, legal special collections librarians, and the papers of lawyers. See *supra* note 2.

8. As I am no longer affiliated with that institution, the guidelines and my writing on them must be seen as reflecting my own views and not those of Manuscripts & Archives or Yale University.

9. Brown, *supra* note 2, at 8.

10. "The Proposed Legal Education Library," 71 *Law Library Journal* 619 (1978) (panel discussion).

11. Brown, *supra* note 2, at 10.

12. *See id.* at 19. See also Karl Llewellyn, *Bramble Bush*, 151-153 (1930); James Williard Hurst, *The Growth of American Law* 335-338 (1950).

13. *See* Thom Weidlich, "The World According to . . . ," *National Law Journal* (May 24, 1993); Kenneth J. Lipartito, *Baker & Botts in the Development of Modern Houston* (1991). Nancy Lisagor and Frank Lipsius, *A Law Unto Itself: The Untold Story of the Law Firm of Sullivan & Cromwell* (1987). These and a number of other firms have cooperated in the writing of these firm histories, including by allowing access to client files. Robert Nelson, for his book *Partners with Power* (1988), was given access to the client files in many law firms with the understanding that he not name the firms of the clients in his sociological research. *See* R. Michael McReynolds, The Archivist and Lawyers' Records, at 8 (unpublished paper delivered at the Society of American Archivists' Annual Meeting, Washington, D.C. (October 2, 1988) (copy on file with author).

14. *See Model Code, supra* note 5, Canon 4, DR 4-101, EC 4-1, 4-6. See also *Swidler & Berlin, supra* note 3, at 403, where the "testamentary exception" is discussed.

15. For an excellent review of the history of the privilege, see Geoffrey C. Hazard, Jr., "A Historical Perspective on the Attorney-Client Privilege," 66 *California Law Review* 1061 (1978).

16. For the most recent developments in this realm of the law, see Margaret Graham Tebo, "Parent Privilege: Lawmakers Seek to Protect Parent-Child Conversation," 86 *A.B.A. Journal* 18 (2000).

17. For an excellent commentary on the social implications of this privilege and the impact that such traditions have on the legal profession, see Sissela Bok, *Secrets: On the Ethics of Concealment and Revelation* (1982).

18. Professional and Personal Responsibilities of the Lawyer (1997) at 107.

19. *See id.* at 107.

20. *See id.* at 108.

21. *See also Federal Rules of Criminal Procedure* 26(b)(3).

22. George W. Conk, "Court Holds Attorney-Client Privilege Survives Even Death," *Hartford Courant,* June 27, 1998, A10; Terry Lemons and Jane Fullerton, "Decision Keeps Lawyer's Notes on Foster Private," *Austin American-Statesman,* June 26, 1998, 10; Stephen Labaton, "Lawyer-Client Privilege Affirmed; Supreme Court Says," *International Herald Tribune,* June 26, 1998, 1; Brian Knowlton, "Court Upholds Lawyer Privilege Even After Death; Ruling Stops Starr From Acquiring Notes About Late Presidential Aide," *The Scotsman,* June 26, 1998, 13.

23. *Swidler & Berlin, supra* note 3, at 403-410.

24. *Model Rules, supra* note 5, Rule 1.6, Comment 4.

25. It is, however, important to note the limitations inherent in the *Swidler & Berlin* opinion. The notes in question that Foster's lawyer took specify that Foster asked whether what he was saying was privileged, and he was assured that it was in fact a privileged conversation. *See Swidler & Berlin, supra* note 3, at 402-403. This element of the attorney-client conversation likely does take place on a regular basis. Also, Chief Justice Rehnquist's majority opinion and Justice O'Connor's dissent repeatedly emphasize that the holding of the case is based on its context in "a criminal proceeding," "criminal cases," or "a criminal context." *See id.* at 403, 409, 411. In addition, the first footnote in the majority opinion specifies the limitation of the ruling that "Because we sustain the claim of attorney-client privilege, we do not reach the claim of work product privilege." *See id.* at 403.

26. *See id.* at 410.

27. *See id.* at 402.

28. *Id.* at 403 (quoting *Upjohn Co. v. United States,* 449 U.S. 383 at 389 (1981)).

29. For further discussion, *see* Hobbs, *supra* note 2, at 183.

30. *Model Code, supra* note 14.

31. *See id.* DR 4-101(A). A number of states have incorporated the Model Code into their state codes, and thus they do carry the weight of law, but are generally only applied by state bar associations and not state courts. *See* Hobbs, *supra* note 2, at 183.

32. This is often the means by which medical historians and other writers on issues related to medicine and related endeavors gain access to otherwise sealed records. *See* Diane E. Kaplan, "The Stanley Milgram Papers: A Case Study on Appraisal of and Access to Confidential Data Files," 59 *American Archivist* 288 (1996). For a recent review of the law in this subject area, *see* Patricia I. Carter, "Health Information Privacy: Can Congress Protect Confidential Medical Information In The 'Information Age'?," 25 *William Mitchell Law Review* 223 (1999).

33. *Law Governing Lawyers, supra* note 5, at 282.

34. *Model Code, supra* note 5, DR 4-101(A).

35. Prof. Hazard also served as, among many other leading posts in the profession, reporter for the ABA's Special Commission on the Evaluation of Professional Stan-

dards; as a member of the ABA's Committee on Lawyer's Responsibility for Client Protection; as a member of the ABA's Committee on Professional Discipline; and as Executive Director of the American Bar Foundation.

36. See *Law Governing Lawyers, supra* note 5, at xxii.

37. *Id.* at § 112.

38. *See* McReynolds, *supra* note 13; and David A. Kaplan, "A Matter of Truth or Confidences: Does Attorney-Client Privilege Outweigh Demands of History?," *National Law Journal,* July 4, 1988, 36.

39. *See* Kaplan, *supra* note 38, at 36.

40. *See id.*

41. Hazard is the author, editor, or co-editor of the following books on this subject, among many others he has written: *Ethics in the Practice of Law* (1978); *The Legal Profession: Responsibility and Regulation* (3d. ed., 1994, with Deborah Rhode); *The Law of Lawyering: A Handbook on the Model Rules of Professional Conduct* (2d. ed., 1990, with William Hodes); *The Law and Ethics of Lawyering* (2d. ed., 1994, with Susan Koniak & R. Cramton).

42. Letter from Geoffrey C. Hazard, Jr., Director, American Law Institute (4 December 1997).

43. *See* Gertner, *supra* note 2, at 77.

44. *See id.*

45. *See id. See also* R. Michael McReynolds, The Organization of American Historians Report on Historians and Access to the Files of Lawyers–An Archivist's Review (unpublished paper delivered at the Society of American Archivists' Annual Meeting, Indianapolis, Indiana (September 3, 1995) (copy on file with author).

46. *See* Morris L. Cohen Preliminary Proposal for a Study on Collecting Lawyers' Professional Papers 2 (1984) (unpublished manuscript, on file at Yale Law Library) at 2; Hobbs, *supra* note 2, at 179, 211; Kaplan, *supra* note 38, at 36; Trimble, *supra* note 2, at 442.

47. See Cohen, *supra* note 46.

48. Again, please note that others, particularly Trimble and Hobbs cited so many times above, provide extensive analysis of these provisions, and I will not replicate that work here. It is important, however, to address this matter to a somewhat lesser extent in order to frame the remainder of this discussion and provide context for my guidelines.

49. *Model Code, supra* note 5, Canon 4.

50. *Id.* at DR 4-101.

51. *Id.*

52. *See* Hobbs, *supra* note 2, at 206.

53. *Model Rules, supra* note 5, Rule 1.6. It is important to note, as Gillers and Simon point out, that "The legislative history and the selected state variations for each [of the ABA's Model] Rule[s] should thus dispel any misconception that the ABA Model Rules are 'the rules.' The Model Rules are important and influential, but they have been and continue to be the subject of considerable disagreement." Stephen Gillers & Roy D. Simon, Jr., *Regulation of Lawyers: Statutes and Standards* iii (1989).

54. *See* Kaplan, *supra* note 38, at 36; McReynolds, *supra* note 45, at 7. *See also Library of Congress Acquisitions, Manuscript Division, 1987* 15-19 (1989). [hereinafter DR 4-101(A) *Library of Congress*]. For Rauh on Rauh, *see* "Historical Perspectives: An Unabashed Liberal Looks At a Half-Century Of The Supreme Court," 69 *North Carolina Law Review* 213 (1990).

55. *See* McReynolds, *supra* note 45, at 7.
56. *See* Library of Congress, *supra* note 54, at 19.
57. Access to the Joseph L. Rauh, Jr., Papers, Manuscript Division, Library of Congress (1989) (unpublished; available from the Library of Congress).
58. *See* Hobbs, *supra* note 2, at 209.
59. Archivists, for example, do have an ethics code that governs their behavior when it comes to disclosure of information contained in materials under their care. Archivist/lawyer Menzi Behrnd-Klodt draws together the various relevant elements of the ethics codes of the Society of American Archivists, the American Library Association, and the American Records Management Association. *See* Behrnd-Klodt, "Privacy Concepts and Definitions" (unpublished paper delivered at the Midwest Archives Conference, Chicago, Illinois (May 14, 1999) (copy on file with author). The Society of American Archivists' website provides a copy of the guiding principles in archival ethics. *See* <http://www.archivists.org/governance/handbook/app_ethics.html>.
60. *See* Hobbs, *supra* note 2, at 190, 200.
61. *See* James S. Toedtman, "Landmark Rulings/Lawyer-Client Privilege Lasts, Even After Death," *Newsday,* June 26, 1998, A5. McCormick had originally favored releasing the file to the local Fall River Historical Society, but was rebuked by the chief lawyer for the Massachusetts Board of Bar Overseers. *See* Lisa Brennan, "Lizzie Borden's Papers; Whitewater Spillover," *National Law Journal,* June 1, 1998, A4; Jeff Donn, "Borden Trial Papers Stay Sealed 105 Years Later," *Legal Intelligencer,* May 12, 1998, 4.
62. *See* Trimble, *supra* note 2, at 434.
63. *See* Charles L. Knapp & Nathan M. Crystal, *Rules of Contract Law* §205 Duty of Good Faith and Fair Dealing (1993).
64. *See* Gertner, *supra* note 2, at 77.
65. *Id.*
66. *Id.*
67. *See* Elizabeth W. Matthews, *Lincoln As a Lawyer: An Annotated Bibliography* (1991); Martha L. Bennner, "The Lincoln Legal Papers and the New Age of Documentary Editing," 30 *Computers & the Humanities* 365 (1996). Of course, the legal papers of other American leaders, such as John Adams and Thomas Jefferson, have also been published.
68. 20 U.S.C. 1232g (1994); see also 34 C.F.R. 99.1-99.67 (1996) (Family Educational Rights and Privacy). The Buckley Amendment is part of the General Education Provisions Act. *See* 20 U.S.C. 1221-1235 (1994). It was in 1976 that Buckley regulations were first issued by the federal government. *See* Family Education Rights and Privacy Act, 41 Fed. Reg. 24,662 (1976) (codified at 45 C.F.R. pt. 98). Major revisions were adopted to this Act in 1988. *See* Family Educational Rights and Privacy Act, 53 Fed. Reg. 11,942 (1988) (codified at 34 C.F.R. pt. 99). Regulations were recently finalized to implement statutory changes made in 1994. *See* Family Educational Rights and Privacy Act, 61 Fed. Reg. 59,292 (1996) (codified at 34 C.F.R. pt. 99).
69. *See* Exec. Order No. 12958, 3 C.F.R. 333 (1995), reprinted as amended in 50 U.S.C. 435 (1996).

## APPENDIX

## ATTORNEY-CLIENT COMMUNICATIONS IN MANUSCRIPT COLLECTIONS*

Here are guidelines to follow when dealing with attorney-client communications that may be subject to confidentiality restrictions. In all three of the scenarios below, "attorney-client communications" are defined as:

- any form of communication between attorney and client directly related to the client's representation; or
- any form of communication to or from the lawyer directly related to the client's representation; or
- any internal document created by the lawyer directly related to the client's representation.

"Attorney-client communications" do not include official, published documents, such as court opinions, pleadings, and the like, which are public and not subject to confidentiality restrictions. However, drafts of such official documents, as well as those that are annotated by the lawyer, are subject to confidentiality restrictions.

*Scenario I: Collection already possessed by library, no living donor or executor*

In the case of a collection that is already possessed by the library and for which there is no living donor or executor, attorney-client communications identified during processing will be closed for a period of fifty (50) years from the last inclusive date of the materials. These materials will be separated into their own boxes. After the fifty (50) years have elapsed, there will be no additional restrictions on access to these materials.

*Scenario II: Collection already possessed by library, living donor or executor*

In the case of a collection that is already possessed by the library and for which there is a living donor or executor, attorney-client communications identified during processing will be brought to the attention of the donor or executor.

The donor or executor will be notified that, in the absence of a response from her or him within ninety (90) days, the attorney-client communications will be closed for fifty (50) years from the last inclusive date of the materials.

Should the donor or executor not want to implement the default closure of fifty (50) years, she or he can (A) waive any restrictions on access and give blanket permission for all researchers to use all materials in the collection, including the attorney-client communications; or (B) for a specified number of years, grant access permission to individual researchers on a case-by-case basis, after which time all materials in the collection will be open without restriction to all researchers.

If either option A or B is chosen and there is an existing deed of gift, then the deed of gift will be amended to reflect these altered access restrictions. If there is not an existing deed of gift, then the donor or executor will be offered the opportunity to sign one.

*Scenario III: New solicitation by library of a collection likely to contain attorney-client communications*

In the case of a new solicitation of papers from a living lawyer, a lawyer's executor, or some other person likely to have attorney-client communications, the person in question will be asked if there are any materials in the papers that may be attorney-client communications and subject to confidentiality restrictions.

If the lawyer or executor answers yes, the following paragraph should be added to the standard deed of gift, at the appropriate location:

> "With the assistance of the donor or the donor's appointed executor, 'Attorney-client communications' will be separated. In order to have access to or to quote from these materials, permission must be received in writing from the donor or executor. This restriction will expire on [date supplied]."

If the lawyer or executor answers no, that there are no such attorney-client communications that are subject to confidentiality restrictions in the papers, then the lawyer or executor, using the standard legal device, will initial in the margin of the deed of gift, making it clear that all the materials contained in the donated collection are "available for research use." If during arrangement and description such materials are discovered within the collection, then the steps listed under "Scenario II" above should be followed.

---

*In 1998, these guidelines became departmental policy on the subject of collecting and providing access to lawyers' papers for Manuscripts & Archives at Yale University Library. As I am no longer affiliated with that institution, the guidelines and my writing on them must be seen as reflecting my own views and not those of Manuscripts

& Archives or Yale University. Despite the fact that I have discussed various elements of these guidelines throughout this article, for ease of reference, I am including the complete text in this Appendix. These guidelines were proposed as possible national guidelines to the Privacy & Confidentiality Roundtable of the Society of American Archivists and endorsed by leading members of that Roundtable in August 1999. The current status of the guidelines as policy at institutions beyond Yale is pending.

# Lawyer-Client Files: A Historical Source, But Can We See Them?

## Victor Tunkel

**SUMMARY.** Private lawyers' files can be of the first importance for legal, social, and local history. In common-law jurisdictions, however, lawyer-client communications are shielded behind the two walls of privilege and confidentiality. The article discusses the legal underpinnings for privilege and confidentiality, with an emphasis on British law, and the implications for the preservation of historic lawyers' files. It concludes with a "Proposed Model Legal Confidentiality Act" that aims to address the needs of lawyers, clients, and archivists. *[Article copies available for a fee from The Haworth Document Delivery Service: 1-800-342-9678. E-mail address: <getinfo@haworthpressinc.com> Website: <http://www.HaworthPress.com> © 2001 by The Haworth Press, Inc. All rights reserved.]*

Anyone interested in rare and archival law materials must at some stage come to ponder this question: what happens to all the files of documents, statements, correspondence, pleadings, legal advice, maps, plans, diagrams, and so forth, created in the course of handling a

---

Victor Tunkel is Senior Lecturer in the Faculty of Laws, Queen Mary & Westfield College, University of London. He is also Secretary for the Selden Society, the only learned society and publisher devoted entirely to English legal history.

[Haworth co-indexing entry note]: "Lawyer-Client Files: A Historical Source, But Can We See Them?" Tunkel, Victor. Co-published simultaneously in *Legal Reference Services Quarterly* (The Haworth Information Press, an imprint of The Haworth Press, Inc.) Vol. 20, No. 1/2, 2001, pp. 181-189; and: *Public Services Issues with Rare and Archival Law Materials* (ed: Michael Widener) The Haworth Information Press, an imprint of The Haworth Press, Inc., 2001, pp. 181-189. Single or multiple copies of this article are available for a fee from The Haworth Document Delivery Service [1-800-342-9678, 9:00 a.m. - 5:00 p.m. (EST). E-mail address: getinfo@haworthpressinc.com].

© 2001 by The Haworth Press, Inc. All rights reserved.

client's affairs, which a law firm retains long after the litigation or advisory work concerned is over and forgotten? We in the Selden Society have laboured for 112 years discovering and editing the manuscript sources of English legal history. But these have been courts' records, law reports, judges' notebooks, professional literature and similar official or authoritative materials. The custody and care (or otherwise) of private lawyers' files have not been our concern. Yet in England, we have some law firms that have practised continuously for two centuries or more. And of course there are plenty of firms in all countries who have acted for famous (or infamous) clients or in causes célèbres. Such firms' retained documents could be of the first importance for historians. But equally the legal documents of more ordinary folk may be a rich source, with all sorts of incidental information for social and local history.

The fact that lawyers may be willing to deposit and archivists happy to receive should be all that is necessary to ensure the preservation and accessibility of this important material. Unfortunately the matter is more complicated. In our common-law world, lawyer-client communications are shielded behind the two walls of privilege and confidentiality. It may be helpful if we look in turn at the scope of these two doctrines, and then see how they may be overridden, if at all.

## *PRIVILEGE AND CONFIDENTIALITY*

These two overlapping concepts need to be distinguished. Privilege (in England confined to lawyer and client communications) is a common law right. It confers on a client the ability to refuse to answer questions in court, or to produce documents concerned with seeking or giving legal advice, without being guilty of contempt; and also to prevent his lawyer answering such questions. Confidentiality, supported by equity, is primarily a professional-ethical duty on the lawyer to not reveal a client's confidences. It is more general in that it covers all manner of client matters, and every possible outlet of leakage. The client may deliberately waive his claim to privilege or to confidentiality, in which case the lawyer must disclose, for he has no privilege.

## LEAKAGE TO OUTSIDERS

Since we are supposing that we would like documents, originally between lawyer and client, to be deposited with a third party for preservation and wider study, we need to know what the law says about third parties getting such documents without the client's waiver. Here it seems that U.S. and English practice has parted company. The older rule, still applicable in England, is that once a third party has gained access to a privileged document (or conversation) the privilege is to that extent destroyed: *Calcraft v. Guest* [1898] 1 Q.B. 759; *R. v. Tompkins* (1977) 67 Crim. App. 181. In the U.S., however, the Federal Rules and state codes have in recent years been extended so as to prevent third parties who have unauthorisedly acquired privileged information (e.g., eavesdroppers, interceptors, etc.) making further disclosure or use.

But the most frequently occurring interference with privilege, in both our jurisdictions, is not of the third party initiating disclosure but of the careless lawyer allowing privileged documents to be seen by opposing parties. Here our two jurisdictions have much the same approach: to invoke the residual confidentiality remedy. A lawyer who unexpectedly receives materials which appear to be confidential, and not intended for him, is supposed to not read them and to inform the sending lawyer: *Berg Electronics v. Molex Inc.* (1995) 875 F.Supp. 61; *English & American Insurance v. Herbert Smith* [1988] FSR 232. Where the receiving lawyer is not aware of the mistake until after reading the documents there is no breach of ethics, according to the D.C. Bar Legal Ethics Committee, Opinion 256 (1995). Where the receiving lawyer reasonably assumes that there has been voluntary discovery by the sending lawyer, there is no remedy for the negligent sender: *Pizzey v. Ford Motor Co.* (*The Times,* Mar. 8, 1993). So in *IBM v. Phoenix* [1995] 1 All E.R. 413, 424, the test applied was: would the mistake be obvious to the hypothetical reasonable lawyer? If it would be, then an injunction may be granted to prevent use of the documents or information.

## EFFECT OF THE CLIENT'S DEATH

Since confidentiality appears to back-up and outlast privilege in this way and to be readily invoked, the next question for present archival purposes is: how long does it last? Surely if the client is long dead, his papers can be safely handed over to a responsible depository by his former lawyers? Again, alas, the matter is not so straightforward.

You may recall the recent affair of Vince Foster. In 1993, seven members of the White House travel office staff were peremptorily dismissed, at the behest, it was rumoured, of Mrs. Clinton herself. A congressional investigation was launched into these dismissals. Vince Foster, a member of the White House staff presumably concerned in the affair, spent two hours with his lawyer, James Hamilton, at which interview Hamilton took hand-written notes. Nine days later Foster committed suicide. In December 1995, the Independent Counsel, Mr. Starr, sought to subpoena Hamilton and his firm, Swidler & Berlin, to provide his notes for the federal grand jury inquiring into the affair. Hamilton claimed privilege. The district court upheld his claim. The Court of Appeals reversed this, on the ground that once a client is dead the claim to privilege must be balanced against the importance of disclosure for the needs of a subsequent criminal case. But the Supreme Court, by 6 votes to 3, upheld the claim: *Swidler & Berlin v. U.S.* (1998) 118 S.Ct. 2081. They said that the justification for the privilege is the willingness of the client to confide in his lawyer in the knowledge that his confidences will be protected; a willingness that might be diminished if the client knew that posthumous revelation was possible. The only exception acknowledged by the court was the "testamentary exception": where a lawyer might be required to reveal a deceased client's communications so as to settle any disputes between beneficiaries.

Pausing to look at English law in these matters, it seems well-settled. The privilege certainly survives the death of the client: *Bullivant v. A-G* [1901] AC 196, 206. So does the power to waive it: *Re Molloy* [1997] 2 Crim. App. 283. The "testamentary exception" also exists: see, e.g., *Re Williams* [1985] 1 All E.R. 964, where it was taken for granted that a letter sent by the testatrix to her lawyers was properly revealed to assist in construing her home-made will. However, we in the U.K. would define it more widely. From *Conlon v. Conlons Ltd.* [1952] 2 All E.R. 162, a commercial case, it seems that a court may infer that a client's communication to his lawyer was intended to be passed on, in the event of certain subsequent circumstances, and will so order. And indeed, this generalised approach seems to be gaining professional acceptance in the U.S.:

> A lawyer shall not reveal information relating to representation of a client . . . except for disclosures that are impliedly authorized in order to carry out the representation . . . (Rule 1.6 of ABA Model Rules of Professional Conduct 1996)

## THE DURABILITY OF PRIVILEGE

If death does not terminate the privilege, what does? The traditional answer of English courts is "once privileged always privileged." So in *Crescent Farm v. Sterling* [1972] Ch. 553, a successor in title was held to be entitled to withhold a document containing the legal advice given to his predecessor and passed on to the successor. The interval of years was not very long but could have been generations, presumably. But would our courts countenance a balancing exception of the sort argued for in the U.S. Supreme Court case? Supposing it is very many years afterwards and supposing there is someone representing the long-dead client and purporting to invoke the privilege, may a court take into account the evaporation of the rationale, the time elapsed, the public or historic interest, the lack of any adverse effect on any individual, the availability of some of the information in the public domain, and such similar factors?

To all such arguments the House of Lords have given a resounding "no." In *R. v. Derby Magistrates ex parte B* [1995] 4 All E.R. 526, Lord Taylor C.J. said:

> ... if a balancing exercise was ever required ... it was performed once and for all in the sixteenth century. No exception should be allowed to the absolute nature of legal professional privilege.

The dire effect was to prevent an accused on trial for murder establishing his innocence. The decision has been criticised: for one thing, there are other exceptions already; and the Lords relied on purely civil precedents. But the law must be taken as settled, subject to a small window left open by Lord Nicholls' *obiter dictum* in the case: that where a client no longer had any interest in maintaining his privilege, it might be treated as spent.

## THE DURABILITY OF CONFIDENTIALITY

In the *Swidler* case, the Supreme Court was concerned only with privilege, and had to decide just the limited question of whether lawyer-client privilege survives the client's death, not the wider one of how long it may last. As to this, various American authorities have suggested that it should be capable of expiration by, e.g., effluxion of time, or by the winding-up of a deceased client's estate. Since in England the privilege seems to be everlasting, such innovations in U.S. law would pass us by. But they could be helpful by analogy in suggesting limits on the confidentiality aspect. Much depends on the comparative effect of the two duties. In privilege the client is saying, "even in defiance of a court I can prevent my lawyer from answering." Can he add, as to confidentiality, "*how much more so* can I prevent him from disclosing to all and sundry"? ("And if I, then also my successors")? Or is the duty of confidentiality innately more vague, weak and transitory?

It is not difficult to find dicta stating that it, too, is permanent and absolute. Thus in *U.S. v. Standard Oil Co.* (1955) 136 F.Supp. 345, 355:

> The confidences communicated by a client to his attorney must remain inviolate for all time if the public is to have reverence for the law and confidence in its guardians . . . The client must be secure in the belief that the lawyer will be forever barred from disclosing confidences reposed in him.

In the recent English "Chinese walls" case, *Bolkiah v. KPMG* [1999] 2 W.L.R. 215, 225G, Lord Millett reasserted the lawyer's duty in the strongest terms:

> Whether founded on contract or equity, the duty to preserve confidentiality is unqualified. It is a duty to keep the information confidential, not merely to take all reasonable steps to do so. The former client . . . is entitled to prevent his former solicitor from exposing him to any avoidable risk; and this includes the increased risk of the use of the information to his prejudice . . .

The particular prejudice in both these cases was the prospect of the lawyer's making use of information acquired while acting for a client when subsequently acting for a new client adversely to the former client. But the strictures may hold good for all situations that are potentially prejudicial.

## THE DISPOSAL OF HISTORIC FILES

Suppose an old firm of lawyers, clearing out their basement, found dusty files concerning some major public figure or event for which they had acted in the dim past. Would they be safe to deposit these with an archive? If a putative descendant of the client were to appear and to demand non-disclosure, claiming perhaps to protect the reputation of the long-departed, what would be the lawyers' proper course? Should they shred, or hand over to the descendant, or apply to the court to be released from their duty, or return the files to their oubliette, or deposit and be damned? And if they decide to deposit, what should be the response of the depositees when the descendant turns up there and demands the files be withheld from popular gaze or that they be surrendered?

The final draft (1996) of the *American Restatement: The Law Governing Lawyers* states: "The duty of confidentiality continues so long as the lawyer possesses confidential client information. It extends beyond the end of representation and beyond the death of the client." It goes on to say that the lawyer must provide for "the return, destruction or continued safekeeping of client files" in the event of the lawyer ceasing for whatever reason to practice. It does not advise further on which of these actions should apply in which circumstances; nor does it consider the conservation of historically important materials.

In England, the Law Society, our governing body for the solicitors' profession, publishes similar professional instructions or recommendations. In their *Guide to Professional Conduct of Solicitors* (7th ed. 1996) they offer some guidelines on this problem. The lawyer is to retain all files for at least six years because of the possibility of claims. After that the position may be reviewed. Where there are documents belonging to the client, these must be offered back, or destroyed with permission. But the Law Society takes the view that lawyers' files, including original letters from clients, are the property of the lawyer. No authority is stated but this may be in reliance on *Re Thomson* (1855) 20 Beav. 545 (obiter, Romilly, M.R.) and *Re Wheatcroft* (1877) 6 Ch.D. 97 (ratio, Jessel, M.R.). That being so, they recommend that those that (in the estimation of the lawyer) are of historical value may be deposited with the county archivist. What restrictions may be imposed on the archive as to access are not stated, save for the possibility of a subsequent claim of ownership. Those files which the solicitors consider to have no such value may be shredded.

## *THE NEED TO PROTECT DOCUMENTS AND LAWYERS*

This sounds like "if in doubt, shred." Destruction is of course the ultimate guarantee of non-disclosure. But much valuable material may be lost in this way. One would think that an archivist is a better judge of these things than a lawyer, save perhaps where it is a leading case with its background, rather than major public events or personages, that the documents would reveal. To offer an extreme example, some years ago I saw in auction a large box containing all the court documents, pleadings, correspondence, counsel's opinion, etc, in the case of *Ashford v. Thornton* (1819), 106 E.R. 149, the last case in which the right to trial by battle was claimed. These probably came ultimately from some lawyer's custody. There must be many similar collections from venerable *causes célèbres* in lawyers' hands, of great value to legal and social historians. Yet in our unsettled state of law, depositing these with an archive may itself amount to a breach of confidentiality, inclining the lawyers to destroy. What is needed is a clear rule of law or of established practice, protecting both documents and lawyers. There are analogies. In England, for official records in the Public Record Office, we have an initial thirty-year rule with exceptions and extensions. In copyright, we have seventy years from the death of the author. In the U.K. we are not as liberal as the U.S. has been in freeing up official information sources, but we are learning. Perhaps the U.K. government might give thought to adding this in the long-promised Freedom of Information Bill, now being drafted. But on both sides of the Atlantic, it seems to me, a more specific Legal Confidentiality (Termination) Act is desirable. Other professions may wish to come within it, but for present purposes I would offer something of this sort. The legislative style and content is of course that of the U.K., but I hope may be adaptable for other countries.

## *PROPOSED MODEL LEGAL CONFIDENTIALITY ACT*

1. Documents, records and all other communications or information in whatever form, which are protected by the principles of professional confidentiality between lawyer and client, shall cease to be so protected after a period of ___ years calculated under the next section.

2. The period of ___ years shall (a) in the case of a client who is an individual, run from the date of death of the client, or where there are joint clients, from the date of death of the last such client; and (b) in the case of a corporate client or partnership or other association, run from the date of its winding up or other dissolution, but subject to the right of any person to seek protection of confidentiality as for an individual.

3. Nothing in this Act shall affect:

   a. the application of legal professional privilege;
   b. the right of any client or other person so entitled to make voluntary disclosure of confidential matters or to authorise any other person or body to do so;

c. the confidentiality of any governmental or official information or communication;
   d. the confidentiality of any communication by or to any member of the Royal Family;
   e. the right of any person or body representing the interest of a former client after the said period of ___ years to apply to the court for an order to maintain confidentiality or to restrict disclosure in whole or part; but the court in deciding such application shall have regard to any public or historic interest in favour of disclosure.

4. It shall be lawful for confidential documents and other records to which this Act applies to be deposited in an approved archive before the expiration of the said period of ___ years provided that:
   a. where such deposit is made by the lawyers, it shall be expressly subject to the continuance of the confidentiality for the remainder of the said period; and
   b. where such deposit is made by a client or by a person representing the interest of a client, it may be made subject to conditions affording restricted access as may be expressly attached to the deposit; and the authority responsible for the archive shall from then to the expiration of the said period maintain the confidentiality accordingly.

5. Nothing in this Act shall operate to create confidentiality for any matter which was not protected by professional confidentiality before the passing of this Act.

6. This Act shall come into force on [date] and shall apply retrospectively so as to release from protection any documents, communications or other information to which confidentiality previously applied if on that date the said period has already expired, but subject to this Act.

# Index

A. H. Robbins/Dalkon Shield litigation, 124
*AB Bookman's Weekly*, 2
Abilene Christian University, 146
Access to archives. *See also* Attorney-client privilege
  general, 121-122
  judicial papers, 139-147
Accursius, 75,108
Ad Hoc Committee on Access to Lawyers' Files. *See* Attorney-client privilege
American Association for tate and Local History, 7,8
American Bar Association, 73,163
  Model Code of Professional Responsibility, 159-160,164-165,170
  Model Rules of Professional Conduct, 157,159,162,164-165,170,184
*American Bar Foundation Research Journal*, 20
American Council of Learned Societies, 6
American Historical Association, 21
*American Historical Review*, 21
*American Journal of Legal History*, 21
American Law Institute
  Restatement (Third), The Law Governing Lawyers, 155,159-160,162,187
American Memory Project, Web site, 57,58
American Radicalism Collection, Michigan State University, Web site, 71
American Society for Legal History, 5-10,20,22,162

Ames Foundation, 72
Ames, James Barr, 24
Archives. *See also* Collection development; Law school archives
  bibliography, 83
  in legal education and research, 155-156
  of organizations, 24
  archivists, 118,121-122
  attorneys, 118-119,155,159-160
*Ashford v. Thornton*, 106 E.R. 149 (1819), trial by battle case, 188
Attorney work product, 123,157
Attorney-client privilege, 122-123,151-189
  access guidelines at the Library of Congress, 165-166
  access guidelines at Yale University, 152-154, 166-167,168-171,177-179
  access to archives and, 123, 152-154,159-160,162-172,181-182,186-188
  Ad Hoc Committee on Access to Lawyers' Files, 162-163
  American Bar Association guidelines, 157,159,162, 163-165,170,184
  American Law Institute guidelines, 155,159-160, 162,187
  case studies, 152-154,160-162
  definition, 122-123, 156-159,182-186
  Law Society (U.K.) guidelines, 187

Proposed model legislation for the
U.K., 188-189
United Kingdom court decisions,
183-187
United States court decisions,
154,157-158,164,183-186
views of legal experts, 156,162-163
Avalon Project, Yale Law School,
Web site, 71-72

Bach Digital Project, Web site, 58
Baker, John H., 24
Baldo degli Ubaldi, 108
Barrow, Charles, 146
Bartolo of Sassoferrato, 108
Baylor University, 146
Bentham Project, Web site, 72
Bentham, Jeremy, 72
*Berg Electronics v. Molex Inc.*, 875
F.Supp. 61 (1995),
attorney-client privilege
case, 183
Bibliographic instruction, 30
Bird, Rose, 142
Blackstone, Sir William, 23,88,91,95
Boalt Law Library Catalog, 101
*Bolkiah v. KMPG*, 2 W.L.R. 215 (1999),
attorney-client privilege case, 186
Bologna, Italy
as medieval center for legal studies, 108
Boniface VIII, pope, 110
Borden, Lizzie, 167
Bowdoin College, 73
Bracton, Henry of, 72,88,95
Bracton: De Legibus Et Consuetudinibus
Angliae, Web site, 72-73
Brooke, Sir Robert, 95
Brown, Louis M., 155,163-164
*Bullivant v. A-G*, AC, 196 (1901),
attorney-client privilege
case, 184

*Calcraft v. Guest*, 1 Q.B., 759 (1898),
attorney-client privilege
case, 183

California Digital Library, 101
Cameron, James Duke, 142
Canon law. *See also* Corpus Juris
Canonici
reference tools, 101-102
sources, 104-105,108-111
use in legal research, 102-104
Canonists, 111
Carle, Susan D., 20
Centre for the Study of the Civil
Law Tradition, University
of Aberdeen, 75
Chiorazzi, Michael, 4
Cino da Pistoia, 108
Civil litigation process, 114-117
discovery, 115-116,
119-120,124-129
parties, 114-115
pleadings, 115
role of archivists and librarians,
116-118,129-132
role of lawyers, 118-120
subpoenas, 116-117
summons, 115
trial, 117
Clark, Tom C., Papers (Tarlton Law
Library, University of
Texas at Austin), 135-138
Clement V, pope, 110
Clinton, Hillary Rodham, 158,184
Code of Judicial Conduct, Texas,
141
Codex Juris Canonici, 111
Cohen, Bill, 3
Cohen, Morris L., 163-164,170
Coke, Sir Edward, 88,91
Collection development
archives and manuscripts,
22-25,155,171-172
rare books, 88-89
Columbia University, Library School,
33
*Conlon v. Conlons Ltd.*, 2 All E.R. 162
(1952), attorney-client
privilege case, 184

Cornell Law Library, 93-94,97
*Corpus authenticorum*, 107
Corpus Juris Canonici, 99,105,108-111
  Clementines, 110
  Decretals of Gregory IX, 110
  Decretum of Gratian, 106,108-109
  *Extravagantes*, 110
  *Extravagantes communes*, 110
  form of citation, 110-111
  *Liber Sextus*, 110
  *Quinque compilationes antiquae*, 110
Corpus Juris Civilis, 75,95,99,105-108
  Code, 105,106-107
  Digest 105,106
  form of citation, 106-107
  Institutes, 105-106
  Novels, 105,107
Court of Criminal Appeals, Texas, 140
Court system, U.S., 114
*Crescent Farm v. Sterling*, Ch. 553 (1972), attorney-client privilege case, 185

D.C. Bar Legal Ethics Opinion 256 (1995), 183
Dallachiesa, Arleen, 4
Daniel, Price, Papers (Sam Houston Regional Library & Research Center), 147
Dauer, Edward A., 163-164
Dawson, Edwin S., Rare Book Room (Cornell Law Library), 94
Decretalists, 111
Decretals, 108-111
Decretists, 111
*Digestum novum*, 106
*Digestum vetus*, 106
Dyer, Sir James, 96

*Effector*, 73
Electronic Frontier Foundation, 73
Encoded Archival Description (EAD), 26

*English & American Insurance v. Herbert Smith*, FSR 232 (1988), attorney-client privilege case, 183
Ernst, Dan R., 19,21
Ethics. *See also* Attorney-client privilege
Evangelista, Donato A., 94
Exhibits. *See also* Outreach
  audience, 44-45
  bibliography, 64-65
  construction and design, 48-50
  documentation, 47-48
  expenses, 53
  importance of, 41-42
  loans and traveling exhibits, 53
  location, 45-47
  mission statement and, 42-43
  online exhibits, 57-59,76-77
  policy, 43
  preservation, 48,51-52
  security, 52-53
  topics, 44-45,63

Family Education Rights and Privacy Act (Buckley Amendment), 170
Family papers, 24
Federal Judicial History Office, 143
Finding aids, online, 56-57,73,74,76-77
Fisher, Terry, 19
Fitzherbert, Anthony, 95
Foster, Vincent W., Jr., 154,157-158,164,184
Frankfurter, Felix, 23
Friedman, Lawrence M., 13,20,162

Genealogy, 6
George Mitchell Papers Project, Web site, 73
Gillers, Stephen, 162
*Glossa ordinaria*, 108

Glossators, 108
Gordon, Robert W., 21
Graduate Theological Union, 101
Grant, Barbara, 94
Grant, Marshal, 94
Gratian, 108-109
Greenleaf, Simon, 23
Gregory IX, pope, 110
Grossberg, Michael, 20
Grossman, George, 32
*Guide to Professional Conduct of Solicitors*, 187
*Guide to the Preservation of Federal Judges' Papers*, 143

H-Law, 22
Hall, Kermit L., 162
Hamilton, James, 164,184
Hartog, Hendrik, 18
Harvard Law Library, 19,23-24,72,143
Harvard Law School, 23,72
Hazard, Geoffrey C., Jr., 160,162-163
Historians. *See* Legal historians
Historical Documents Study, 5-14
Hoeflich, M. H., 89-90
Holdsworth, Sir William, 18
Hurst, J. Willard, 18,21,24
Hutchinson, Dennis, 135

*IBM v. Phoenix*, 1 All E.R. 413 (1995), attorney-client privilege case, 183
*Infortiatum*, 106
Inns of Court, 95
Inter-library loan, 10
*Internet Scout Report*, 59
Irnerius, 108

JavaScript, 68
John XXII, pope, 103,110
Johns Manville asbestos litigation, 124

*Journal of American History*, 21
*Journal of Legal History*, 21
JSTOR, 21
Judicial confidentiality, 140-142,144-146
Judicial papers
  definition, 140
  federal judges' papers, 142-143
  importance of, 18,143,146
  State appellate judges' papers, 140-147
  U.S. Supreme Court justices' papers, 135-138,142-143
Justinian I, Byzantine emperor, 105

Kaplan, Diane E., 152
Karsten, Peter, 20
Kilgarlin, William, Papers (Texas State Archives), 143-144,146
Kimball, Bruce, 24

Langdell, Christopher Columbus, 23,24
LaPlante, Chris, 144
*Law & History Review*, 20,22
*Law & Social Inquiry*, 20
Law French, 91,96,97
Law librarians
  training for rare books and archives, 30-31,33-39
Law libraries
  use by legal historians, 9,13-14
Law school archives, 22-25
  faculty papers, 22-23
  institutional records, 22
  student notebooks, 23-24
Law Society, 187
Law-related Internet Project, 75
Lee, Sul, 3
Legal historians
  experience and training, 7-8,12-14

research methods courses, 30-33
research techniques, 10-14
research topics, 8,13,18-21
types of libraries used, 9-10
types of sources used,
    10-11,18,23-24,32
Legal history
    current trends, 18-20
    historiography, 18-22
    journals, 20-22
    online resources, 21-22
Legal Information Institute, Cornell
    University, Web site, 72
Legal Journals on the Web, Web site, 73
*Legal Research: Historical Foundations
    of the Electronic Age*, 32
Lewis F. Powell, Jr. Archive, Web site,
    74
*Liber authenticorum*, 107
Library of Congress,
    10,57,143,165-166,169
*Libri feudorum*, 107
Lindsay, Matthew J., 20
*Literature of American Legal History*, 19
Lyndwood, William of, 100


Maitland, Frederick W., 24
*Mapp v. Ohio*, 367 U.S. 643 (1961),
    exclusionary rule case, 138
Marshall, Edwin, collection of books on
    equity (Cornell Law Library),
    94
Mauzy, Oscar, Papers (Tarlton Law
    Library, University of Texas at
    Austin), 144-146
McCarthy, Mary, 153
McCormick, Jeffrey F., 167
MELVYL, 102
Mersky, Roy M., 4
Metzger, Ernest, 75
Mexican American Legal Defense and
    Educational Fund, 74
Mitchell, George, Papers (Bowdoin
    College), 73-74

Moak, Nathaniel, collection of trials
    (Cornell Law Library), 94
Morales, Dan, 141,147


Napoleonic Code, 96
National Archives and Records
    Administration, 9-10,142
    Legislative Archives Division,
        162
National Council on Public History,
    7,8
National Digital Library Project, 57
National Genealogical Society, 7
National Historical Publications and
    Records Commission, 2,6
National Study Commission on
    Records and Documents of
    Federal Officials, 143,146
Nelson, William, 19
Nobunaga, Wendy, 73
Noonan, John T., 156
Northwestern University, 74
*Novellae Constitutiones Post Codicem*,
    107


Online Archive of California, Web
    site, 58
Organization of American
    Historians, 7,8,9,21,162
Outreach. *See also* Exhibits
    as development tools, 41-42,47
    bibliography, 64-65
    donor relations, 54
    mission statement and, 42-43
    online outreach, 55-60,67-77
    patron relations, 55
    techniques, 53-55
Oyez, Oyez, Oyez, Web site, 74


Painter, Richard W., 156
*Palingensia of Latin Private
    Rescripts*, 75

*Pandecta*, 106
Phillips, Thomas R., 144-145
*Pizzey v. Ford Motor Co.* (1993),
    attorney-client privilege case, 183
Pope, Jack, 142,145-146
Powell, Lewis F., Jr., Papers
    (Washington and Lee
    University), 74
Project Muse, 21
Public Record Office, 188
Public relations, 41-42

*R. v. Derby Magistrates ex parte B*, 4 All
    E.R. 526 (1995), attorney-client
    privilege case, 185
*R. v. Tompkins*, 67 Crim. App. 181
    (1977), attorney-client privilege
    case, 183
Rare Book School, University of
    Virginia, 29,31,33-34
*Rare Books & Manuscripts*
    *Librarianship*, 38
Rare books. *See also* Collection development
    annotated copies, 88
    bibliography, 80-83
    bindings, 88
    in law libraries, 85-92
    in legal education and research,
        86-87,89-92,94-96
    preservation, 97
    training for librarians, 30-31,33-39
"Rare Law Books and Manuscripts"
    course, Rare Book School, 33
*Ratio Juris*, 103
Rauh, Joseph L., Jr., Papers (Library of
    Congress), 165-167,169
Raymond of Peñafort, 110
*RBM: A Journal of Rare Books,*
    *Manuscripts, and Cultural*
    *Heritage*, 38
*Re Malloy*, 2 Crim. App. 283 (1997),
    attorney-client privilege case, 184
*Re Thomson*, 20 Beav. 545 (1855),
    ownership of client files case, 187

*Re Wheatcroft*, 6 Ch.D. 97 (1877),
    ownership of client files
    case, 187
*Re Williams*, 1 All E.R. 964 (1985),
    attorney-client privilege
    case, 184
*Records Management in Federal*
    *Courts*, 143
Records management, 124-129
Reeve, Tapping, 23
Reference needs
    historians, 9-14
    law students, 136-138
    lawyers, 119-121,129-132
"Research Methods in American
    Legal History" seminar, Yale
    Law School, 31-33,34
Rehnquist, William H., 157-158
*Reid v. Covert*, 354 U.S. 1 (1957),
    military court jurisdiction case,
    137
Reid, John Philip, 19,146
Research Analysis Corporation,
    Princeton, N.J., 6
Research Guide to the Records of the
    Mexican American Legal
    Defense and Educational
    Fund (MALDEF)
    (1968-1983) at Stanford
    University, Web site, 74-75
*Reviews in American History*, 21
Robbins Collection, University of
    California at Berkeley,
    99-102,104
Robbins, Lloyd M., 100-101
Roman Law Homepage, Web site, 75
Roman Law Resources, Web site, 75-76
Roman law. *See also* Corpus Juris
    Civilis
    reference tools, 101-102
    sources, 104-108
    use in legal research, 102-104

Sacred Roman Rota, 103
Sam Houston Regional Library &
    Research Center, 147

*Scales v. United States*, 360 U.S. 924 (1959), Communist Party case, 137
Schaadt, Robert, 147
Selden Society, 3,182
Shakespeare, William, 88
*Sicurella v. United States*, 438 U.S. 285 (1955), conscientious objector case, 137
Simpson, Kenneth Farrand, Papers (Yale University), 152-153,165,168
Sixtus IV, pope, 110
Smedley, Graham, Papers (Tarlton Law Library, University of Texas at Austin, 147
Smith, Daniel, 94
Society of American Archivists, 2
South Carolina Legal History Index, Web site, 76
Spector, Rose, 145
*Stanford Law Review*, 19
Stanford University Library, 74
Starr, Kenneth W., 157-158,184
State Bar of Texas
    Committee on History and Traditions, 147
    Daniel Center for Legal History, 147
Story, Joseph, 23
Studies in Legal History (monograph series), 22
Supreme Court of Texas, 3,139-140,143-147
Supreme Court of the United States, 74,141
    papers of Supreme Court Justices, 135-138,143
Swarthmore College Peace Collection, Web site, 76-77
*Sweatt v. Painter*, 339 U.S. 629 (1950), school desegregation case, 137
*Swidler & Berlin and James Hamilton v. United States*, 524 U.S. 399 (1998), Vincent Foster case on attorney-client privilege, 154,157-158,164,184,185

Tarlton Law Library, University of Texas at Austin, 135,139,140,143-145
Taylor, Lord, 185
Texas Government Code, 143
Texas History Internet Consortium, 58
Texas Judicial Council, 147
Texas Open Records Act, 141-142,147
*Texas Open Records Handbook*, 141
Texas Penal Code, 144
Texas State Archives, 3,139,140,146
Texas Supreme Court Historical Society, 147
Thomas, Brook, 20
Thompson, E. P., 18
Thorne, Samuel, collection of books on English legal history (Cornell Law Library), 94
Tobacco litigation, 124
*Tractatus de consecratione*, 109
*Tractatus de penitentia*, 109
*Tres libri*, 107

*Uniform System of Citation: The Bluebook*, 105
*United States v. Seeger*, 380 U.S. 163 (1965), conscientious objector case, 137
*United States v. Standard Oil Co.*, 136 F.Supp. 345 (1955), attorney-client privilege case, 186
University College London, 72
University of Aberdeen, 75
University of California at Berkeley, 101
University of Saarbrücken, 75
University of South Carolina Law Library, 76
University of Southern California Law Library, 73
User studies, 6

*Volumen*, 107

Wallace, James P., Papers (Daniel Center for Legal History, State Bar of Texas), 147
Warrington, David, 31,33
Washington and Lee University, 74
Web sites
   as outreach tools, 55-59
   design, 57-59,67-70
   evaluation criteria, 68-70
   evaluation of selected sites, 71-77
Weinberger, Harry, Papers (Yale University), 153-154

White, Byron, 135
Widener, Emma Molina, 4
Widener, Michael, 136
William the Conqueror, 95
Willis, Bill, 144,146
Wilson, Edmund, 153
Wilson, Mary Blair, 153

*Yale Journal of Law & the Humanities*, 21
*Yale Law Journal*, 21
Yale Law School, 31
Yale University, 151
Year Books, 95